Emotions in research and practice

AALBORG UNIVERSITY PRESS

Emotions in research and practice

Edited by:
Francisco Pons,
Marc de Rosnay
and Pierre-André Doudin

Emotions in research and practice

Edited by Francisco Pons, Marc de Rosnay and Pierre-André Doudin

© Aalborg University Press, 2010

Layout: Pernille Guldbæk, Guldbæk Grafisk
Printed by: Toptryk Grafisk ApS, 2010
ISBN: 978-87-7307-995-9

Published by:
Aalborg University Press
Skjernvej 4A, 2. floor
9220 Aalborg
Denmark
Phone: (+45) 99 40 71 40, Fax: (+45) 96 35 00 76
E-mail: aauf@forlag.aau.dk
forlag.aau.dk

This book is financially supported by The Department of Communication and Psychology, Aalborg University, Denmark.

All rights reserved. No part of this book may be reprinted or reproduced or utilized in any form or by any electronic, mechanical, or other means, now known or hereafter invented, including photocopying and recording, or in any information storage or retrieval system, without permission in writing from the publishers, except for reviews and short excerpts in scholarly publications.

Content

Introduction
Emotions in research and practice:
An introduction
Francisco Pons, Marc de Rosnay and Pierre-André Doudin 7

Chapter 1
On the cognitive nature of emotions
and the emotional nature of cognitions
Francisco Pons, Marc de Rosnay,
Frédérique Cuisinier and Patrick Bender 17

Chapter 2
Entertainment, emotions and personality:
Why our preferences for media entertainment differ?
Christian Jantzen and Mikael Vetner 39

Chapter 3
Understanding children's tendencies
to hide their feelings: The roles of emotion
understanding and impulsivity
Selene Succar, Karli Beswick and Marc de Rosnay 65

Chapter 4
Mental states, emotion and culture: A pragmatic
proposal of the mentalistic understanding of culture
Laura Quintanilla, Lina Arias and Encarnación Sarriá 97

Chapter 5
Study of the evolution of children's social
representations of emotions at ages five and six
Marie-France Daniel, Emmanuelle Auriac and Lee Londei 127

Chapter 6
Emotion and emotion regulation in typical and atypical development: Implications for affect education
Hedy Stegge and Mark Meerum Terwogt 145

Chapter 7
Emotional experiences at the elementary school: Theoretical and pragmatic issues
Frédérique Cuisinier, Céline Clavel,
Marc de Rosnay and Francisco Pons 177

Chapter 8
Emotional competences: Development and intervention
Francisco Pons, Marc de Rosnay,
Bettina Gamskjær Andersen and Frédérique Cuisinier 205

Chapter 9
Violence at school:
Emotional control and risk of burnout in teachers
Pierre-André Doudin, Denise Curchod and Bernard Baumberger 241

List of contributors 257

Emotions in research and practice: An introduction

Francisco Pons, Marc de Rosnay and Pierre-André Doudin

This edited volume is the result of a collaboration by twenty-one researchers in psychology and educational sciences working in a dozen of different universities from Europe (Denmark, France, Netherlands, Norway, Spain and Switzerland), North America (Canada), and Oceania (Australia). At the heart of this book lies a single theme: The integration of research and practice concerning the emotional lives of persons, with a particular emphasis on children. In fact, the Editors of this volume all work within the domain of emotional development within institutions that explicitly mandate research and educate future practitioners.

The balance between research and practice is not unproblematic. Their integration is even more challenging. So it is not rare to hear researchers say of practitioners that all they want are solutions to specific problems, and they are filled with prejudice or indifferent to theory. Practitioners, on the other hand, do not mince their words: they often blame researchers for pursuing questions that are not useful, speaking unintelligibly and avoiding solutions to real problems. These different approaches and attitudes result in several problems, such as the distorted, contorted or non-existent communication between researchers and practitioners. Perhaps more profoundly, however, the researcher rarely confronts him- or herself with the compelling necessity faced by the practitioner to evaluate the validity of his or her research outcomes. While the practitioner only rarely seeks support or criticism for his or her practice, and, when such validation is sought, it is often very incomplete. Thus, both research and practitioner are poorer, or at least they miss very real opportunities to enrich their occupation.

It is all very well to espouse the virtue of integrating the worlds of research and practice but it is altogether more difficult to show how it is possible and to bring it about. Nevertheless, in the domains of research and practice covered by this volume, and concerning emotions, it is abundantly clear why this difficult goal should be pursued; and that is the function of this volume. It brings together researchers from different cultures, language groups and intellectual traditions who nonetheless straddle the divide between fundamental research and practice because of a shared interest not only in the nature of emotion, but also in the origins and impact of emotional experience. By bringing these different perspectives together, it is our intention to find out how it is possible for the researcher to integrate elements from the world of the practitioner, and for the practitioner to integrate elements from the world of research. It is our hope that such integration will result in enhanced communication and a better grasp of the phenomena discussed in the different chapters of this volume.

As a caveat, we would like to emphasize some points. We recognize that the respective worlds of research and practice, even within the domains represented in this volume, are not culturally uniform. So, just as all researchers do not hold equivalent views about practitioners, the reverse is also true. Equally, many researchers and practitioners consider themselves part researcher, part practitioner, or they see themselves on a continuum with fundamental research at one end and practice at the other.

Nevertheless, we think that the dichotomous split between research and practice is a sufficiently accurate characterization of reality, and it provides a useful framework to help understand how further integration of these two worlds can be achieved. Below, therefore, we begin by setting out the ways in which the worlds of research and practice differ, particularly in terms of their aims, and how they might be better integrated. We then introduce the contributions of this volume and show how they are grappling with the tension between what is true and what is important.

The worlds of research and practice

A first essential difference between the worlds of research and practice lies in their goals and relations to knowledge, which are revealed in the questions that are asked and the answers that are sought. Broadly speaking, the aim of research is to understand the world (reality); researchers are usually, to their own minds, grappling with the idea of reality and trying to pin down its truths. By contrast, the aim of practitioners and practical life more generally is to change the world (reality), to bring about some positive influence or effect. The researcher seeks, more or less explicitly, for truth and objectivity, whereas understanding the world from the point of view of a practitioner is part of the process of changing it efficiently. For example, the affective scientist may wish to understand the emotion system of mammals and its specific manifestations in humans, whereas the clinical psychologist or psychotherapist seeks to transform the emotional realities of a specific person and establish a practice or method that can reliably do so in more persons. In other words, for the researcher knowledge about the world is a goal (and the impact of this knowledge on the world a consequence), whereas for the practitioner knowledge is co-opted to change the world.

A second essential difference between the worlds of research and practice lies in the way the validity of knowledge is evaluated. Most researchers evaluate the validity of their knowledge in an empirical and/or analytical manner, and most practitioners do it in a pragmatic way. To a researcher knowledge is valid if it empirically corresponds to the world and/or if it analytically connects with other insights about the world. To the researcher, something is valid if it is objectively observable, and logically true. To a practitioner knowledge is valid if it facilitates the achievement of a legitimate aim; for example, when knowledge contributes to the solution of a problem it thereby becomes valid. These empirical inductions (validity defined as accordance with reality or as objectivity), analytical deductions (validity defined as logical coherence, truth) and pragmatic evaluations (validity defined as success) can, to the individual researcher or practitioner, be more or less uncertain or certain, contestable or incontestable, timely or untimely, changeable or unchangeable, specific or general, and individual or universal (see Doudin, Pons, Martin, Lafortune, 2003 for a discussion). Our purpose is not to evaluate such empirical, analytic or pragmatic validity. Rather, our purpose is to identify a range of that characterise research and practice approaches that are meaningful in the sense that they promote mutual integration, which we believe to be important. Nevertheless, we hope that the definitions of the phenomenon of validity which we use somehow corresponds to the world, that they possess a certain internal coherence and that they are sufficient to help us achieve the aims that motivates the present work.

Before we go further, it is important to recognize a few points. First, what is commonly called applied research is often taken as an example of successful integration between research and practice. In our opinion, however, this is often not the case. Applied research generally concerns change or success; it is a form of practice that falls under empirical methodologies. This is commonly seen in investigation of certain psychotherapies or teaching methods, which are evaluated in terms of effectiveness. It is true that an attempt is often made to equate effectiveness with truth, but this does not affect the basic practice-based orientation of most applied research. The same can often be said of action research, which seeks to change the world rather understand it. Action research aims to promote success; truth and objectivity are subordinate in this context. In fact, applied and action research do more to perpetuate separation between the worlds of research and practical life rather than actually attempting to integrate them. Second, in this Introduction, we limit ourselves to an humanistic definition of the immediate aims of research and practice. Regarding practice, such a definition entails enhancement of the individual's or the group's well-being (biological, psychological, social). Regarding research, such a definition is centered on truth and objectivity. It is self-evident that the practitioners pursue other aims (e.g., fortune) and this is also true for researchers (e.g., funding), but these are aims we are not going to address. Third, there are of course other differences between the worlds of research and practice which we shall not discuss in this Introduction.

Relations between the worlds of research and practice

Based on Berry's (1999) definition of acculturation, we identify four kinds of relations between the worlds of research and practice; that is, four possible ways to integrate (or not integrate) their aims, relations to knowledge and evaluations of the validity of knowledge. These are separation, assimilation, marginalization and integration. We think that the first approach is at present by far the most widespread, whereas the last is, in our opinion, the most desirable.

Separation is the practitioner's rejection of the fruits of research or the researcher's rejection of the concerns of practical life. A separation-relation is to negate the value of the other's culture, typically because one considers one's own culture significantly more valuable (idealization of our own culture). While this position may seem extreme, it is not uncommon to encounter sentiments that are wholly consistent with such a view (e.g., "there's no such thing as objectivity or truth", "the goals justify the means"). Assimilation is the researcher or the practitioner abandoning their respective culture in favor of the other. An assimilation-relation is to reject your own culture because you regard the other to be far more valuable (idealization of others' culture). This relationship is less commonly observed but can be observed from time to time (e.g., "my research is meaningless, it won't change the world", "my practice is useless, it won't improve our understanding of the world"). While it may seem that the assimilation view is trivial, we hasten to point to an increasing shift at the institutional level (e.g., universities and their associated funding agencies) which resembles an ultra-liberal assimilation-stance: whereas universities maintain that they are founded on the pursuit of knowledge and truth, in reality research and teaching are increasingly controlled by actual practical needs or outcomes that in most cases are financial and not, for example, social, humanitarian or religious. Marginalization occurs when one rejects one's stance, but does not adopt the other (desidealization of both cultures). A marginalization-relation is both the denial of the value of your own culture and the value of the others culture, since both cultures, cynically or fearlessly, are considered worthless (e.g., "Truth is an illusion, and don't bother trying to change the world").

In contrast to these three kinds of relations, integration occurs when the practitioner and the researcher combine their respective worlds. An integration-relation implies that you not only appreciate your own culture, but also the culture of the other. Of course this can occur in various ways. We identify three integration-relations between the world of research and the world of practical life: A-linear, B-linear and circular. In the A-linear integration-relationship the world of practical life matters more than the world of research. This relationship can be illustrated by the following statement: "To understand the world you first have to change it, since practical success causally precedes truth and objectivity". In the B-linear integration-relationship it is the world of research that matters more than the world of practical life. This relationship can be illustrated by the following statement: "To change the world you first have to understand it, since truth and objectivity causally precedes practical success". Whereas the A/B-linear integration-approaches are really just mirrors of one another, in the circular integration-relationship the worlds of research and practical life mutual define each other. This relationship can be illustrated by the following statement: "To change the world you have to understand it, and to understand it you have to change it, since truth, objectivity and practical success mutually define each other". We favor this final stance, even if it may often be beyond the reach of a single researcher or practitioner.

For now we have defined what we understand by the world of research and the world of practice based on a description of their respective aims and relations to knowledge, and in light of the ways in which these two cultures evaluate the validity of their knowledge. We claim that making insights (knowledge) relative, making their empirical, analytic, and pragmatic validity inter-dependent, will encourage fruitful integration of disciplines. In our view, and we think it is a view shared by many, the integration of research and practice not only enhances communication between researchers and practitioners but also enhances the validity of their respective insights and practices. As a consequence, a valid evaluation of research should be representative of the diversity of the goals of research (e.g., to improve our understanding of the world and/or to change the world for the better). It should also be representative of the diversity of publication goals (e.g., from experimental articles in blind peer-reviewed international scholarly journal in English with a "high" impact factor to books in a non-English language which is going to change professional practice in a specific country) and dissemination channels (from scientific articles to editorials in magazine or newspapers, from papers to scientific conferences to interviews in the media, and so on)

The organization of the volume

In this volume we bring together contributions from various research traditions that attempt such integration within the contexts of emotional competence development, the relation between cognition and emotion (including emotion understanding), emotion regulation in various contexts, Emotional Pedagogy, and cultural influences on emotion. Below, we finish by providing a brief overview of these contributions. Despite the fact that this volume brings together very different perspectives, the individual contributions share a common concern to marry research and practice, and to be relevant both to science and society. To put order on these contributions, they can be broadly classified into three, albeit overlapping groups.

The first group, chapters 1 and 2, provides a macroscopic perspective on the nature of emotion and its relation to mental processes, self-regulation and culture. Pons, de Rosnay, Cuisinier and Bender (Chapter 1) start by setting out a classical distinction between emotions and cognition. The distinction goes back to the Greeks and to a very great extent persists to the present day. This initial chapter, primarily drawing on fundamental research but also integrating clinical and educational perspectives, explores the nature of the relations between cognition and emotion, asks whether such relations can be construed as causal, and emphasizes the need to accommodate both domains in the study of the human, particularly if such study is likely to yield practical insights. Jantzen and Vetner (Chapter 2) similarly provide us with a broad view but their's starts with phenomena that are immediately recognizable and important to virtually all people, entertainments and diversions, and the construction of these forms in such a manner that their appeal is remarkably encompassing. In their subtle analysis of media preferences they, like Pons and colleagues, quickly arrive at a functional conceptualization of emotion that serves the needs of persons and is inexorably connected with their understanding of the world and themselves. Their exploration of our relationship with entertainments reveals that our preferences for specific kinds of diversions to some extent lie in basic physiological needs, as well as our more self-conscious identities (which are underpinned by personality). Thus, entertainment becomes an important feature of human existence that taps directly into our idiosyncratic yearnings for a sense of subjective well-being. Jantzen and Vetner explain that seeking entertainment, exploring its parameters as a form of play and finding gratification therein, is in fact an act of emotion regulation sufficiently detached from the real world to allow a diverse range of experience and arousal that is in need of expression. Indeed, throughout the ensuing chapters, and particularly in Chapter 6, the importance of emotion regulation is continually touched upon. Thus, Jantzen and Vetner take ubiquitous human behaviors and provocatively suggest that they are motivated and sustained by, amongst other things, the organization of the emotion system, underlying personality constructs, and the needs that extend from these realities.

The second group, chapters 3 through 7, takes a predominantly microscopic perspective: these chapters focus on detailed issues and empirical questions about the emotional competence and development of children. Thus, Succar, Beswick and de Rosnay (Chapter 3) make a careful analysis of the determinants of 7-year-old's abilities to hide their feelings in a social deception paradigm, the disappointing gift task, and to maintain that deception under conversational pressure. Quintanilla, Arias and Sarriá (Chapter 4) present new research from various studies exploring the extent to which conversational interactions and other social contexts can influence young children's emotion understanding, and they interweave these empirical insights into a broader developmental account of the mastery of mental state understanding and its relation to culture. Daniel, Auriac and Londei (Chapter 5) provide a detailed exploration of the kinds of representations that 5- and 6-year-old children develop about specific emotions and the fundamental ways in which these shift with development and, critically, social experience. Cuisinier, Clavel, de Rosnay and Pons (Chapter 7), in keeping with the qualitative orientation of Chapter 5, engage school-aged children in novel and intriguing interviews about their own emotional experiences in relation to pedagogical settings (Study 1), and examine the relations between these feelings and children's actual school performance and subject preference (Study 2). These chapters address quite different issues but they share a focus on the richness of children's emotional experience and understanding; each chapter in its own way illustrating the remarkable emotional sensitivity of children both in terms of what they are capable of understanding and their awareness of the relevance of contextual factors. These chapters also identify and confirm lawful structures/processes in children's emotional development, but there is no sense in which such structures/processes offer an adequate account of a given child's emotional experience. Indeed, the profundity of individual experience against a backdrop of reliable developmental change and structure forms the basis of Stegge's and Meerum Terwogt's chapter (Chapter 6) on children's emotion regulation. This chapter stands alone in presenting a unified theory of emotional organization and its relation to emotional experience and well-being (see also Chapter 2, which grapples with such issues). The authors acknowledge and explore the tension between emotional responses to objects (situations, persons, things, etc), which at their most basic are experienced as unbidden changes in one's orientation and appraisal, and the gradual acquisition by children of the knowledge that emotion can be treated as a to-be-regulated phenomenon. They also entertain ways in which changing habits of interaction and socialization might allow children, particularly children with difficulties, to bring about some changes in the ways that they manage their emotional responses.

The final group, chapters 8 and 9, has a more pragmatic orientation, clearly focusing on the importance of children's emotional lives within a pedagogical context, and the practicalities of introducing Emotional Pedagogy. Despite the pervasive nature of emotion in human life and the rich history of emotion research in early childhood, it is currently difficult to find an integrated view on how the different domains of emotional competence develop in young children. In their chapter, Pons, de Rosnay, Andersen and Cuisinier (Chapter 8) present a synthesized view of various domains of children's emotional competence before asking how such competence can be cultivated through intervention. Finally, Doudin, Curchod and Baumberger (Chapter 9) move the spotlight from children to the teacher-child(-class) relationship and explore the ways in which violence creates an emotional atmosphere that to a very great extent subverts the learning framework.

In sum, the chapters presented in this volume traverse many issues, questions and perspectives but they are unified in their preoccupation with the need to bring about a proper integration between domains that have traditionally been the exclusive focus of researchers (e.g., the nature of the emotion system, including its dimensions, properties and structure) and domains that have traditionally been viewed as needing pragmatic intervention or having only practical consequences (e.g., classroom intervention, media choice, social integration, etc). It may be that our focus on emotion, which presents humans with so many contradictions and surprises, forces such integration. Or it may just be a prudent way to proceed as a research community, to find a balance between our need to understand and affect the world.

Reference

Berry, J. (1999). Intercultural relations in plural societies. Canadian Psychology, 40, 1, 12-21.

Doudin, P.-A., Pons, F., Martin, D., & Lafortune, L. (2003). Croyances et connaissances: analyse de deux rapports aux savoirs. In L. Lafortune, C. Deaudelin, P.-A. Doudin & D. Martin (Eds.), Conceptions, croyances et representations (pp. 1-26). Sainte-Foy: Presses de l'Université du Québec.

Chapter 1

On the cognitive nature of emotions and the emotional nature of cognitions[1]

Francisco Pons, Marc de Rosnay, Frédérique Cuisinier and Patrick Bender

1. Introduction

What is the relation between the quality of children's emotional attachments to their caregivers and their intellectual development? Is there a relation between the emotional valence or content of a text and its comprehension by a pupil? How are emotional disorders such as depression and anxiety related to memory and attention? These are the kinds of questions that both researchers and practitioners in psychological sciences might address when confronted with the issue of the relation between emotion and cognition. This issue provides a framework within which researchers and professionals in cognitive and affective sciences can meet, share and discuss their knowledge.

In today's psychological literature, it is impossible to find a cohesive outline of the possible answers to the question of the relation between cognition and emotion. In this chapter we address the form that such an answer might plausibly take.

Importance of the question

To begin with, it is necessary to ask why it is important to grapple with the nature of the relation between cognition and emotion. There are numerous reasons depending on your starting point, but we address four.

First, the question itself is intriguing because very few have tried to undertake an impartial investigation of this question. In a search of the psychological literature we found that more than 200 000 publications (articles, book chapters, and books) include the terms cognition or emotion in their title; or equivalent terms such as intelligence, intellect, feeling, mood or af-

---

[1] We would like to thank Geir Overskeid for his enlightening and constructive comments.

fect. However, less than three percent of these publications include both terms in the title (PsycINFO and Medline, January 2009). Furthermore, nearly all publications that do include both terms look at the role of cognition and emotion in relation to a third phenomenon, such as the impact of emotion and cognition on music, or the impact of gender on cognition and emotion. By contrast, the psychological investigation of causal relations between cognition and emotion is rarely undertaken. Moreover, studies that do examine such causal relations usually presume a fixed order of influence, ignoring potentially reciprocal (circular) influences between cognition and emotion. Also, it should be noted that, to the best of our knowledge, there is only one international peer reviewed journal in psychological sciences that combines the two terms in its name: Cognition and Emotion.

Second, gaining a better understanding of nature of the relation between cognition and emotion may improve our comprehension of the nature of each. In other words, by forcing simultaneous consideration of both these domains, we may gain insight into what could be called the emotional nature of cognition and the cognitive nature of emotion.

Third, a better understanding of the relation between cognition and emotion may contribute to the development of more holistic methods for the simultaneous assessment of these phenomena; which might more closely mirror human experience. Likewise, such an understanding may enable us to devise combined interventions for the improvement of both cognitive and emotional competences. Such assessment methods and interventions could prove to have a positive impact not only on people with psychological difficulties but on typical people as well.

Finally, most researchers and practitioners in psychology working in the respective areas of emotion and cognition do recognize that the two phenomena are in some sort of causal relationship. However, more often than not they do not collaborate with each other and may not even know each other when they are working in the same institution (university, hospital, etc.). Thus, by addressing the nature of the relation between cognition and emotion we may be able to contribute to a meeting of cognitive and affective researchers and practitioners within psychological sciences.

Origins of the schism between cognition and emotion

What are the reasons for the schism between cognitive psychology and affective sciences? There are at least two explanations. The first explanation concerns the fact that emotions are still often considered as problematic for the study of cognition. Even today, emotions are typically excluded from cognitive sciences, omitted from research on cognitive mental states and processes, and taught as a separate area of psychology. In fact, emotion is often considered as a potentially confounding variable, which is to be neutralized (frequently by randomization). Why do most researchers and practitioners in cognitive sciences still consider cognition a cold phenomenon disconnected from emotion? There may be quite a few reasons but ignorance is not one of them. Indeed, most cognitive scientists recognize the existence of emotions, as well as the causal impact of emotions on cognition. Nevertheless, this recognition is almost never implemented explicitly in their actual research or practice. Perhaps the best candidate to explain the exclusion of emotion from cognitive research is methodology. When employing experimental research designs, one relies heavily on existing paradigms and has to make difficult choices about what variables belong in a given study. Since it is impossible to examine everything at once and devise studies that are both wide-ranging and in-depth at the same time, one could argue that studying emotion and cognition simultaneously is not expedient. Another reason could be entirely pragmatic in nature: it takes time to specialize as a researcher or practitioner and the prospect of putting yourself in unfamiliar research or practice terrain may not be appealing, especially given the likelihood that you will have to argue with both cognitive and affective researchers/practitioners, and take the risk of not being recognized by either of them! Furthermore, cognitive scientists are also under the influence of social representations: the idea that emotion is an additional burden and inferior to cognition is frequent among cognitive researchers and practitioners (Solomon, 2000). Often, they hold the Platonic (emotions are inferior), Darwinian (emotions are a phylogenetic atavism), or Freudian (emotions have to be tamed) beliefs that emotion interferes with cognition (if not always at least most of the time). The belief that emotion and cognition are two incompatible systems is also quite common. As Pascal (1670/1998) so eloquently put it, "The heart has its reasons that the reason does not know". Cognition is about truth (and falseness) and emotion about pleasure (and displeasure). Many see these two principles as incompatible. And finally, for many centuries and in many cultures and societies, emotion has been considered as too close to the viscera/body and, consequently, our animal nature. Experiences arising from emotion, therefore, have been considered too problematic for systematic or rational enquiry: Emotions are just too hot.

The second explanation of the schism between cognitive psychology and affective sciences concerns the relatively recent upsurge in research within the affective sciences (see Davidson, Scherer & Goldsmith, 2003; Lewis & Haviland-Jones, 2000; Manstead, Frijda & Fischer, 2004 for reviews). Half a century ago, a revolution took place within cognitive psychology that provoked the downfall of some of the behaviorist diktats, such as the excommunication of first person introspection and the censure on "internal" mental states and processes as scientific objects (versus "external" third person observation of the individual's responses/behaviors). Since then, cognitive researchers have again been allowed to investigate what is happening in the black box, which stands between environmental stimuli and the individual's responses/behaviors; namely people's mental states and processes. More recently, about thirty years ago, a second revolution took place: the affective revolution. Indeed, many serious psychologists had previously given emotion close consideration (e.g., Sigmund Freud, Silvan Tomkins) but the study of emotion had never really penetrated psychological research. However, now researchers in psychology have also been given the green light to investigate what is happening in the heart: emotion too, albeit by a different route, has come to the forefront as a mediator between the environment and the person. Thus, emotion has become a valid object of study and it is increasingly called upon to describe, explain and alter the human condition. With this latter revolution, individuals are no longer considered as merely cognitive machines, whether that be a computers, neural network or dynamic system.

Today, most researchers and professionals in affective sciences would consider emotion, to have the same importance as cognitive mental states and processes, both being necessary to understand the mind and the person. The affective revolution came about for many reasons. For one, private, subjective experiences such as feelings and moods, as well as self-reports of these experiences obtained by introspection, are now again considered legitimate scientific topics and methods. Relatedly, affective scientists allowed themselves to investigate people's conscious experience of their feelings and moods, namely their subjective emotional experiences. Of course the affective revolution also owes much to yet another methodological revolution that is neuroscience. With the onset of wide spread neurosciences, ushered in by a dramatic improvement of the technologies made available to measure the activity of the body, and especially the brain (e.g., fMRI, PET, second generation EEG), scientists gained a new opportunity to observe the physical correlates of peoples' subjective experiences. What followed was a legitimization of the status of feelings and moods as scientific objects because they were now seen as variables that could be objectively measured. Today, new technologies are beginning to undermine the dominant dualistic attitude within the psychological sciences regarding the mind-body relationship (e.g., Vogt & Devinsky, 2000). These technologies have opened a space in which the study of emotions can take place, as the missing link between the mind and the body. Finally, over the last few decades, many societies and cultures have attenuated the negative representation of emotions. In line with some of Sigmund Freud's hypotheses, emotions are increasingly recognized as one of the most important dimensions of the individual's mind.

The rest of this chapter is divided into five sections. First, we discuss the meaning of the terms emotion and cognition. We then examine three possible conceptions of a causal relation between cognition and emotion: no causal relationship, cognition causing emotion, and emotion causing cognition. In the conclusion, we speculate about a circular relation between these two domains.

2. Defining cognition and emotion

Since the beginning of psychological sciences, and stretching back to their philosophical roots, scholars have wondered about the definition of cognition and emotion. Even today, definitions of these terms are sometimes considered impossible, or at least as manifold as the people trying to define them. While it is not our aim to offer a final definition of the two terms, it is necessary to develop some sort of understanding of their meaning in order to investigate the causal relationship between the two. Indeed, much of the controversy and conflict around this issue is related to the absence of an explicit definition of cognition and emotion (which may ultimately prove insoluble).

In this chapter, the term cognition refers to the different forms of knowledge (belief, percept, idea, thought, etc.) that we have about ourselves, others and the world, both perceived and imagined, as well as to our cognitive functions that make possible the acquisition, storage, retrieval, transformation and use of this knowledge (i.e., memory, attention, language, thought, perception, etc.). Our knowledge can be empirically or logically true or false, more or less certain or uncertain, temporary or permanent, general or specific. It can also be more or less real or unreal, simple or complex, sensorial or symbolic, conscious or unconscious, controllable or uncontrollable, as well as universal or idiosyncratic. In this chapter our, knowledge and cognitive functions are considered as interrelated states and processes of the mind (e.g., the subjective experience of the color red), the body (e.g., neuronal correlates associated with the perception of the color red), and the culture (e.g., words representing the color red—red, rød, rojo, rot, rouge, etc—and its connotations—danger, alarm, fire, anger, etc).

The term emotion refers to our feelings and moods directed toward our selves, others and the world, both perceived and imagined. These feelings and moods can be more or less pleasant or unpleasant, intense or moderate, temporary or permanent, general or specific. They can also be more or less basic or complex, sensorial or symbolic, conscious or unconscious, controlled or uncontrolled, as well as universal or idiosyncratic. In this chapter our feelings and moods are considered as interrelated states and processes of the mind (e.g., subjective experience of happiness), the body (e.g., peptide release, heart rate, respiration rate, blood pressure, muscle tension, etc), and the culture (e.g., the display rules for the expression of anger; the social and cultural norms related to the feeling of anger).

Having set forth a working understanding of the two phenomena, we will now focus on the question of the causal relationship between the two, starting with the view that is no causal relationship.

3. No causal relation

With the understanding of emotion and cognition outlined above it seems difficult to imagine the two as being completely separate phenomena without an influential interrelation. Both share similar properties and are properties of the mind, body and culture. In addition, keeping in mind the inherent directedness of emotion (but perhaps not moods), it seems that emotion in itself contains cognitive processes, in the sense that our emotions have to be "cognitively connected" to the stimuli causing them (e.g., Solomon, 2000).

Nevertheless, experimental studies have shown that some emotional responses appear to take place in the absence of any cognitive process. For example, LeDoux (1996) showed that some emotional reactions, taking place within only a few milliseconds (e.g., the fear of an already known stimulus), are the result of a purely biological reaction; in the sense that they appear to occur before any cognitive processes could take place. Such a reaction to a familiar stimulus can be produced without the involvement of the cortex where cognitive processes are assumed to predominantly reside. Also, in line with evolutionary theory, certain internal and external stimuli are believed to be naturally connected to specific emotions without the involvement of any cognitive processes (i.e., phylogenetically known; Cosmides & Toby, 2000; Darwin, 1872/1899; Ekman 1999).

It should be noted, however, that LeDoux (1996) also showed that learning a new emotional reaction, and thus connecting an emotional response to a certain stimulus, requires the (sensory) cortex until the emotional reaction is completely automatic, and therefore implies some cognitive treatment. Thus, it could be argued that it is unfeasible to train an emotional response without the involvement of cognitive processes.

Interestingly, to the best of our knowledge, no experimental study has yet tried to demonstrate that cognitive responses can be shaped without the involvement of emotion. Maybe the reason for the lack of such studies is the fact that it seems to be a non-issue; we tend to perceive of ourselves as being able to act rationally, free of an emotional taint. Given the automaticity of emotional responding and the apparent genetic predisposition to be emotional, this is a non-issue that may have to be revisited.

4. Cognition as a cause of emotion

Until thirty years ago most of the causal explanations of emotions were related to the body. Two hypotheses were then in competition: the James-Lange and the Cannon. In brief, whereas the first postulated that emotions arose as a result of bodily activity (i.e., we are subjectively sad because our body cries), the second hypothesis postulated almost the opposite (i.e., our body cries because we are subjectively sad). These two theories spawned other hypotheses, such as the Neo-Jamesian somatic markers theory by Damasio (1994), and the facial feedback hypothesis (e.g. McIntosh, 1996). Whereas, the debate about the relation between emotions and their bodily correlates is still very much alive (e.g., Cacioppo et al., 2000; Ekman & Rosenberg, 2005), we can now also investigate how cognition may function as a cause of emotional experience. We discuss this below with respect to adults and children.

Cognition as a cause of emotion in adults

With the affective revolution another causal explanation emerged, cognition as the cause of emotion. This Neo-Cannonian hypothesis holds that cognitive appraisal or evaluation of both internal and external stimuli is a cause of emotion. Schachter and Singer (1962) were among the first to give an empirical demonstration of the existence of this kind of appraisal. In their study, they injected two groups of participants with adrenaline. While they told the first group that the injection would have an impact on their heart rate (which was true), the second group was told that the injection would have no impact whatsoever (which was not true). Although, the two groups experienced the same physical changes (increase of heart rate), only the second group of participants reported emotional reactions. Moreover, when the second group was exposed to a happy research confederate, the participants in that group reported positive feelings, whereas they reported negative feelings when exposed to an angry research confederate.

The cognitive appraisal hypothesis, and more precisely the necessity of cognitive appraisal for emotion to occur, has been the object of vivid debates, such as that between Zajonc (1980, 1984) and Lazarus (1982, 1984). While the latter argues in favor of the necessity of cognitive appraisal for emotions, the former has questioned this necessity (for a similar view see LeDoux, 1996). According to Zajonc, cognition, and thus cognitive appraisal, takes place exclusively in the form of conscious processes. Consequently he argues that (conscious) cognitive appraisal cannot account for emotional responses since these do not require the consciousness of the stimulus that causes or changes them; he states "[emotional] preferences need no [conscious cognitive] inferences" (Zajonc, 1980). In line with Zajonc's argument and the limitation of cognition to consciousness, some studies have claimed to show that emotions can be elicited and modified without involving any kind of conscious treatment (Li, Zinbarg, Boehm & Paller, 2008). By contrast, in line with Lazarus' position, others continue to argue that there is always a trace of consciousness at the origin of our emotional experience and its modification (Pessoa, Japee, Sturman, & Ungerleider, 2006).

Notwithstanding this ongoing debate, it has been shown that cognition is not always conscious (see, for example, studies on implicit learning, memory, etc.) and numerous studies have demonstrated that more or less conscious or unconscious cognitive appraisals often have an impact on emotional valence and arousal; both prior to the emotional experience, as antecedents, and also during the experience, as modulators (e.g. Fridja, 1986; Roseman, 1984; Scherer, 1984; Smith, 1989). The impact of cognitive appraisal on emotional reactions also lends support to cognitive psychotherapy theories. These therapeutic approaches aim to treat emotional illnesses, such as depression and anxiety, via cognitive intervention seeking to correct or alter the individual's inadequate or maladaptive cognitive appraisal processes (e.g., Beck, 1976).

Several dimensions of the cognitive appraisal of stimuli have been identified as having importance for emotional responses, such as novelty (sudden, familiar, predictable, etc.), valence (pleasant, unpleasant, etc.), goal/need significance (relevant, urgent, etc.), coping potential (controllable, adjustable, etc.), and compatibility with personal and cultural norms (acceptable, unacceptable, etc.) (see Kappas, 2006; Scherer, Schorr, & Johnstone, 2001, for reviews). For example, stimuli that are evaluated as pleasant and acceptable will commonly result in feelings of happiness or pleasure. In contrast, a sudden, unpredictable, unpleasant and uncontrollable stimulus would more often than not result in a feeling of fear.

Cognition as a cause of emotion in children

Numerous studies have also shown that children develop a certain understanding of the impact of cognitive appraisal on emotions early on in life (see Harris, 1989; Pons, Harris & de Rosnay, 2004, for reviews). For example, at around 4-5 years of age, children begin to understand the effect of memories on emotions. They realize that the intensity of one's anger decreases over time, that looking at a picture of a lost loved one can cause sadness or that thinking about a positive event in the past can cause joy. At approximately 5-6 years of age, children also begin to understand the role of knowledge on emotions (beliefs, perceptions, etc.). They come to understand that a person can feel sad because he or she believes a favorite object has been lost, when in reality it has just been misplaced. Likewise, they are able to grasp the full measure of Little Red Riding Hood's naiveté; they understand that she not only fails to realize that a wolf is waiting for her with the intention of eating her, but she also feels no fear on account of her misaprehension of reality. Before this age, children have the tendency to say that Little Red Riding Hood either knows that the wolf is waiting for her and that she is scared, or that she does not know about the wolf but feels scared nonetheless. From about 8-9 years of age, children also begin to understand how feelings can be regulated via the use of cognitive strategies, such as the cognitive re-evaluation of a given situation or the re-orientation of one's focus of attention. Before this age children have the tendency to report more behavioral and external strategies, such as doing something else to stop feelings of sadness, or to ask for parental help. Such evidence shows that children gradually develop an understanding of how cognitive processes can influence their emotional reactions and experiences. In fact, a substantial number of studies have identified a link between emotional well-being and the understanding and use of strategies for emotion regulation. For example, individuals who use strategies such as rumination and passivity in order to deal with negative emotions rather than re-evaluation of the situation or re-focusing show more depressive symptoms than individuals who employ those latter strategies (e.g., Endrund & Vikan, 2007; Haga & Kraft, 2006). This begs the question of the extent and implications of individual differences in children's emotion understanding (Pons & Harris, 2005) and, more generally, of whether improvement in emotion understanding and regulation could lead to enhanced emotional well-being, resilience and mental health (see Borge, 2007; de Rosnay, Harris & Pons, 2008; Monsen & Monsen, 1999, for discussions).

Furthermore, an increasing number of studies show that children's knowledge about emotions (including their nature, causes, consequences and possibilities of regulation) has an impact on their emotional experiences in a social context. This impact has been identified in both preschool-aged and school-aged children (see de Rosnay et al., 2008; Pons, Harris & Doudin, 2002 for reviews). For example, young children who have a good comprehension of the impact of situational variations on emotions (e.g., that someone should feel happy or surprised when receiving an unexpected gift or sad or angry when breaking a favorite toy) are also more likely to be popular with their day-care playmates. Further, children between three and four years of age with a well-developed understanding of emotion are less likely to have behavioral problems, such as aggressiveness or limited empathy, and children who are skilled at recognizing basic emotions, such as happiness, anger, fear and sadness at five years of age, are also more likely to be popular amongst peers one or two years later. Finally, children between nine and thirteen years of age with a good understanding of emotions and emotion regulation strategies are considered the most socially competent by their classmates and teachers.

Surprisingly, it is difficult to find empirical research that explores the impact of school achievement on emotions. Some studies show a complex pattern of relations between positive and negative emotions, motivation, school performance and self-evaluation of academic competences. For example, the link seems to be stronger between emotions and self-evaluation of academic competencies than between emotions and actual school achievements (Gumora & Arsenio, 2002). It seems that for some pupils good marks at school do not necessarely result in positive feelings; the self-evaluation by the pupil of his or her academic competencies being a better predictor of his or her feelings.

5. Emotion as a cause of cognition

Arguably, one of the functions of emotions is to provide us with a meaningful relationship to ourselves, others and our environment. In other words, emotions allow us to distinguish between different stimuli, to which we attach specific meanings that have some kind of motivational salience to us. Emotion allows apperception and provides a reason to respond to the world in meaningful ways (that are usually adaptive). In this sense, emotions are means by which we make sense of and relate to the internal and external world. How, then, does this relational mechanism impact our cognitive processes? The answer to this question is twofold: Emotional arousal is considered to be motivational/energetic, whereas emotional valence is considered to be a compass, guiding our cognitive processes. We elaborate this perspective below.

Emotion arousal as an energizer for cognition

At a general level, emotional arousal has an impact on cognition because it mobilizes the mind, the body and the culture to act and react. For example, fear prepares the mind, the body and the culture for fight or flight. This motivational function of emotional arousal is the only one recognized by Piaget (1954/1981), the creator of modern cognitive developmental psychology. He acknowledged that cognition needs emotional arousal, which can either speed up or slow down the processes of the intellect and therefore its development. However, since Piaget considered cognitive disequilibrium to be at the origin of emotional arousal, it would be more accurate to say that, according to Piaget, emotional arousal is a consequence, rather than a cause of cognition. Yerkes and Dodson (1908) proposed a more precise description of the impact of emotional arousal on cognition. They postulated that an appropriate level of emotional arousal is needed in order to achieve an optimal level of cognitive performance. A level of emotional arousal which is either too high (e.g., too much anxiety) or too low (e.g., not enough interest) may have a negative impact on cognitive performance. They also suggested an operational relation between emotional arousal and cognitive functions, which states that the more difficult the task (i.e., the higher the cognitive demand), the lower the level of emotional arousal necessary in order to achieve the optimum level of cognitive performance.

Emotional valence as a compass for cognition

According to this second view, emotion not only makes cognition move but it also orients its movement. Whereas emotional arousal drives cognitive processes, emotional valence dictates the direction of cognition, a function that is also important for development. Without emotional valence, most behavioral conditioning would not be possible; such conditioning produces a specific behavior in response to a certain stimulus. Naturally, behind the required behavior lies a cognitive process that determines the elicitation of the behavior in question. In the absence of an emotional value attached to the outcome of this action, the behavior itself would become meaningless and the cognitive processes would fail to produce that particular behavior. In other words, our emotional reaction to a particular stimulus (more or less positive or negative, intense or mild, permanent or punctual, etc.) determines the nature of our cognitive response to that stimulus to some extent, and thus the appearance, disappearance, prioritization or transformation of certain behavior (Overskeid, 2007). Freud (e.g. 1905/2002) recognized this compass function of emotional valence, together with the mobilizing force of emotional arousal, as being the most important aspect of emotion in relation to cognition: the expressed or repressed drive coming from the emotional Id not only gives its energy to the cognitive Self, it also orients its functioning (e.g., activation and inhibition) and development (in collaboration with the cognitive Super-ego).

Emotion as a cause of cognition in adults

Numerous experimental studies have demonstrated the impact of emotional arousal and valence on memory, attention and creativity (e.g., Braisby & Gellaty, 2005). For example, when shown a list of positive and negative words, most people will recall more positive words. However, people who are clinically depressed tend to recall more negative words, especially when these are clearly negative (e.g., Death, Cancer, War, etc.). Likewise, anxious people (with the diagnosis of PTSD) have the tendency to have more negative false-memories than non anxious people (Brennen, Dybdahl & Kapidzic, 2007). Similarly, people tend to recall more elements of a story when the emotional valence of the story matches their own mood at the time of reading the story, especially when the story is sad and they themselves are in a sad mood. When in a neutral mood, people tend to remember more positive than negative details from the story (e.g., Matt, Vasquez & Campbell, 1992 for a review). It is as if our memory is biased towards positive information when we are in a neutral emotional state or, in the case of non-clinical populations at least, our resting emotional state is actually quite positive.

Additional studies have shown that the recall of information is facilitated when the person asked to recall information is in the same mood as he or she was when the information was first learned; at the time of encoding. This effect holds up irrespective of the emotional valence of the information in question and is particularly strong when the information is autobiographical. For example, the recall of a list of neutral words is facilitated if the person is in a sad mood both when trying to encode and to recall this same list (see Eich & Forgas, 2003, for a review). Such findings may explain why the recall of traumatic autobiographical events is facilitated when we are already in a negative mood. The recall of such events, in turn, may reinforce our negative mood, thus starting a vicious cycle recognized by many schools of psychotherapy (Beck, 1976).

Emotional arousal and valence also have an impact on another important cognitive function, our attention (see Eysenck, Derakshan, Santos & Calvo, 2007; MacLeod, 2005, for reviews). For example, people with mood disorders tend to pay more attention to information (words, pictures, faces, etc) with an emotional valance matching their mood. Further, when explaining their failures, depressed people have the tendency to pay more attention to their personal characteristics (internal locus of control; e.g., "I failed because of who I am, what I did or what I said"), whereas they tend to pay more attention to their environment when explaining their success (external locus of control; e.g., "I succeeded because of luck, fate or external events"). In contrast to non-anxious people, individuals who are clinically anxious direct their attention more towards threatening words (Cancer, Evil, Death, etc) than neutral words (House, Picture, Chair, etc.). Also, when confronted with homonym words (e.g., Batter [pancake] versus batter [assault]) non-anxious people have the tendency to activate the neutral meaning of the word whereas anxious people have the tendency to activate the negative meaning. An additional feature of emotional valence and arousal is that it may play an important role in relation to our ability to construct new information. Projective tests such as the CAT/TAT and the Rorschach are partially built on this assumption; that is, people's emotions determine, via a process of projective identification, their interpretation of reality, especially when this reality is ambiguous (e.g., inkblots could be interpreted as a loving mother, a threatening father, a lost child, an unfaithful partner, etc.). Of course, emotions may also have an impact on other aspects of memory, attention and creativity (see, for example, research on flashbulb memories and autobiographical memory), as well as other aspects of cognition or of the mind, such as intelligence, language, perception and morality (e.g., Skoe, Eisenberg & Cumberland, 2002).

Emotion as a cause of cognition in children

It should be noted that the majority of studies investigating the impact of emotion on cognition are conducted with adults. However, studies that do investigate this relationship in children seem to confirm the findings obtained with adults. For example, inducing a positive mood in children (e.g., providing a compliment or a gift) increases their performance on classic IQ measures, such as block design tasks from the WISC. Also, numerous studies have demonstrated that the quality of children's emotional experiences has an impact on their conceptualization of both emotions and cognitions. For example, de Rosnay and Harris (2002) found that children in secure emotional attachment relationships with their mothers display a higher level of knowledge about others' psychological states (i.e., theory of mind) than children in insecure attachment relationships. Secure children are also more independent and critical when they have to evaluate what other people (mother versus stranger) are saying about ambiguous objects (Corriveau et al., 2009). It should be noted that the quality of the attachment relationship of the child to the mother—or other parenting behaviors that such security entails—is not the only factor having an impact on children's theory of mind, or on their capacities to deal with what other people are saying. Their cognitive inhibition (and more generally their executive functions) are also related to their theory of mind (Melinder, Endestad & Magnussen, 2006), as well as their language (Pons, de Rosnay, Harris & Lecce, 2009).

A substantial number of studies have also shown that emotions such as anxiety, but also joy, pride, shame, and fear, have an impact on several aspects of learning at school (e.g., achievement, motivation, interest and goal setting). For instance, anxiety that is too intense can prevent pupils from living up to the best of their potential and can in some cases prevent them from being able to apply metacognitive reasoning altogether. When being presented with mathematical explanations, for example, some students feel as if a veil suddenly appears in front of them, stopping them from reaching the concentration level necessary to comprehend what they are being shown; anxiety thus prevents them from evaluating their knowledge and from engaging in the metacognitive processes necessary to solve the problems. More generally, these studies show that pupils' emotional competences (i.e., their capacity to experience, recognize, express, control the expression of, regulate the experience of, and understand emotions) have an impact on their school achievement (see Govaerts & Grégoire, 2004; Lafortune & Pons, 2005 for a review).

6. Conclusion

The different findings presented in this chapter can be summarized into three main results. (1) Some previously encoded or naturally conditioned emotional reactions may be able to be elicited without the intervention of cognition; via a direct biological appraisal of the stimulus and without the involvement of the cortex in this appraisal. Surprisingly, the reverse function has not been so well documented; maybe because the notion of cognition being caused by emotion seems too far-fetched. In any case, the possibility of the occasional occurrence of either emotional or cognitive reactions, void of the influence of the other, does not mean that these two functions do not (usually) interact. (2) In fact, numerous studies have demonstrated that many emotional reactions are caused by the individual's cognitive appraisal of the stimuli coming from his/her body, mind and environment. Also, many studies show a robust relation between children's cognitive understanding of emotion and their emotional experiences in a social context, as well as between children's understanding of emotion regulation and their own emotional well-being. (3) Correspondingly, another line of studies has shown that emotional arousal and/or valence have an impact on, for example, memory, attention, and creativity. This impact is neither linear nor symmetrical: emotional arousal has to be neither too low nor too high to have an optimum impact and the impact of negative emotions seems clearer than the impact of positive emotions.

Continuity and circularity between cognition and emotion

The findings of such studies suggest that the impact of emotional and cognitive processes on each other may not be linear, but rather have circular characteristics. Emotion and cognition may be described as two languages present in each individual to represent and communicate about the world in an inter-dependant manner; each individual being emotionally and cognitively bilingual, these two languages interact with one another continuously. Indeed, when looking at the different ways in which one can influence the other, it seems difficult to identify either cognition or emotion as the unique driving force in the so-called causal relationship. The allocation of cause, in many cases, may depend on the moment you are taking the snapshot in the continuous flow of the person's subjective experience (e.g., "I am depressed which makes me focus my attention on depressive information, which in turn reinforces my depression, which in re-turn makes me focus on negative information, etc."). Moreover, as a function of the situation (context, circumstances, etc.) and the individual (personality, level of development, etc.), an individual's mental functioning may be dominated by cognitive or emotional processes. We can speculate that the absence of this circularity between cognition and emotion could even be dysfunctional for the individual. Indeed, we may even speculate that any theoretical attempt to reduce this cognitive and emotional circularity to a linear relationship would ultimately result in a conceptual cul-de-sac both for the researcher and the practitioner in psychological sciences.

Continuity and circularity between research and practice

Finally, although most of the studies reported in this chapter have been conducted in laboratories an increasing number of scientific studies seems to confirm, with some nuances, the continuous and circular impact of cognition and emotion at school and in the clinical context. In the future, it would be interesting to further investigate this continuous and circular impact of cognition and emotion in the world of education and the clinical world. Such investigations could have a positive influence on pupils' school achievement, patient's psychological well-being and on the quality of teachers' and psychotherapists' competences. In return, such investigations would also test the validity of our understanding of the relation between cognition and emotion. Indeed, it is one thing to demonstrate the logical coherence (the truth) and the empirical correspondence (the objectivity) of this understanding but it is another thing altogether to demonstrate that such an understanding can result in pragmatic changes and improvements in the world of educational and clinical practice. Any attempt to break the continuity and circularity between research and practice would then result in a conceptual and practical dead end (Pons, Doudin & Cuisinier, 2007).

References

Beck, A. (1976). Cognitive therapy and the emotional disorders. New York: Meridian.

Borge, A.-I. (2007). Resiliens i praksis - teori og empiri i et norsk perspektiv. Oslo: Gyldendal Akademisk Forlag.

Braisby, N., & Gellatly, A. (Eds.) (2005). Cognitive psychology. Oxford: Oxford University Press.

Brennen, T., Dybdahl, R., & Kapidzic, A. (2007). Trauma-related and neutral false memories in war-induced Posttraumatic Stress Disorder. Consciousness and Cognition, 16, 877-885.

Cacioppo, J., Berntson, G., Larsen, J., Poehlmann, K., & Ito, T. (2000). The |psychophysiology of emotion. In M. Lewis & J. Haviland-Jones (Eds.) Handbook of emotions (pp. 173-191). New York: The Guilford Press.

Corriveau, K. H., Harris, P. L., Meins, E., Fernyhough, C., Arnott, B., Elliott, L., Liddle, B., Hearn, A., Vittorini, L., & de Rosnay, M. (2009) Young children's trust in their mother's claims: Longitudinal links with attachment security in infancy. Child Development, 80(3), 750-761.

Cosmides, L., & Tooby, J. (2000). Evolutionary psychology and the meotions. In M. Lewis & J. Haviland-Jones (Eds.) Handbook of emotions (pp. 91-115). New York: The Guilford Press.

Dalgleish, T., & Power, M. (1999). Handbook of cognition and emotion. Chichester: John Wiley.

Damasio, A. (1994). Descartes' error: Emotion, reason and the human brain. New York: Putnam.

Darwin, C. (1872/1899). The expression of the emotions in man and animals. New York: D Appleton and Company (Plain Label Books).

Davidson, R., Scherer, K., & Goldsmith, H. (Eds.) (2003). Handbook of affective sciences. Oxford: Oxford University Press.

de Rosnay, M. & Harris, P. L. (2002). Individual differences in children's understanding of emotion: The roles of attachment and language. Attachment &

Human Development. 4 (1). 39-54.

de Rosnay, M., Harris, P., & Pons, F. (2008). Emotion understanding and developmental psychopathology in young children. C. Sharp, P. Fonagy & I. Goodyer (Eds), Social Cognition and Developmental Psychopathology (pp. 343-385). Oxford: Oxford University Press

Eich, E., & Forgas, J. (2003). Mood, cognition, and memory. In A. Healy & R. Proctor, Robert (Eds.). Handbook of psychology: Experimental psychology, Vol. 4. (pp. 61-83). Hoboken: John Wiley.

Ekman, P. (1999). Basic Emotions. In T. Dalgleish and M. Power (Eds.). Handbook of Cognition and Emotion. Sussex, U.K.: John Wiley & Sons, Ltd.

Ekman, P., & Rosenberg, E. (Eds.) (2005). What the face reveals? Basic and applied studies of spontaneous expression using the facial action coding system. (FACS). Oxford: Oxford University Press.

Endrerud, M., & Vikan, A. (2007). Five to seven year old children's strategies for regulating anger, sadness, and fear. Nordic Psychology, 59, 127-134

Eysenck, M., Derakshan, N., Santos, R., & Calvo, M. (2007). Anxiety and cognitive performance: Attentional control theory. Emotion 7(2), 336-353.

Freud, S. (1905/2002). The joke and its relation to the unconscious. London: Penguin Books.

Frijda, N. (1986). The emotions. Cambridge: Cambridge University Press.

Govaerts, S. & Grégoire, J. (2004). Stressful academic situations: Study on appraisal variables in adolescence. European Review of Applied Psychology, 54, 261-271.

Gumora, G., & Arsenio, W. (2002). Emotionality, emotion regulation and school performance in middle school children. Journal of School Psychology, 40, 395-413.

Haga, S., & Kraft, P. (2006). The role of emotion-regulation and personal self-consciousness for subjective well-being and depressed mood. Psychology and Health, 21. 61-71

Harris, P. L. (1989). Children and emotion: The development of psychological understanding. Oxford: Blackwell.

Kappas, A. (2006). Appraisal are direct, immediate, intuitive, and unwitting… and some are reflective… Cognition and Emotion, 20(7), 952-975.

Lafortune, L., & Pons, F. (2005). The role of anxiety in metacognition in mathematics. In F. Pons, D. Hancock, L. Lafortune & P.-A. Doudin (Eds.), Emotions in learning (pp. 139-161). Aalborg: Aalborg University Press.

Lazarus, R. (1982). Thoughts on the relation between emotion and cognition. American Psychologist, 37, 1019-1024.

Lazarus, R. (1984). On the primacy of cognition. American Psychologist, 39, 124-129.

Lazarus, R. S. (1991) Emotion and adaptation. Oxford: Oxford University Press.

LeDoux, J. (1996). The emotional brain: The mysterious underpinnings of emotional life. New York: Simon & Schuster.

Lewis, M., & Haviland-Jones, J. (Eds.) (2000). Handbook of emotions. New York: The Guilford Press.

Li, W., Zinbarg, R. E., Boehm, S. G., & Paller, K. A. (2008). Neural and behavioral evidence for affective priming from unconsciously perceived emotional facial expressions and the influence of trait anxiety. Journal of Cognitive Neuroscience, 20, 95-107.

MacLeod, C. (2005). The Stroop Task in clinical research. In A. Wenzel & D. Rubin (Eds.). Cognitive methods and their application to clinical research. (pp. 41-62). Washington: American Psychological Association.

Manstead, N., Frijda, N., & A. Fischer (Eds.) (2004). Feelings and emotions: The Amsterdam Symposium. Cambridge: Cambridge University Press.

Matt, G., Vasquez, C., & Campbell, W. (1992). Mood-congruent recall of affectively toned stimuli: A meta-analytic review. Clinical Psychological Review, 12, 227-255.

McIntosh, D. (1996). Facial feedback hypotheses: Evidence, implications, and directions. Motivation and Emotion, 20, 121-147.

Melinder, A., Endestad, T., & Magnussen, S. (2006). Relations between episodic memory, suggestibility, theory of mind, and cognitive inhibition in the preschool child. Scandinavian Journal of Psychology, 47. 485-495.

Monsen, J., & Monsen, K. (1999). Affects and affect consciousness - A psychotherapy model integrating Silvan Tomkins' affect and script theory within the framework of self psychology. In A. Goldberg (Ed.), Pluralisms in self psychology. Progress in self psychology (pp. 287-307). Hillsdale: The Analytic Press.

Overskeid, G. (2007). Looking for Skinner and finding Freud. American Psychologist, 62, 590-595.

Pascal, B. (1670/1998). Œuvres complètes. Paris : Gallimard.

Pessoa, L., Japee, S., Sturman, D., & Ungerleider, L. G. (2006). Target visibility and visual awareness modulate amygdala responses to fearful faces. Cerebral Cortex, 16, 366-375.

Piaget, J. (1954/1981). Intelligence and affectivity. Their relationship during child development. Palo Alto: Annual reviews.

Pons, F., de Rosnay, M., Harris, P., & Lecce, S. (2009). Theory of Mind and language in children. Impuls, 3, 30-41.

Pons, F., Doudin, P.-A., Cuisinier, F. (2007). Er integrering af forskning og praksis en utopi? In S. Brinkmann & L. Tanggaard (Eds.). Psykologi: Forskning og profession (pp. 49-68). Copenhagen: Hans Reitzels Forlag.

Pons, F., & Harris, P. (2005). Longitudinal change and longitudinal stability of individual differences in children's emotion understanding. Cognition and Emotion, 19(8), 1158-1174.

Pons, F., Harris, P., & de Rosnay, M. (2004). Emotion comprehension between 3 and 11 years: Developmental periods and hierarchical organizations. European Journal of Developmental Psychology, 1(2), 127-152.

Pons, F., Harris, P., & Doudin, P.-A. (2002). Teaching emotion understanding. European Journal of Psychology of Education, 17(3), 293-304.

Roseman, I. (1984). Cognitive determinants of emotions: A structural theory. In P. Shaver (Ed.), Review of personality and social psychology. Volume 5. (pp. 11-36). Beverly Hills: Sage.

Schachter, S., & Singer, J. (1962). Cognitive, social and physiological determinants of emotional state. Psychological Review, 69, 379-399.

Scherer, K. (1984). On the nature and function of emotion: A component process approach. In K. Scherer & P. Ekman (Eds.), Approaches to emotion (pp. 293-318). Hillsdale: Lawrence Erlbaum.

Scherer, K., Schoor, A., & Johnstone, T. (Eds.) (2001). Appraisal processes in emotion: Theory, methods, research. New York: Oxford University Press.

Skoe, E., Eisenberg, N., & Cumberland, A. (2002). The role of reported emotion in real-life and hypothetical moral dilemmas. Personality and Social Psychology Bulletin, 28, 962-973.

Smith, C. (1989). Dimensions of appraisal and physiological response in emotion. Journal of Personality and Social Psychology, 56, 339-353.

Solomon, R. C. (2000). The philosophy of emotion. In M. Lewis & J. M. Haviland-Jones (Eds.). Handbook of Emotions (2nd Ed) (pp. 3-15). New York: The Guilford Press.

Vogt, B. A. & Devinsky, O. (2000). Topography and relationships of mind and brain. In Mayer, E. A. & Saper, C. B. (Eds.). Progress in Brain Research Vol. 122: The Biological Basis for Mind Body Interactions. Amsterdam: Elsevier.

Yerkes, R. M., & Dodson, J. D. (1908). The relation of strength of stimulus to rapidity of habit-formation. Journal of Comparative Neurology and Psychology, 18, 459-482.

Zajonc, R. (1980). Feeling and thinking: Preferences need no inferences. American Psychologist, 35, 151-175.

Zajonc, R. (1984). On the primacy of affect. American Psychologist, 39, 117-123.

Chapter 2

Entertainment, emotions and personality: Why our preferences for media entertainment differ?

Christian Jantzen and Mikael Vetner

1. Entertainment is 'serious business'

A very substantial portion of our media fare is in some way entertaining. The total turn over of Hollywood, the video game industry, porn, music labels, publishing houses, in TV production, on-line betting and other entertainment products adds up to a tremendous amount. The more 'main stream' parts of the entertainment industry (i.e. excluding e.g. porn and betting) is thus expected to reach a turn over of $1,8 trillion in 2010 and is currently growing with 6,6% each year (Price Waterhouse Coopers 2006). Nonetheless research in entertainment is still relatively sparse both in regard to issues of industrial production and distribution (e.g. media concentration and globalization) and when it comes to the actual uses of entertainment by viewers, listeners and players. Only the critical perspective on the cultural and social impact of entertainment can rely on a long and continuous tradition (e.g. Adorno and Horkheimer 1997/1945).

Entertainment is serious business, not only for the industry or society at large but also for its users. This article deals with the gratification TV viewers or video game players derive from entertainment programs. Our basic assumption is, that people are motivated for entertainment not least because this activity is pleasurable and emotionally satisfying. The experiential qualities generated by being entertained have a significant impact on individuals' physical, psychological and social well-being.

It seems obvious that not all individuals are motivated by or are motivated for the exact same experiential qualities or the same entertainment programs. What some people find thrilling is anxiety provoking to others. Some users may evaluate a program as evocative and moving whereas others perceive it as boring or trivial. Such differences in taste and preferences are to a large extent systematic. They are firstly founded in socially learned or biologically based dispositions towards a range of functionally equivalent situations or objects. Secondly, large groups of individuals are more or less imbued with almost similar dispositions. This constitutes segments, each characterized by a distinct set of motivations and an identifiable behavioral style. Systematic dispositions are largely determined by situational factors and personality traits. Personality traits stabilize behavior across different situations, in different domains and at different times. They predict what a person "will do when placed in a given situation" (Catell 1965, p. 118), and which pleasures, emotions or actions a person will be motivated for.

It is hence our intention to contribute to an understanding of the influence of personality factors on differences in users' preferences for entertainment and in their actions in regard to entertaining programs. Little research has been done in this particular field (Hartmann and Klimmt 2006, Weaver 2000). We address this issue by presenting a typology of pleasures and relating these experiential qualities to subjective well-being and emotions. Emotions, understood as "activation readiness" (Frijda 2007), are crucial for individuals' motivation for and dispositions towards entertainment programs. By arguing for this connection we furthermore try to illustrate how mass mediated entertainment aims at bridging the dispositional differences between segments to reach large audiences. This is typically done, by crafting the aesthetic structure in such a way that the program appeals to different emotional dispositions simultaneously. We start our discussion by defining the aesthetic and play-like character of entertainment.

2. Entertainment as a form of play

Wanting to entertain others and taking delight in being entertained is a very human urge. Some evolutionary psychologists go so far as to suggest that this ability is a specific human trait contributing to the survival and success of our species (Ohler and Nieding 2006). In contrast to other mammals, entertainment appears to be an independent goal for humans throughout their whole life span. A relatively simple explanation for this is that evolution has created a considerable amount of spare-time for our species. Entertainment is a leisure activity that helps to fill the non-working hours in an attractive way (Zillmann 2000a).

The weak spot in this argument is, that it does not sufficiently explain why precisely entertainment is such an attractive activity for passing the time. Why not indulge in quite different actions? Like so it seems reasonable to assume that entertainment serves other evolutionary purposes than just being a mere pastime. Such a suggestion is in line with Dissanyake's (1992) argument for the role of aesthetics in the development of the human species. According to her, the ability of aesthetics to regulate emotions and moods has been paramount to human evolution. By mitigating negative emotions, promoting positive ones and increasing social coherence aesthetics contributes to physiological, psychological and social well-being, which is precisely why people are motivated to seek out aesthetically pleasing objects and experiences.

The fact, that this universal aesthetic competence is expressed in many different cultural forms furthermore implies that there is no ontological difference between 'high' and 'low' culture. Art and entertainment share the same aesthetic premises. Firstly, aesthetics is an operation characterized by "making special": certain features of the object are exaggerated, beautified, repeated or otherwise overemphasized. Secondly, aesthetics de-contextualizes the object by framing it differently from ordinary use. Aesthetics concerns issues and depends on actions other than those characterizing quotidian life. In this way aesthetics establishes another reality, outside the realm of everyday life. An aesthetic object resembles ordinary ones, albeit some of the object's features are presented in an artificial way. The effect is, that aesthetic objects are perceived as if they where 'real', although their users are conscious of the fact, that they are not (Vaihinger 1952/1911). Audiences for example interact "para-socially" with actors on the screen: as if both parties share the same reality (e.g. being in the same room), but the audience is well aware that this is not actually the case (Horton and Wohl 1956).

Our way of perceiving and responding to aesthetic objects is no different from ordinary objects. But this does not keep us from relating aesthetically to those objects. This has made evolutionary psychologists suggest that entertainment (as well as art in general) must be conceived as play (Vorderer 2001). Three aspects define play (Oerter 1999):

1. Play is intrinsically motivated and as such highly attractive
2. Play involves a change in our perception of reality by establishing another reality
3. Play is highly suited for numerous repetitions.

We have already dealt with the second aspect, and it seems equally obvious that the serial production and fixed program formats of mediated entertainment promote the third aspect. Moreover, by being repeated the roles of both entertainer and the entertained (i.e. the audience) become ritualized (Rubin 1984). The first aspect emphasizes, that being entertained by a media program is not a simple response to an entertaining stimulus. Entertainment presupposes – just like play – active participation from the entertained. Furthermore this aspect stresses that seeking and wanting entertainment is primarily done for internal purposes. It is "autotelic": i.e. an activity not defined by external factors (like e.g. work) or done to obtain external rewards (e.g. money or status).

The perceptions, feeling and insights, that may be promoted by participation in this other reality of entertainment (the second aspect), adds to the attractiveness of the activity (the first aspect). Comedies, crime series, thrillers, horror movies, talk-shows, quizzes and game-shows, sports programs, reality-television, music programs, lifestyle formats and many other are first and foremost meant to be entertaining. Even informative programs – the news, documentaries or public debates – often have to be entertaining in some respect. This gamut of entertaining products is aiming at various perceptions, feelings and insights, and quite different pleasures are derived from these products. Pleasure is in no way a simple quality (see below). In fact, the quality and quantity of pleasure may vary remarkably during the program, and there may be considerable difference between the internal effects during and after the program.

'Good' entertainment is often characterized by generating positive emotions while watching e.g. a show, but sadness (a negative emotion) when the show is over. This is typical for other types of play as well: post coitam omne animal triste est. The narrative structure or sequence in the entertaining program itself is moreover marked by perpetual fluctuations in the quantity of pleasure. Excitement in- or decreases, leading to shifts in attention and involvement (Pfaff 2006). And emotionally a program may often be composed of antagonistic feelings ranging from fear to relaxation (a horror movie) or from disgust to excitement (a jack ass program). The dominant experience produced by 'good' entertainment may in addition even be quite the opposite of pleasure. The tragic fate of the heroines in Flaubert's Madame Bovary or Tolstoy's Anna Karenina does not disqualify these products as 'good' entertainment. Obviously, this goes for modern works of fiction as well. The lack of a 'happy ending' might in such cases lead to emotional reactions quite distinct from anger or frustration – i.e. to purification – precisely because the viewer or reader has consciously invested emotions in another reality. This is due to the playful qualities of entertainment, as stressed by Vorderer (op.cit. p. 258): "So, what exactly is entertainment? It's an experience that helps media users to cope with their everyday life. [...] It's what media users seek very often, and to their own advantage."

The experiences generated by entertainment may be quite versatile: "For some, it's pleasure seeking in boring situations or compensation in burdening situations; for others it's compensation in a depriving situation, fulfillment of needs in unsatisfactory situations, and self-enhancement or even self-realization when they are – for whatever reason – ready for it" (ibid.). Before such differences in entertainment preferences can be accounted for more systematically, we have to clarify various experiential qualities.

3. Entertainment and experiences

Experiences are bodily, mental and social effects produced in and by the user. Dealing with entertainment from the perspective of experiences implies changing the focus from the stimuli transmitted by the producers of entertainment programs to the intrinsically motivated responses generated by the audience (the first aspect of play). Enumerating such experiences produces a long list of different qualities: e.g. happy, boring, stimulating, relaxing, stressing, monotonous, depressing, sad, disappointing, etc. Such a list easily becomes just as pointless as the enumeration of entertaining programs (see above).

Actually, only few attempts have been made at categorizing fundamental experiential qualities. One of the attempts is made by Bosshart & Macconi (1998), and is inspired by Tiger's (1992) typology of pleasures. We have elaborated on this categorization, firstly to distinguish more efficiently between physiological types of pleasure related to changes in the organism's state of arousal. Secondly, our classification aims at capturing those 'good' experiential qualities of programmes or products, which at first glance seem pain rather than pleasure related (e.g. tragic or certain melodramatic forms).

Feeling entertained means to be moved sensually/bodily and emotionally and/or to be addressed on concerns of more profound importance for one's personal or social well-being rather than the issues provided by the daily stream of information. Entertainment is hence related to physiological as well as identity-oriented experiences. Physiological experiences are caused

by changes in the organism's state of arousal. Such changes can go in two different directions:
- Stimulation, which increases the state of arousal and may be experienced as both pleasurable (e.g. excitement, elation or alternation) and painful (e.g. stress, tension or anxiety)
- Relaxation, which decreases the state of arousal and may be experienced as both pleasurable (e.g. tranquility, evocation or harmony) and painful (e.g. boredom, monotony or sadness).

Entertainment programs can cater for stimulation or relaxation or both of them. But it is the mood and motivation of each viewer or reader that decides whether 'good' experiences will be produced or not. A simple logic generalized by "mood management theory" (Zillmann 2000b) suggests that stressed users will prefer relaxing programs, while bored users will strive for stimulating programs. Pleasurably excited viewers will furthermore attempt to elongate their enjoyment by opting for stimulation, just like a pleasurably relaxed audience most probably will try to prolong their harmonic state. The actual mood of the user is hence a good indicator of, which programs will be chosen in a given situation. But so are earlier experiences (by way of reinforcement) and personality traits (more on this below). We are not always that interested in X-factor or gardening programs, and such programs are not equally relevant for all audiences.

Identity-oriented experiences come in two main categories too:
- Ego-pleasures confirming or destabilizing the agent's (i.e. viewer's) competences, wit and autonomy
- Socio-pleasures confirming or destabilizing the agent's ability to relate emotionally to others and to identify with others' attitudes and behavior.

These types of experiencing presuppose agents: i.e. individuals who can act skillfully in respect to the media fare and use programs for identity affirming or developing purposes. As viewer of Britain's Got Talent each member of the audience may become an integral part of the Paul Potts' fan or hate groups (socio-experiences) or on the other hand take pleasure in discerning the motives, arguments or gestures of Simon Cowell, the creative genius of the program as well as one of its jurors (ego-experiences). Or watching TV chef

Keith Floyd preparing meals while mocking French pronunciation on BBC may elicit socio- (the mockery) as well as ego-pleasures (e.g. knowing more than Floyd).

But what pleasures may be derived from the agony of watching other persons' despair and suffering? This question cannot be readily answered within the framework of "mood management", which favors explanations based on physiological pleasures (Oliver 2003). But the play-perspective on entertainment might be helpful here. Knowing that the tragedy is acted out some other place (i.e. in other people's life or in a fictional universe), without the viewer being explicitly affected by it or able to control it might elicit quite different responses:

- Ideo-pleasures confirming that anger and activism are justified (when harm is done to 'heroes' or 'innocents') or that revenge or justice is righteous (when 'villains' are brought down)
- Purification pleasures involving the audience in the protagonist's despair, thus giving the viewer or reader an emotional insight into more profound aspects of existence.

Purification and justification could be labeled the moral experience of entertainment. The punishment of scoundrels is justified, just like the audience's activism spurred as it is by the viewers insight into injustice. Purification is a well-known effect in tragedy: namely catharsis, the 'purgatory' climax of the plot accompanied by strong emotions (e.g. pity or sorrow) caused by the audience's involvement in the hero's tragic fate, and leading to the acknowledgement of virtue and a feeling of revitalization on the part of each viewer or reader (Aristotle 1996). Tragedy thus teaches its audience to feel emotions in the proper way and to learn lessons about their own way of life. This emotional resolution of the plot is pleasurable (cf. Scheele and DuBois 2006). Unresolved conflicts are either unpleasant (tension, stress) or they spur the audience to take action themselves (ideo-pleasures) – a technique utilized in social(ist) realism and in those early Bolshevist experiments with the theatrical form, Agitprop and Proletkul't (Fokkema and Kunne-Ibsch 1979, p. 94 ff.).

Ideo- and purification pleasures show how entertainment as a type of play enables agents to cope with negative aspects of existence and thereby generate positive experiences. Anxiety, frustration and sorrow and other negative emotions are transformed into fundamental insights into the human condition or a specific acknowledgement of social injustice. This might promote a reversal of emotions: anxiety may turn into joy (e.g. malice), sorrow into relief (in tragedy) or frustration into anger (injustice). These pleasures are thus connected to physiological pleasures of in- or decreased arousal. But they also have identity effects. Activism may for example enhance social identity (cf. Tajfel 1978), whereas purification as well as malicious pleasures may teach the agent lessons on personal identity by overcoming or emphasizing discrepancies between the actual, the ideal and the normative self (cf. Higgins 1987).

From an experiential perspective entertainment hence functions as "emotion regulation" (Dissanyake 1992) or "mood management" (Festinger 1957, Zillmann 1988, 2000b). It elongates positive moods or turns negative emotions into positive ones. But secondly, entertainment also functions as "identity facilitation". Entertainment enables agents to actualize hitherto hidden potentials (ego-pleasures) and/or to affirm their social belonging (socio-pleasures). Specific entertainment programs typically invites to physiological as well as identity-oriented pleasures. In addition, a 'good' experience often consists of multiple pleasures. As shown in some of the mentioned examples, different types of pleasure interrelate in producing such 'good' experiences. The structure of experiencing should therefore be understood as a dynamic relation between instantaneous changes in arousal (physiological pleasures) and much more long-lasting identity effects, mediated by emotionally based changes in behavior and cognitively based alterations in attitude (Jantzen and Vetner 2007). By influencing the arousal as well as the identity pole in this structure, entertainment contributes crucially to subjective well-being.

4. Experiences and well-being

The emergence of "positive psychology" in the last decades has made the increase or maintenance of well-being and happiness a topic of serious research as well as therapeutic interventions (e.g. Csikszentmihalyi 1993, Peterson and Seligman 2004). In this respect entertainment is much more than superficial pastime, because well-being depends crucially on both physiological and identity-related pleasures – the key attractors in entertaining experiences. But how 'the good life' should precisely be conceived is an ancient matter of debate. Two main traditions have emerged in the history of ideas. The first, named "hedonic well-being", stresses that sensual pleasure is paramount to happiness (cf. Bentham 2007/1789). Well-being is characterized by the absence of physiological needs. This position is criticized as being simplistic and reductive (cf. Nozick 1974, p. 43 ff). It might even prove harmful to real psychological well-being, according to followers of the second tradition (Ryan and Deci 2001). This tradition, named "eudaimonic well-being" (from Greek daimon: "little god"), stresses the importance for well-being of actualizing inner capabilities and deeper longings (Aristotle 1998). The pursuit of more 'simple' pleasures would from this perspective cloud the quest for self-development, which is seminal to actualizing the self's potentials.

Modern psychology has predominantly focused on the hedonic tradition (cf. Schreier 2006). The presence of positive emotions, absence of negative ones and the cognitive evaluation of life satisfaction are the determinant factors of subjective well-being (Kahneman, Diener and Schwarz 1999). In this perspective, individuals are – whether cognizant of this or not – motivated by an urge to maximize or maintain pleasure and minimize or alleviate pain. They will actively avoid situations or objects that may elicit negative emotions and prefer options that promise gratification and positive emotions. In regard to entertainment, mood management theory predicts behavior according to this hedonic conception of motivation.

In comparison, the eudaimonic perspective is less developed in psychology, although it has a strong and well-established tradition in moral philosophy. This perspective stresses the importance of both personal and social development for subjective well-being. But there is as yet no theoretical agreement on how these two sides should be balanced. One of the dominant theories, "self-determination theory" suggests that the satisfaction of three psychological needs is decisive for psychological growth, inner motivation, personal integrity, experiences of vitality and self-congruency (Ryan and Deci 2000):

- Autonomy: i.e. the ability to exert own free will
- Competence: i.e. the ability to utilize own capabilities
- Relatedness: i.e. the ability to connect to other people.

These needs are by and large related to ego-pleasures. Other theories have stressed the importance of socio-pleasures by pointing at the impact of having a sense of belonging, feeling accepted and partaking in a collective fate for subjective well-being (Keyes 1998). A series of indicators may be used to measure social well-being:

- Social integration expressing the individual's relationship to society and community
- Social acceptance expressing the individual's trust in others
- Social contribution expressing the individual's evaluation of his or hers contribution to society and community
- Social actualization expressing the individual's evaluation of a society's potentials for development and its ability to determine its own fate
- Social coherence expressing the individual's appraisal that society is discernible, sensible and predictable.

Personal and social well-being are both related to identity-oriented pleasures. Ego-pleasures find gratification in self-actualization (personal well-being). Socio-pleasures, on the other hand, are satisfied by experiencing interdependence and by sharing consciousness with others. These two ways of conceptualizing eudaimonic well-being thus point at two different ways of defining identity: i.e. either in terms of self-development or in terms of social development. These are extremes on the eudaimonic (or identity-defining) dimension, which is one of the guidelines in the individual's decision-making on and evaluations of the supply of entertainment (and, more generally, in regard to the options in life). This dimension is one of the two main axes in the psychographic segmentation model, we will outline below.

5. Positive and negative emotions

The identity-defining dimension expresses how an individual is motivated by personal or social well-being in striving for 'the good life'. Entertainment may contribute to strengthen or weaken an individual's sense of autonomy and competence (i.e. the ego-pole). It may also increase or decrease the sense of being integrated in and accepted or valued by a community (i.e. the group-pole).

But the physiological pleasures related to hedonic well-being are of equal importance for understanding psychographic differences in preferences. Such differences are partly situational: i.e. depending on the actual setting of the media use (e.g. morning, noon, evening or weekday, weekend, holiday) and on the actual state of arousal of the user (bored, stressed, relaxed, excited, etc.). But personality traits also contribute to these differences. Some individual's are generally more motivated for challenging entertainment, while others typically prefer relaxing programs. Individuals who frequently indulge in first person shooter games will find this product more interesting and relevant than e.g. Facebook, historical novels, fantasy, or programs on interior decoration. This interest and relevance is to a wide extent determined by their personality.

Such differences in interest and relevance illustrate how entertainment functions as emotion regulation, because entertainment programs are selected and evaluated for their ability to adjust the organism's arousal to a preferred state and thereby produce an attractive emotional response. Emotions are automatic reactions triggered by evaluations of changes in the environment, but controlled to make the response match social norms (Frijda 2007). First person shooter games might be attractive for their target audience precisely by allowing the player to exert violence without this having serious consequences for his or her social position. In the other reality of the game aggression - prohibited in ordinary reality - is adequate behavior: it is part of the game's own (but special) set of norms.

While emotional psychologists tend to agree on the function of emotions, there is more disagreement on the role of emotions in the processing of stimuli. We adhere to those theories, inspired by modern neuroscience, which assume that emotions are responses that aim at changing behavior and that they may be activated in advance of cognitive processing (Damasio 1994, LeDoux 1996, Zajonc 1980, Öhman and Wiens 2004). Very little agreement exists on the issue of how many emotions may be discerned and how they are to be classified (cf. Ortony and Turner 1990). The following diagram, suggested by Rolls (2005, p. 14), shows the relation between some fundamental emotions:

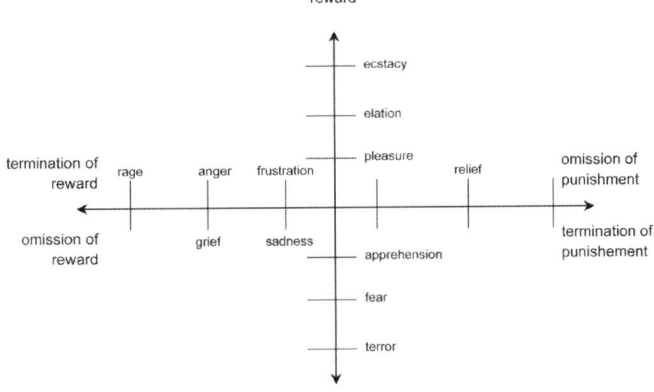

Figure 1. Rolls' diagram of emotions

This diagram illustrates primary, i.e. biologically based emotions – not secondary, and i.e. socially or culturally informed emotions like shame, guilt, jealousy, pride or shyness. The point of this model is, that the intensity of the emotion increases the further away it is from the diagram's centre. The vertical reward/punishment-axis is the primary dimension. Reward elicits positive emotions, whereas punishment produces negative emotions. The termination of reward or its absence also produces negative emotions in various degrees. Absence of punishment generates relief, a positive emotion.

To long for positive emotions (rewards or absence of punishment) is a very human trait. But negative emotions are seminal for survival by protecting the organism against too audacious actions (anxiety) and by making the organism react appropriately in dangerous situations (fear) or in cases of abuse (anger). They are warning systems increasing the state of arousal to a high level (alarm), which in the longer run becomes painful (stress). Entertainment hence functions to reduce tension (leading to relief) and to increase reward (joy, elation). 'Bad' entertainment is characterized by frustrating this longing for reward (leading to frustration) or by leaving the audience behind in unresolved tension when the program is over (anxiety, fear). The sadness experienced when a favorite program is terminated is on the other hand, and as stated above, an indication of positive experiences, while the program was running.

6. Emotion regulation and personality

It is obvious that all media users at times are motivated for arousing entertainment (reward orientation) but at other moments select relaxing programs (i.e. are oriented towards absence of punishment). It seems equally obvious that some groups of users more often prefer reward than other groups. Such differences are to a wide extent caused by personality traits, which stabilizes individual behavior and contributes to behavioral consistency across various domains. The psychology of personality has contributed to seminal knowledge on individual differences. According to Gray (1981) two opposite systems predict differences in personality traits: a behavioral activation system (BAS) characterized by impulsivity and a behavioral inhibition system (BIS) characterized by anxiety. Individuals who have high impulsivity as a dominant trait are sensitive to reward, while individuals with high anxiety are sensitive to punishment or the absence of reward. Impulsive individuals are thus oriented towards the upper right corner in Rolls' diagram, whereas anxious individuals are oriented towards the lower left corner.

Gray's BAS/BIS-axis is derived from the dominant dimension in Eysenck's typology of personality, i.e. high vs. low extraversion (Eysenck 1967, Eysenck and Eysenck 1985). Indicators of extraversion are pro-social behavior, assertion, liveliness and high self-esteem. Extraverts are easy-going, motivated by sensual pleasure, and, as in Gray (1981), impulsive. Introverts, on the other hand, are less motivated by sensual pleasure, and have an introspective character. Eysenck's model has two additional dimensions:

- Neuroticism, characterized by anxiousness, depression, social isolation and shyness
- Psychotism, characterized by egocentricity, stimulation seeking, autonomy, creativity and socially deviant behavior.

These three dimensions are independent of one another, implying that individuals can score high measures on e.g. both extraversion and neuroticism, which can be shown in this figure:

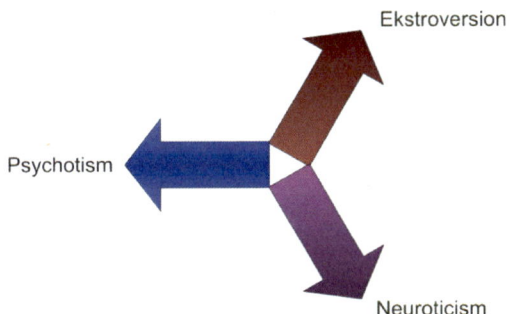

Figure 2. The three dimensions in Eysenck's theory of personality.

Eysenck's model is based on neurophysiology: i.e. on differences in the brain's energetic level. It assumes that a high degree of extraversion is caused by a low innate base-level of arousal. Individuals with this trait easily feel bored (understimulated). They are hence motivated to seek excitement and the company of others. In contrast, introverts have a high base-level of arousal, causing a tendency towards anxiety and irritability (overstimulation). This produces a disposition towards harmonic and relaxing experiences. To sum up: extroverts typically strive for stimulating physiological pleasures, while introverts find greater pleasure in less stimulating activities.

Recent research in behavioral endocrinology has produced new insights in the effects of hormones and neurotransmitters on individual differences. Panksepp's (1998) identification of seven independent emotional systems seems especially promising also for describing differences between various types of media entertainment (see Miron 2006): the seeking, fear, rage, lust, care, panic and play systems. The organizational psychologist Häusel (2004) has simplified this theory with the purpose of developing a segmentation tool for marketing and organizational change. Häusel has identified two fundamental emotional themes: a stabilization theme directed at protecting the organism against punishment and the destructive effects of continuous fear of punishment, and a spontaneity theme directed at reward and hence explorative in regard to various options life offers. The stability theme is derived from Panksepp's panic and fear systems and motivates the organism for:

- Avoiding risks (an urge for safety)
- Avoiding unnecessary alarm against risks (an urge for balance)
- Grasping control of risk (an urge for power).

The stability theme is fundamentally oriented towards establishing or maintaining balance and can thus be called preserving and pessimistic. The spontaneity theme on the other hand is optimistic and innovative. It is derived from Panksepp's seeking and play systems and motivates the organism for:

- Actively striving for risks (an urge for excitement)
- Accepting risks (an urge for stimulation)
- Warding the self against the effects of risks (an urge for comfort)

The spontaneity theme is fundamentally oriented towards stimulation. The urge for comfort is also related to the stability theme, because it is motivated by a belief that increasing care for oneself and others may minimize the workings of external risks. The urge for power (a stability theme) and the urge for excitement (a spontaneity theme) are derived from Panksepp's rage system. Individuals imbued with this trait strive for control, status and competition – for dominance. It is hence possible to sketch a model with three antagonistic forces and three additional sub-themes in the emotional processing of and motivation for stimuli:

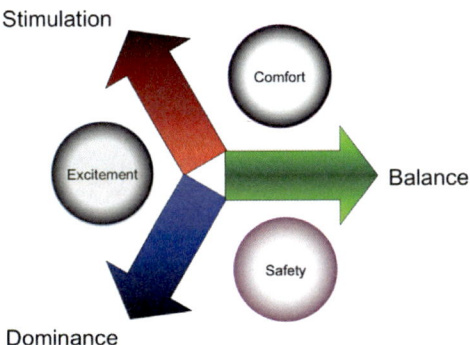

Figure 3. A behavioral endocrinology model of emotional systems inspired by Panksepp (1998) and Häusel (2004).

From the theories presented above some assumptions follow. Firstly, stable personality traits cause a more optimistic or pessimistic attitude towards life. Secondly, entertainment preferences are affected by these differences, because a main purpose of entertainment is to regulate emotionality. Users may seek entertainment to have exciting experiences, or on the contrary to mitigate or control the effects of negative emotions, so the level of arousal decreases – which also generates 'good' experiences.

The more optimistic attitude is marked by impulsivity and characterized by spontaneous decision-making. Individuals with such traits will appear to be extravert and motivated by sensual pleasure. They are physical active and seek personal challenges (stimulation), or they are socially active and value-based in their behavior (comfort). The more pessimistic attitude is marked by a higher degree of anxiousness and characterized by carefully planned decision-making. Individuals with such traits will appear to be introvert and motivated by an urge for social and/or personal stability: i.e. as privately and socially more insecure (safety) or as control and status oriented (dominance).

A more optimistic attitude hence correlates with the extravert trait in Eysenck's personality theory and the spontaneity theme in Häusel's segmentation model. On the other hand, a more pessimistic attitude correlates with the anxiety trait in Eysenck's theory (i.e. neuroticism) as well as the dominance theme in Häusel's model.

Our discussion of personality traits has produced a dimension with extraversion and introversion as its extremes. This insight can be combined with the dimension emanating from our discussion of eudaimonic well-being: i.e.

the identity-defining axis having ego- and socio-pleasures as its extremes. But our discussion has implicitly also shown a connection between these two dimensions. The extravert personality type can be either group-oriented and hence more motivated for socio-pleasures (i.e. as comfort, defined as caring for the community; cf. Keyes, above) or self-oriented and hence motivated for ego-pleasures (i.e. as stimulation, defined as self-development and vitality; cf. Ryan and Deci, above). Correspondingly, the introvert personality may be motivated either by an urge for safety (group-orientation) or by an urge to control the situation (self-orientation).

The correspondence between these two dimensions is illuminated by the fact, that the balance trait in Häusel's model combines the extravert strive for comfort with the introvert for safety. Both urges are directed towards social norms and socially defined normality. Moreover, Eysenck's personality trait with the unflattering label "psychotism" covers the extravert personality's urge for stimulation and creative expression and the introvert urge for upholding autonomy. In a positive vein, psychotism is characterized by a headstrong will to defy impeding social norms to reach own goals – i.e. a creative form of socially defiant behavior. The two dimensions produce four quadrants, shown in the following figure:

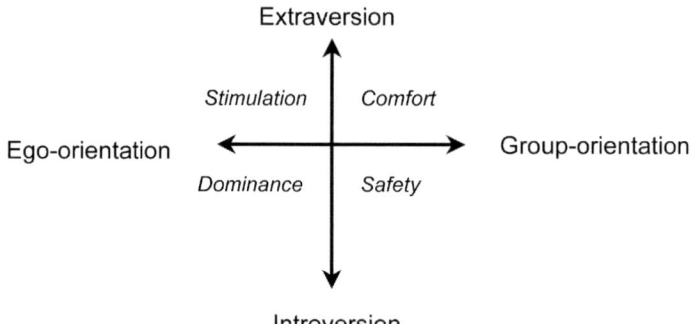

Figure 4. The two dimensions in our psychographic model constituting four elementary types of motivation.

This model is a hypothetical construct, composed of insights from various theories on personality, each based on extensive empirical research. It illustrates our hypothesis: viz. that even though most individuals will be motivated for the whole spectrum of experiential qualities that entertainment programs offer, there are significant individual differences as to which qualities are most often preferred. In other words, the four quadrants define separate behavioral styles (or dispositional patterns of expression), each more or less appealing to actual individuals. Mapped on the field of entertainment, this means, that different user segments have their own preferred set of entertainment genres (i.e. objects), their distinct ways of and reasons for seeking entertainment (motivation) and their specific types of gratification derived from entertainment programs ('good' experiences). These differences mark distinct entertainment styles.

7. Entertainment styles

A profound reason for the attraction exerted by entertainment is that it creates another reality, which produces the same emotional responses as those actions and events occurring in everyday life. Entertainment is a form of play in an autonomous universe. By consequence, our responses to entertainment are without real impact on our social standing or our sanity (cf. Geertz 1973). Closing our eyes during the most gruesome scene in a horror movie will not kill us. And weeping while watching a melodrama will rarely ruin our public reputation. Such strong emotions are facilitated by the aesthetics of entertainment. By being made special entertainment – like art – presents stimuli in a purer and more closed or finalized form than ordinary objects (cf. Dissanyake op.cit.). Closure implies an outlet for those tensions that the narrative of the entertainment program has helped to build up. Such tensions are in addition more crystallized than in ordinary life, because of 'purification': i.e. actions and events are carefully selected and magnified to fit the narration. Much of the 'noise' that often disturbs and diverts our attention in everyday life is absent.

Entertainment is useful to individuals' physical and/or social survival, because it allows them to cope with situations and emotions in a way that everyday life rarely does (cf. Vorderer op.cit.). Among other things, entertainment serves as:

- A refuge for responses, that are subdued in everyday life
- A 'time out' in regard to ordinary obligations, allowing for contact with emotions of profound character
- Self-oblivion, leading to proximity with other individuals who usually are kept at a distance
- A training course for experimenting with responses, different from those typically experienced in quotidian life

- A social mirror, where individuals can take joy in their own righteousness when confronted with others' misfortune.

Entertainment is hence a matter of having one's appetites and morals reaffirmed, of rediscovering forgotten aspects of one's identity, of transgressing one's limitations and of expanding one's social and emotional competences. A quiz-show like The Weakest Link (BBC) appeals to dominance-oriented individuals by affirming that knowledge is power, that it is worthwhile to make an effort and that ignorance should rightfully be punished: the weakest link is deservedly humiliated in public and expelled from the show. At the same time this show tells the safety-oriented individual, that wanting to stand out from the crowd is risky, and that those participants who try to excel without having the qualifications for doing so must receive their just punishment from the headmaster-like host. Stimulation-oriented individuals perhaps enjoy that victory not solely depends on barren factual knowledge but also on social skills – not least: the competence to detect opponents' motives and to decipher their calculations. More often than not, it is not the most knowledgeable but the cleverest player who turns out victorious. The comfort-oriented individual will be disgusted by the barbaric punishment theme of the program and by those flaws of character exposed by the players in their quest for scrappy prize money. Such an individual will perhaps be particularly disgusted by his or her own pleasure in watching these motives of punishment, revenge and treason displayed on the screen. In such cases, entertainment confronts users with their darker sides.

Increased knowledge of own tendencies and competences is one of the main attractions of entertainment. The life transmission of sport events on public screens and for huge audiences gratifies those individuals motivated by competition (the stimulation segment) as well as those spurred by community feelings (the comfort segment). But it is attractive for the dominance and safety segments too, because it allows such individuals to loosen self-control and to be carried away by collective enthusiasm. By being immersed in the mass of spectators these segments may learn that it is sometimes safe to let go. They may even act in ways that ordinarily seems prohibited by social standards (the safety segment) or by personal norms (the dominance segment). This illustrates how entertainment may promote self-oblivion or function as a training course.

A concept like the Dutch program Spoorloos ("Without a trace", KRO), which helps people to trace lost relatives, will presumably be attractive for the comfort-oriented segment, because it gives the viewer ample opportunity to relate empathically to other people's concerns and because the solution of the conflict – i.e. the finding of the lost relative – presupposes collaboration between many sympathetically inclined individuals. The program moreover confirms the safety-oriented segment in their conviction, that family is a social nucleus and that even a long-lasting social disorder may be overcome. For the dominance-oriented segment the idea that a problem may be solved by headstrong will and logical reasoning is a gratifying one. That logic often needs creativity and spontaneous decisions to reach a solution confirms the stimulation-oriented segment's attitude.

These examples illustrate how an entertainment program may appeal to distinctive experiential qualities in different segments. Entertainment can bridge differences between segments not by being emotionally bland or indistinct but on the contrary by being aesthetically constructed in such a way that the program offers tailored emotional gratification for distinct dispositions. This tailoring is in no way a simple matter. It is not the program genre that determines its emotional relevance: e.g. there does not exist such a thing like a 'crime-series-stimulus' evoking precise and predictable 'crime-series-satisfaction'. But there may exist a personality-based readiness to respond positively or negatively – i.e. to make emotional evaluations – to certain stimuli, which typically are found in crime-series, and that by reinforcement have generated motivation and preferences for precisely this kind of program. Crime series may for example meet the safety-oriented urge to see order restored and culprits punished. But The Weakest Link and many other programs may also satisfy this urge. A crime series like the award winning Danish Rejseholdet ("Unit One", DR), may in the same vein emotionally substitute quite different entertainment genres, for example the Dutch concept Spoorloos, by stressing a similar emotional theme: in this case the socio-pleasures of mutual collaboration as well as social coherence and actualization, typical of the comfort-oriented segment.

At best, program genres serve as an indication of whether the program will contain pleasurable stimuli or not. We know by experience that the theme of crime series is the destruction and restoration of social order and norms. That is precisely why this genre seems an obvious choice if we are catering for experiences that may reaffirm safety. But our examples also illustrate, that entertainment preferences not solely are a matter of confirming pre-existing motivational structures. Prior to the restoration of order, crime-series may have provided safety-oriented individuals with a titillating insight in a realm of pleasures that they would prefer to avoid in 'real' life. A quiz show like The Weakest Link may display darker sentiments in the comfort-oriented individual than he or she would like to admit, while more pessimistically inclined individuals may utilize entertainment as an outlet for optimistic reactions (e.g. enthusiasm generated from watching sport in a crowd). The effect of entertainment could in this respect even be called therapeutic. It produces opportunities for integrating underdeveloped emotional aspects in our motivational structure. In line with our argument on the positive outcomes of apparently negative experiential qualities, this therapeutic effect may function to increase awareness and consciousness (catharsis) as well as to instigate action (activism).

The consequences of being entertained are of course rarely that drastic. But by allowing us to view the world from a different perspective or with somebody else's view, these programs generate an emotional insight that contributes to our knowledge of the world (Clore and Gasper 2000). Travel programs like Lonely Planet and Global Trekker (both BBC) are probably so immensely popular, because they produce such vicarious experiences. While we follow in the footsteps of Ian Wright we partake in a world, in which we could have been physically present if only we had dared or been able to do so. We are activated and get excited, without having to leave the comfort of our couch. By being a form of play entertainment allows for actions and emotions that would have been most unwelcome in 'real' life. One is invited to experiment with one's taste, feelings, mind-set, expressions or reactions without risking too much personally or socially. Entertainment facilitates such experiments by affording its users an opportunity either to put themselves in the protagonist's place (empathy, typical of fiction), to submerge in an anonymous crowd (immersion), or to act according to norms that would otherwise be perceived as deviant (acting out, typical of some computer games).

From this perspective entertainment functions as a training course. It offers relatively safe frames outside the realm of everyday life for transgressing or developing specific aspects of our identity. It nonetheless seems obvious that individuals neither wish to develop in the same manner nor are motivated by exactly the same personality traits. A psychographic view on entertainment thus stresses the following aspects of entertainment:

- Not everything is just as entertaining to everybody: what some people

for example find boring or trivial is exciting and challenging to others
- Those programs that nearly everybody enjoys are entertaining to different segments for distinctive reasons, determined by personality traits
- Because entertaining experiences are the outcome of emotional processing of input (stimuli) different entertainment programs can substitute one another: it is not the specific qualities of the input that motivates users but the urge for specific ways of processing
- Entertainment contributes to hedonic as well as eudaimonic well-being, implicating both physiological and identity-defining pleasures; personality traits help determining a motivational hierarchy of pleasures
- Entertainment furthermore contributes to emotionally based experiences with more problematic or more conflict-oriented aspects of an individual's self-concept; entertainment potentially has therapeutic-like effects.

There is no apparent correspondence between psychographic segments and specific preferences for entertainment genres. It may even be misleading, as lifestyle segmentation often does, to suggest a correspondence between segments and preferences for specific programmes. The interesting question is not: who prefers which programs? The questions to be asked are in stead: how does a specific program effect its users, and which qualities or expectations do motivate users for being entertained in a particular way? These questions concern specific entertainment styles: i.e. dispositional differences in preferred objects and in motivations for and evaluations of 'good' experiences. A psychographic approach to entertainment styles is thus characterized by focusing on the dialectics between aesthetic structure (stimuli), pleasure and emotional processing on the one hand and personality traits on the other. These traits motivate users to direct their attention at particular experiential qualities and seek out specific stimuli.

Entertainment is a way of regulating emotions within the frame of playing. But being entertained also implies discovering or developing uncommon, even hitherto unknown pleasures. In this respect entertainment may challenge the regulating principle itself. From a psychographic perspective entertainment is hence more than mere pastime or just distraction from more serious concerns. It is also an aesthetic practice mediating pleasure and cultivation, Bildung, and thereby contributing to identity construction and development (Schiller 2004/1794). This practice puts the issue of individuals' happiness – whether hedonic or eudaimonic well-being – at stake.

References

Adorno, Theodor W. And Max Horkheimer (1997/1945). Dialectic of Enlightenment. London: Verso Books.

Aristotle (1996). Poetics. Harmondsworth: Penguin (orig. ca. 335 BC).

Aristotle (1998). The Nicomachean Ethics. Harmondsworth: Penguin (orig. ca. 350 BC).

Bentham, Jeremy (2007/1789). An Introduction to the Principles of Morals and Legislation. Mineola, N.Y.: Dover.

Bosshart, Louis and Ilaria Macconi (1998). Defining "Entertainment". Communication Research Trends Vol. 18 (3-6).

Catell, Raymond B. (1965). The Scientific Analysis of Personality. Harmondsworth: Penguin.

Clore, Gerald L. and Karen Gasper (2000). Feeling is Believing: Some Affective Influences on Belief. In: Nico Frijda, Antony Manstead og Sacha Bem (eds.), Emotions and Beliefs. How Feelings influence Thoughts. Cambridge: Cambridge University Press.

Csikszentmihalyi, Mihaly (1993). The Evolving Self. A Psychology for the Third Millenium. New York: Harper Collins.

Damasio, Antonio R. (1994). Descartes' Error. Emotion, Reason and the Human Brain. London: Macmillan.

Dissanyake, Ellen (1992). Homo Aestheticus. Where Art Comes From and Why. Seattle: University of Washington Press.

Eysenck, Hans J. (1967). The Biological Bases of Personality. Springfield, Ill: Charles C. Thomas.

Eysenck, Hans J. and Michael W. Eysenck (1985). Personality and Individual Differences. A Natural Science Approach. New York: Plenum Press,

Festinger, Leon (1957). A Theory of Cognitive Dissonance. Stanford, CA: Stanford University Press.

Fokkema, Douwe W. and Elrud Kunne.Ibsch (1979). Theories of Literature in the Twentieth Century. Structuralism, Marxism, Aesthetics of Reception, Semiotics. London: C. Hurst & Co.

Frijda, Nico H. (2007). The Laws of Emotion. Mahwah, NJ: Lawrence Erlbaum.

Geertz, Clifford (1973). Deep Play: Notes on a Balinese Cockfight. I: Clifford Geertz (red.), The Interpretation of Cultures. New York: Basic Books (412-453).

Gray, Jeffrey A. (1981). A Critique of Eysenck's Theory of Personality. I: Hans J. Eysenck (red.), A Model for Personality. New York: Springer Verlag (246-276).

Hartmann, Tilo and Christoph Klimmt (2006). The Influence of Personality Factors on Computer Game Choice. In: Peter vorderer and Jennings Bryant (eds.), Playing Video Games. Motives, Responsens, and Consequences. MahwaH, NJ: Laurence Erlbaum (115-131).

Häusel, Hans-Georg (2004). Brain Script. Warum Kunden kaufen [Brain Script. Why Customers Buy]. Freiburg: Haufe.

Higgins, E. Tory (1987). Self-Discrepancy: A Theory Relating Self and Affect. Psychological Review, Vol. 48 (317-340).

Horton, Donald and R. Richard Wohl (1956). Mass Communication and Para-Social Interaction: Observation on Intimacy at a Distance. Psychiatry, Vol. 19 (185-206).

Jantzen, Christian and Mikael Vetner (2007). Design for en affektiv økonomi [Design for an Affective Econnomy]. In: Christian Jantzen and Tove Arendt Rasmussen (eds.), Oplevelsesøkonomi. Vinkler på forbrug. Aalborg: Aalborg University Press (201-218).

Kahneman, Daniel, Ed Diener and Norbert Schwarz (eds.) (1999). Well-Being. The Foundations of Hedonic Psychology. New York: Russell Sage Foundations.

Keyes, Corey Lee (1998). Social Well-Being. Social Psychology Quarterly, Vol. 61 (121-140).

LeDoux, Joseph (1996). The Emotional Brain. New York. Simon & Schuster.

Miron, Dorina (2006). Emotion and Cognition in Entertainment. In: Jennings Bryant and Peter Vorderer (eds.), Psychology of Entertainment. Mahwah, NJ: Lawrence Erlbaum (343-264).

Nozick, Robert (1974). Anarchy, State, and Utopia. New York: Basic Books.

Nussbaum, Martha (2001/1986). The Fragility of Goodness. Luck and Ethics in Greek Tragedyand Philosphy. Cambridge: Cambridge University Press.

Oerter, Rolf (1999). Psychologie des Spiels. Ein handlungstheoretischer Ansatz [Psychology of Play. An Activity Theoretical Approach]. Weinheim: Beltz.

Ohler, Peter and Gerhild Nieding (2006). An Evolutionary Perspective on

Entertainment. In: Jennings Bryant and Peter Vorderer (eds.), Psychology of Entertainment. Mahwah, NJ: Lawrence Erlbaum (423-433).

Oliver, Mary Beth (2003). Mood Management and Selective Exposure. In: Jennings Bryant, David Roskos-Ewoldsen and Joanne Cantor (eds.), Communication and Emotion. Essays in Honor of Dolf Zillmann. Mahwah, NJ: Lawrence Erlbaum (85-106).

Ortony, Andrew and T. J. Turner (1990). What's basic about basic emotions? Psychological Review, Vol. 97 (315-331).

Panksepp, Jaak (1998). Affective Neuroscience. The Foundations of Human and Animal Emotions. Oxford: Oxford University Press.

Peterson, Christopher and Martin E.P. Seligman (eds.) (2004). Character, Strengths and Virtues. A Handbook and Classification. Oxford: Oxford University Press.

Pfaff, Donald (2006). Brain Arousal and Information Theory. Neural and Genetic Mechanisms. Cambridge, MA: Harvard University Press.

Price Waterhouse Coopers (2006). Global Entertainment and Media Outlook: 2006 2010. New York: Price Waterhouse Coopers.

Rolls, Edmund T. (2005). Emotion Explained. Oxford: Oxford University Press.

Rubin, Alan M. (1984). Ritualized and Instrumental Television Viewing. Journal of Communication Vol. 34 (67-77).

Ryan Richard M. and Edward L. Deci (2000). Self-Determination Theory and the Facilitation of Intrinsic Motivation, Social Development, and Well-Being. American Psychologist Vol. 55 (68-78).

Ryan Richard M. and Edward L. Deci (2001). On Happiness and Human Potentials. A Review of Research on Hedonic and Eudaimonic Well-Being. Annual Review of Psychology Vol. 52 (141-166).

Scheele, Brigitte and Fletcher DuBois (2006). Catharsis as a Moral Form of Entertainment. In: Jennings Bryant and Peter Vorderer (eds.), Psychology of Entertainment. Mahwah, NJ: Lawrence Erlbaum (405-422).

Schreier, Margrit (2006). (Subjective) Well-Being. In: Jennings Bryant and Peter Vorderer (eds.), Psychology of Entertainment. Mahwah, NJ: Lawrence Erlbaum (389-404).

Schiller, Friedrich (2004/1794). On the Aesthetic Education of Man. Mineola, NY: Dover.

Tajfel, Henri (red.) (1978). Differentiation between Social Groups. Studies in the Social Psychology of Intergroup Relations. London: Academic Press.

Tiger, Lionel (1992). The Pursuit of Pleasure. Boston: Little, Brown & Co.

Tomkins, Silvan S. (1980). Affect as Amplification: Some Modifications in Theory. In: Robert Plutchik og H. Kellerman (eds.), Emotion: Theory, Research, and Experience, Vol. 1. San Diego: Academic Press (141-164).

Vaihinger, Hans (1952/1911). The Philosophy of "As If". London: Routledge (translation from German C.K. Ogden).

Vorderer, Peter (2001). It's all Entertainment – Sure. But what exactly is Entertainment? Communication Research, Media Psychology, and the Explanation of Entertainment Experiences. Poetics Vol. 29 (247-261).

Weaver III, James B. (2000). Personality and Entertainment Preferences. In: Dolf Zillmann and Peter Vorderer (eds.), Media Entertainment. The Psychology of its Appeal. Mahwah, N.J.: Lawrence Erlbaum (235-248).

Zajonc, Robert H. (1980). Thinking and Feeling. Preferences Need no Inferences. American Psychologist, Vol. 35 (151-175).

Zillmann, Dolf (1988). Mood Management through Communication Choices. American Behavioral Scientist, Vol. 31 (327-340).

Zillmann, Dolf (2000a). The Coming og Media Entertaiment. In: Dolf Zillmann and Peter Vorderer (eds.), Media Entertainment. The Psychology of its Appeal. Mahwah, N.J.: Lawrence Erlbaum (1-20).

Zillmann, Dolf (2000b). Mood Management in the Context of Selective Exposure Theory. Communication Yearbook, Vol. 23 (103-123).

Öhman, Arne and Stefan Wiens (2004). The Concept of an Evolved Fear Modulen and cognitive theories of Anxiety. In: Anthony Manstead, Nico Frijda and Agneta Fischer (eds.), Feelings and Emotions. Cambridge: Cambridge University Press (58-80).

Chapter 3

Understanding children's tendencies to hide their feelings: The roles of emotion understanding and impulsivity

Selene Succar, Karli Beswick and Marc de Rosnay

1. Introduction

Over the past two decades there has been an expansion of research investigating emotion regulation (ER) in children. This research has linked children's ER to both social competence and psychological functioning (Zeman, Cassano, Perry-Parrish & Stegall, 2006). Despite the proliferation of ER studies, there is no consensus in the literature on a single definition of ER (Bridges, Denham & Ganiban, 2004; Eisenberg & Spinrad, 2004), which currently denotes two types of phenomena: emotion as regulating and emotion as regulated (Cole, Martin & Dennis, 2004). Emotion as regulating refers to changes—typically thoughts and behaviours—that appear to arise from an emotion that is triggered, whereas emotion as regulated refers to changes in the actual emotion that is triggered. Despite the apparent elegance of this putative dichotomy, it remains challenging to provide an account of ER in which such distinctions between different regulatory functions holds (Cole, Martin & Dennis, 2004). Nevertheless, a pragmatic definition can be employed for the purposes of this study, which defines ER as the ongoing process of responding to one's environment with emotions that are both socially acceptable and context-appropriate for a given situation (Cole, Michel, & Teti, 1994). This definition implies that certain situations may require that emotions that would be inappropriate or maladaptive to display be hidden, and incorporates the notion of display rules within the ER construct. Display rules are the expression of culturally appropriate responses to a given social situation, regardless of the real emotion being felt (McDowell, O'Neil, & Parke, 2000). When children conceal how they feel they may hide their emotions but, in keeping with the literature on display rules, they may also express sentiments that contradict their feelings. The existence of this phenomenon in young school-aged children, and the variation occurring between them in its manifestation, are the objects of this study.

Background

Whilst infants' facial expressions reveal their feelings (Hiatt, Campos, & Emde, 1979), it becomes increasingly necessary for young children to inhibit and modify their emotional reactions in response to the demands and intricacies of the social world (Carlson & Wang, 2007); a world in which they and their peers have a growing awareness of situational expectations and other people's psychological view points. Children's abilities to regulate emotions in response to the demands of a social situation has typically been measured using Saarni's (1984) disappointing gift paradigm, which capitalizes on the cultural convention that one should show pleasure and gratitude at receiving a gift, even when it is disappointing. While this paradigm has revealed much about the existence of deliberate concealing of emotion, there is inconsistency concerning the effects of age on children's behaviour. Whereas one might expect an escalation in such behaviour during early childhood, in keeping with the rapid developments in children's advancing understanding of mind and emotion (e.g., Pons, Harris & de Rosnay, 2004), empirical findings have been equivocal: Some groups have found that older children are more likely to display a higher number of positive behaviours (e.g., broad smile, enthusiastic "thank you!") in response to a disappointing gift (Saarni, 1984; Carlson & Wang, 2007), while other studies have found no effect of age in young children (approximately 4 to 6 years of age, conservatively; Cole, 1986; Josephs, 1994; Davis, 1995).

There also appear to be gender differences in the inclination to hide emotions, with girls exhibiting less negative and more positive behaviours than boys, especially in social situations (McDowell et al., 2000; Davis, 1995). Saarni (1984) proposed three reasons to account for gender differences: knowledge of display rules, ability to produce expressions, and motivation to hide the true emotion. Gender differences in knowledge have not been supported by the literature (Friend & Davis, 1993; Gnepp & Hess, 1986) and neither has motivation (Davis, 1995). Davis (1995), however, found gender differences in suppressing a negative expression; boys were not as proficient as girls even when they were explicitly instructed to do so. Based on these findings, Davis concluded that girls' relative skill in hiding emotion was a function of differences in socialization practices. Such a conclusion sits comfortably with findings presented by Saarni (1984), who showed that gender differences in concealing emotion interacted with age, with older girls producing more positive behaviours and younger boys producing the highest frequency of negative behaviours (e.g., avoiding eye contact, shoulder shrug). In addition, older boys used more transitional behaviours; that is, behaviours which were either minimally positive in affect or suggestive of uncertainty, apprehension or tension. In sum, the existing literature using the disappointing gift paradigm suggests that both age and gender may be important determinants of children's tendency (or ability) to hide their true feelings, but it is also clear that these variables do not exert their influence in an unequivocal manner: it seems to be that older girls most reliably hide their feelings, but even this conclusion is far from clear.

Given that age and gender do not sufficiently account for individual differences in children's inclination to regulate their emotional expressions in a disappointing gift paradigm, it remains an important issue to determine what does. Individual differences in two other domains that may be impacting children's proclivity to conceal how they feel are therefore outlined and investigated in this study: (i) emotion understanding; and (ii) behavioural self-control (impulsivity).

The role of emotion understanding

During the pre-school to early primary school years, children's understanding and use of display rules improves (Zeman et al., 2006). Children may learn display rules via a simple reward system, whereby they are punished for displaying a socially inappropriate emotion, such as expressing sadness when receiving a disappointing gift (Josephs, 1994), or praised for successfully concealing their true feelings. In keeping with this operant interpretation, children may apply display rules to social situations without necessarily understanding the underlying basis for such rules. Indeed, there is evidence to suggest that children hide their emotions without fully realizing that they are doing so. In Cole's (1986) study, for example, children were asked if the person who gave them their gift in the disappointing gift task knew how they really felt, and to justify their response (i.e., how was it that the experimenter knew/did not know?). Although about half of the 4-year-olds indicated that the experimenter did know how they actually felt, they were not able to come up with reasons, based on facial expression, for their response. It appears, therefore, that children at this age have difficulties grasping how the emotion one expresses depends on what that person wants onlookers to believe about his or her emotional state (Harris, 1989). As children get older they are more likely to refer spontaneously to expressive control in their justifications (Cole, 1986).

Saarni (1999) suggested that spontaneous expressive control of facial displays might develop in conjunction with children's social-cognitive skills in reasoning about emotion and the perspective of others. Children's understanding of display rules has been examined through tasks that contrast a real emotion with an apparent or expressed emotion. In such hiding emotion tasks, children listen to a set of stories that describe situations in which it would be appropriate for the protagonist to conceal how they really feel. Children are asked the following: how the protagonist would really feel (reality); how the protagonist would look on his or her face (appearance); and how other characters in the story would think the protagonist felt. Children are also asked to justify their answers. Studies using these kinds of stories indicate that children as young as four are able to identify the protagonist's real emotion (Gross & Harris, 1988). However, children's understanding of the distinction between real and apparent emotions at four years of age appears limited to stories where the real emotion involved negative affect, and there are pronounced individual differences (Harris, Donelly, Guz & Pitt-Watson, 1986). By seven years of age, however, many children are beginning to focus on the relevant part of the story when answering each type of question, and can correctly identify the emotion another character would attribute to the protagonist (Gross & Harris, 1988).

More recently, evidence has emerged to suggest that children as young as three years of age can distinguish between real and apparent emotion (Josephs, 1994; Banerjee, 1997; Gosselin, Warren & Diotte, 2002), and that previous studies used measures that were too complex for preschoolers because the methodology relied heavily on verbal abilities and memory span (Gosselin et al., 2002). Josephs (1994) used a feeling thermometer to symbolize real emotions and drawings of facial expressions to symbolize apparent emotions. He found that 4- and 5-year-olds were able to distinguish between real and apparent emotions but only when the real emotion had a negative valence. Also, although these young children performed relatively well, they had more difficultly with the appearance-reality distinction than 6-year-olds.

Negative stories, in which negative feelings were hidden, were understood more readily by all children and this difference was especially true for the younger children. Joseph's (1994) accounted for this by arguing that negative emotions seem to be the target of display rule socialization and this is reflected in children's answers.

Banerjee (1997) obtained similar results using an interview protocol designed to reduce the verbal and memory load of the task. He found that children as young as 3 years performed above chance in a hiding emotion task and that they do understand many of the social display rules governing emotional expression. Such evidence indicates that understanding the distinction between real and apparent emotion emerges from three years of age, but there are profound individual differences (Banerjee, 1997). Indeed, there is evidence that the development of emotion understanding in all domains is characterized by marked individual differences (Pons, Lawson, Harris & de Rosnay, 2003).

No study to date has examined the relation between children's understanding of hidden emotions and their actual ability to conceal their own feelings. Traditionally, one line of research employing the disappointing gift paradigm has examined children's abilities, and another line of research employing the hiding emotion stories has explored their understanding. Although Josephs (1994) examined both understanding and ability in the same sample, he did not analyze the relations between these domains as, "it seemed to be impossible to define a reasonable outcome measure on a subject's level in the behavioural domain" (Josephs, 1994, p. 320). In Joseph's (1994) study, reactions to the disappointing gift were coded using Ekman and Friesen's Facial Coding System (FACS) to derive a positive aggregate and a tension aggregate of children's responding, but these measures did not seem appropriate to contrast with a cognitive task (i.e., hiding emotion stories). In fact, many studies employing the disappointing gift paradigm have relied solely on a behaviour coding system such as FACS (Cole, 1986; Josephs, 1997), or Saarni's (1984; 1992) protocols, as a measure of children's ability to control their emotions (Davis, 1995; Carlson & Wang, 2007). Thus, coding of children's responses has been focused on specific behaviours, rather than a goal; that is, to hide how one feels. Therefore, in response to this problem, specific behaviours were scored in the current study, following accepted protocols, but a global rating scale was also developed, based on how successfully children concealed their disappointment. This novel scoring procedure provides an outcome measure that can be meaningfully compared with children's understanding of hidden emotions.

In this study we seek to establish whether there are meaningful links between individual differences in children's tendency/ability to hide their feelings, and their understanding of hidden emotions. We predicted that children who understand that emotions may be concealed would be more likely to conceal their feelings in the disappointing gift task. Importantly, there is a rich literature on young children's emotion understanding that covers many domains (see Pons et al., 2004). Therefore, in the event that children's understanding of hidden emotion relates to their tendency/ability to conceal their feelings, it is of theoretical significance to establish weather such relations show specificity, or if they extend to broader domains of emotion understanding. In particular, given the demands of successfully hiding one's feelings, as discussed above, it was important to make assessments of children's abilities to: (i) recognize and label emotional expressions, (ii) accurately identify what emotions are appropriate in a given situation, and (iii) understand the connection between belief and emotion, which is inherent in any successful act of deliberate deception. Thus, additional emotion understanding tasks were included in the current study to assess these domains of children's emotion understanding competencies.

Finally, although some attention has been given to subsequent interrogation of children (i.e., like question, "Do you like the gift?"), after the disappointing gift paradigm (Cole, 1994), relatively little has been made of these responses in connection with other variables of interest. The findings of Carlson and Wang (2007) suggested that children's responses to the like question were unrelated to their emotion understanding but the emotion understanding tasks they used were not, on the face of it, theoretically connected to the skills tapped in the disappointing gift paradigm. Further, their findings did not indicate a relation between negative expressions in the disappointing gift paradigm and children's responses to the like question but, as we have noted above, children's responses to the disappointing gift paradigm were not conceptualized in terms of goals. Thus, to further explore children's responses to the like question, a second experimenter interviewed children upon receiving the disappointing gift. It was predicted that children who maintain that they like the disappointing gift would have greater understanding of hidden emotions and be more likely to conceal the way they feel during the disappointing gift paradigm.

The role of impulsivity

Children's abilities to control their behaviour and regulate their emotions both develop rapidly during childhood and are overlapping skills, so it is possible that differences in the ability to control behaviour has an impact on children's tendency/ability to hide their feelings. In support of this, research indicates that poorer ER is linked to disruptive behaviour in general (Cole, Zahn-Waxler, & Smith, 1994). One subset of disruptive behaviours linked to poor ER in children is impulsive behaviours (Walcott & Landau, 2004). Children who are impulsive may find it more difficult to hide their true emotions, being unable to inhibit their natural response to an emotion elicited by a particular situation. It seems sensible then to examine children's performance on behavioural measures that require the inhibition of actions, and compare their performance with a measure that requires inhibition of an emotion. Impulsivity is a multi-dimensional concept, with little consensus on a clear definition. The most practical definition is that of White et al. (1994), who posit that impulsivity has two dimensions, behavioural and cognitive. These two dimensions are supported by a number of other studies (e.g., Luengo, Carrillo-De-La-Pena, Otero & Romero, 1994; Martin, et al., 1994; Olson, 1989). In addition, research has shown that the two impulsivity dimensions are distinct from one another, as correlations between behavioural and cognitive impulsivity measures were found to be quite low, but strong correlations occurred within each dimension (White et al., 1994; Harnishfeger, 1995).

Behavioural impulsivity (BI) is defined as, "behaviour that is socially inappropriate or maladaptive and is quickly emitted without forethought" (Oas, 1985, p.142). Impulsive behaviours include shouting out in class, interrupting others and failing to wait in lines. In the disappointing gift task, a child who displays facial expressions and behaviour in response to their feeling of disappointment can be hypothesized to be acting without thinking about the rules or conventions governing a gift giving social situation, or about the perceptions of the gift giver. As children high on BI act impulsively, it is entirely plausible that there may be a relation between BI and the tendency to conceal, or not to conceal, feelings.

BI is typically measured using questionnaires, as the child's behaviour in a context is of interest. One such measure is the Teacher-Rated Impulsivity Scale (TRIS) designed by White et al. (1994), which asks questions about the child's behaviour in the classroom when they are interacting with others. The TRIS is made up of six items taken from the Child Behaviour Checklist (CBCL; Achnbach & Edelbrock, 1983) and the Self-Report Delinquency (SRD; Elliot, Huizinga, & Ageton, 1985) questionnaires. These items are similar to the criteria used by clinicians to assess impulsivity in children (Munden & Arcelus, 1999) and are variations of symptoms of impulsivity outlined in the DSM-IV-TR (American Psychiatric Association, 2000). As the TRIS includes items that are very similar to the symptoms of impulsivity, in the DSM-IV-TR, it is likely that the TRIS is measuring the construct of impulsivity. In addition, both the CBCL and SRD questionnaires from which the TRIS has been derived have been validated on a large sample of children between the ages of four and 16 years, and are used as diagnostic instruments to identify behavioural problems of children (Achnbach & Edelbrock, 1983; Elliot et al., 1985). Together, these facts suggest that the TRIS is an appropriate instrument for assessing children's BI in a classroom context. We expected that children who are more impulsive, as determined by high scores on the TRIS, would be less likely to conceal the way they feel during the disappointing gift task.

The second dimension of impulsivity, cognitive impulsivity, is defined as mental suppression required to keep task-irrelevant information out of mental sets (White et al., 1994). Cognitive impulsivity reflects one of the executive functions, that is, the internally generated mental control processes (Tannock, 1998). Executive functions include cognitive processes such as planning, working memory, set shifting, error detection and correction and response inhibition (Roberts, Robbins & Weiskrantz, 1998). These processes are essential for goal directed behaviour to solve novel or difficult problems, especially those that require the inhibition of automatic thoughts and responses (Carlson & Wang, 2007).

Executive functions develop in children between 12 months and eight years of age (de Luca et al., 2003). Much of the research investigating the development of executive functions in children has employed children diagnosed with Attention Deficit Hyperactivity Disorder (ADHD; Oosterlaan & Sargeant, 1998). While children with ADHD tend to perform significantly more poorly on a range of tasks measuring executive functions (Sergeant, Geurts & Oosterlaan, 2002), in recent theories such as Barkley's (1997) model of ADHD a defining characteristic of ADHD is the executive function of response inhibition (RI). RI is defined as the mental suppression of responses that are inappropriate (Livesey, Keen, Rouse & White, 2006)[1].

---

1 Lack of RI is synonymous with White et al's (1994) term cognitive impulsivity.

Indeed, there is compelling evidence that children with ADHD perform significantly worse on RI tasks than other children of the same age (Walcott & Landau, 2004; Byrne, DeWolfe & Bawden, 1998; Oosterlaan & Sergeant, 1998; Pennington & Ozonoff, 1996).

In Barkley's (1997) model, RI consists of three interrelated processes: inhibition of an initial pre-potent response; inhibition of an ongoing response to allow for time for behavioural decision making; and protecting this time from disruptions by competing events and responses (i.e., interference control). Barkley (1997) posits that children with ADHD do not use effective self-regulation strategies because poor RI does not allow for the necessary time to do so. Poor inhibitory control may hinder children's ability to delay their response for long enough to consider the rules governing a social situation, in keeping with the ADHD profile (Barkley, 1997).

A number of tasks have been used to measure RI, including the Change Task (Geurts, Verte, Oosterlaan, Roeyers & Sergeant, 2004), the Wisconsin Card-Sorting Task (Barkley, 1997) and the Stroop colour word test (Berlin & Bohlin, 2002). However, these tasks also appear to measure other executive functions (Sergeant, Oosterlaan, & Van der Meere, 1999). By contrast, the Stop Signal Task (SST) was specifically designed to measure RI. In this task, children are required to inhibit a motor response that is being executed. The goal of the SST, from the child's view point, is a simple action based choice under reaction time pressure, known as a go-trial (i.e., the child has to touch the correct figure on a computer screen as quickly as possible; Livesey et., 2006). However, after the onset of the primary action at the go-signal, a stop-signal is sometimes presented, which indicates to the child to withhold their primary response (Sergeant et al., 2002). Unlike other tasks used to measure RI, the SST has been found to have low loadings on factors other than RI (Livesey et., 2006).

Another advantage of the SST is that it is based upon a well-developed mathematical model, the race model (Logan and Cowan, 1984), which posits that the go and stop processes compete to determine whether a response is executed. If the go process is faster than the stop process, the response is executed and if the stop process is faster than the go process, the response is inhibited. However, in practice the speed of the stop process cannot be determined because the stop process results in no overt response. The SST overcomes this problem by considering the speed of the go process and the time interval between the onset of the go-signal to the onset of the stop-signal (stop-signal delay; SSD). The race model allows for the estimation of the speed of the inhibitory process (stop signal reaction time; SSRT) by varying the timing of the SSD (Sergeant, 2002). The shorter the SSD, the greater the likelihood of inhibiting a response (Livesey et al., 2006).

A number of studies employing the SST have compared children with ADHD to their age equivalent peers and found that children with ADHD had significantly slower SSRTs (Alderson, Rapport & Kofler, 2007; Nigg, 1999; Oosterlaan, Logan & Sergeant, 1998). Slower SSRTs suggest poorer RI in children with ADHD. This is consistent with Barkley's (1997) model of ADHD, and can be taken as evidence that the SST is a valid measure of RI. It should be noted that it is as yet unclear which RI process the SST measures. Some researchers posit that it measures the inhibition of a pre-potent response (e.g., Barkley, 1999; Logan, Schachar & Tannock, 1997), whereas other researchers posit the SST measures the inhibition of ongoing responses (e.g., Livesey et al., 2006; Tannock, 1998). Irrespective of this difference in interpretation, the SST has been described as the most current and direct measure of the processes involved in the inhibition of a response (Sergeant, 2000). Therefore, the SST is employed in this study as a measure of RI.

Research on the relationship between impulsivity and emotion regulation, using non-clinical samples is relatively limited. Carlson and Wang (2007) found a significant relationship between the two domains in pre-school children, even after age and verbal ability were accounted for. In addition, a quadratic relationship was found between inhibitory control and ER, with intermediate scores on inhibitory control being associated with more successful ER. Carlson and Wang's (2007) interpretation of this relationship was that children who were relatively over-controlled might have been hindered in the ER tasks due to, "... blunting of affect or increased anxiety" (p.505). Such results are consistent with Liew, Eisenberg and Reiser's (2004) finding that effortful control was associated with a smaller number of negative behaviours, as well as positive behaviours, in the disappointing gift task.

Based on this research, there appears to be a relation between impulsivity and ER. However, the relatively small number of studies that have been conducted have tended to use pre-school aged children and have only measured one dimension of impulsivity. The present study overcomes these shortcomings by exploring the relationship between two dimensions of impulsivity and children's tendency to conceal their feelings in a social situation, in a sample of children between six and nine years of age. It was hypothesized that children who were less impulsive would be more likely to conceal the way they feel in the disappointing gift task. In addition, the possibility of a quadratic relation between impulsivity measures and responses to the disappointing gift was investigated.

Summary

The aims of this study are threefold. First, we examine the effects of age and gender on children's tendency to conceal their feelings in a disappointing gift paradigm, which we consider to be an index of emotion regulation (ER). Second, we explore the relation between children's emotion understanding and their success in hiding their feelings; both in terms of hiding their emotional expressions and maintaining, under questioning, that they like a disappointing gift. Finally, we investigate whether a link exists between the two dimensions of impulsivity outlined above—behavioural inhibition and response inhibition—and the likelihood of children concealing their feelings when receiving a disappointing gift.

2. Method
Participants

Fifty children (M = 7 years, 7 months; SD = 8.3 months) were recruited from two elementary schools in Sydney. The children were drawn from Year 1 through to Year 3. While all children in these classes were invited to participate, parental consent was obtained for 41%. The sample consisted of 33 girls (M = 7 years, 8 months; SD = 8.9 months) and 17 boys (M = 7 years, 5 months; SD = 6.7 months).

Procedure

The tasks were administered over two sessions spaced about one week apart, with each session lasting for approximately one hour. At the first session, children were given two tests of emotion understanding (belief-based emotion and hiding emotion stories) and a measure of response inhibition (SST). The order of administration of the emotion understanding tests and the SST was systematically counter balanced. At session 2, the remaining tasks were given in a fixed order: Assessment of Children's Emotion Skills (ACES), a test of verbal mental age (Peabody Picture Vocabulary Test; PPVT-IV) and the disappointing gift task. All tasks were administered individually in a quiet location within the school, during school hours.

Measures[2]

Peabody Picture Vocabulary Test (PPVT). The Peabody Picture Vocabulary Test (4th ed.; Dunn & Dunn, 2007) was administered to assess children's verbal ability. PPVT raw scores were used in data analyses, as chronological age is an important independent variable.

Belief-base emotion understanding (BBEA). Belief-based emotion attribution tasks required children to make an emotion attribution on the basis of a story protagonist's false-belief. The stories were based on the research of Harris, Johnson, Hutton, Andrews and Cooke (1989) and presented in a simple cartoon format based on the Test of Emotion Comprehension (Pons et al., 2004). In the first item, children were introduced to a character (Molly) who really likes sweets, but dislikes beans. In Molly's absence, another character takes the sweets out of the packet and replaces them with beans. To ensure children understand the scenario, they are asked a control question: How does Molly feel when she returns (hungry) and sees the packet of sweets, but before discovering that they have been replaced with beans. Children are prompted with the aid of four small pictures of Molly, each displaying a different facial expression. Thus, children were asked: "So, how does Molly feel when she first looks at the packet of sweets on the table but before she eats some food from it? Does she feel happy? Does she feel angry? Does she feel just alright? Or does she feel sad?" Finally, children are asked about Molly's (false) belief. The second item was similar to the first item, but was about a male protagonist (Max), who had something he disliked (nuts) replaced with something he liked (chocolates). To succeed on these items, children needed to make the correct emotion attribution as well as correctly identifying the false belief. This scoring was based on previous literature (de Rosnay, Pons, Harris & Morrell, 2004; Bradmetz & Schneider, 1999). Children received a score of '2' if they passed the false belief question and gave the correct emotion, and a score of '1' if they passed the false belief question but chose an emotion with the correct valence, resulting in a 0-4 scale.

Assessment of Children's Emotion Skills (ACES). The ACES (Schultz, Trentacosta, Izard, Leaf, & Mostow, 2004) assesses children's emotion attribution accuracy. Two sections of the ACES, the faces and situations, were modified and used in the study. The ACES-faces were administered first and consisted

---

[2] Details of all measures can be obtained from the final author

of two parts. During part 1, children were required to spontaneously identify the emotions expressed in each picture. In part 2, children had to identify expressions when given an emotion label. There were 15 expressions (three each for happy, sad, angry, scared and surprised) randomly presented in blocks of five (one of each expression). Children received a score of '1' for each expression correctly identified, for both parts, yielding a 0-30 scale.

For the ACES-situations a brief description of an emotionally evocative scenario was described to children with the aide of a simple illustration. Children were asked to identify the emotion in each scenario. There were eight items concerning social situations (e.g., losing a pet, receiving a compliment, etc.). In response to each item, children choose either a happy, sad, angry, scared or no feeling from cartoon facial expressions which they had previously (correctly) identified. Children received a score of '1' for each correct emotion attribution, yielding a 0-8 scale.

Hiding emotions. Four hiding emotion stories were presented to children as story vignettes with accompanying pictures. Two stories depicted situations where it would be appropriate to feel a positive emotion but conceal it, and the other two depicted stories where it would be appropriate to feel a negative emotion, but conceal it. Two of these stories (one positive and one negative) were based on the research by Pons et al. (2004). The other positive story was taken from Banerjee's (1997) stories, while the second negative story was adapted from Gardner, Harris, Ohmoto and Hamazaki (1988). As an illustration, a positive emotion story was as follows: "This is Adam and this is Harry. Harry is showing Adam the new bicycle that he got for his Birthday. But Adam doesn't have a bicycle!" The depiction of this story shows Harry and Adam both with negative expressions on their faces, despite the fact that Harry almost certainly feels happy about his new bicycle. To pass this item, children need to identify that Harry's true feeling (happiness).

Consistent with previous studies (Harris et al., 1986; Gardner et al., 1988; Gross & Harris, 1988; Josephs, 1994; Banerjee, 1997), participants were told that the protagonist wanted to "hide the way they felt". Some previous studies using hiding emotions stories have also revealed the protagonist's true feeling to children (Banerjee, 1997), and provided the reason for the protagonist wanting to hide his or her emotion (Gardner et al., 1997; Banerjee, 1997). In this study, however, because we had an older sample, it was unnecessary to provide children with the protagonist's real emotion and their motivation for concealing it. In the four stories used, the rationale for the character wanting to hide his or her emotion was apparent from the context of the story. To pass the first two items children merely had to identify the correct emotion felt by the protagonist (true feeling). To pass the third and fourth stories, children were required to correctly identify the protagonist's true feeling as well as show an awareness of the discrepancy between the true emotion and the displayed emotion. Final scores were derived from the total number of items passed, yielding a 0-4 scale.

Stop Signal Task (SST). The SST is a computer-based measure of response inhibition developed by Livesey et al. (2006). The task (see Figure 1) was introduced to participants as a game to see how quickly they could touch the shape (circle or square) that matched the shape in Mickey Mouse's box (B); children's responses were registered when they touched the computer monitor (a Diamond View DV154MT-C Touch Screen). Figure 1 illustrates how four squares were presented to participants on the computer screen.

Figure 1. Computer screen layout of the Stop Signal Task (Livesey et al., 2006)

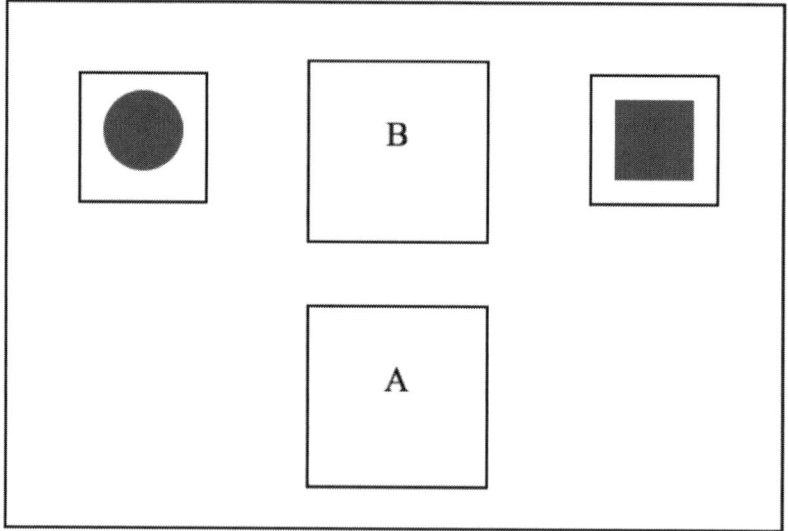

The two smaller squares on the left and right contained a blue circle in one, and a blue square in the other. At the experimenter's initiation, a picture of Mickey Mouse's face appeared in square A. Participants were required to touch Mickey on each occasion to make his shape (either a square or circle) appear in square B. They were then required to touch the shape that was the same as Mickey's shape (in B) as quickly as possible. Both the circle and square were presented an equal number of times in a randomized order. This part of the task was called a go trial.

A stop trial occurred when all shapes in the top three squares turned red and a 500 millisecond, 1 kHz tone was presented. This stop-signal indicated to participants that they were not to touch the shape. The stop-signal delay (SSD) -the time interval between the presentation of the go-signal and the stop-signal- was initially set at 600 milliseconds. This was found to be an appropriate SSD for children of the same age as those participating in this study (Livesey et al., 2006). The SSD automatically adjusted itself by 50 milliseconds depending on the response of the child, increasing if the child was successful in inhibiting their response and decreasing if the child was unsuccessful.

Participants were given feedback on their performance immediately after each trial. When they touched the correct shape on go trials or inhibited their response on stop trials, a smiley face appeared in square B accompanied by a bell. If they touched the incorrect shape on go trials or failed to inhibit their response on stop trials, a frowny face along with a different, flat tone was presented. In addition, responses were recorded as incorrect if participants took longer than 3 seconds to respond for all trials.

The SST consisted of eight blocks of trials. The first block was made up of 12 go trials and was used to practice the go-signal. The second block was also a practice block, comprising of 24 trials used to introduce the stop-signal and to determine the SSD at which the probability of inhibiting a response was 0.5. The remaining six blocks each consisted of 24 trials and were used in calculating the different measures of the SST. In each of these six blocks, 17 go trials and 7 stop trials were presented. This meant that 29% of trials were stop trials, which is higher than the 25% usually presented in the standard SST. This was necessary as a minimum of 40 stop trials is required for reliable data (Ridderinkhof, Bland & Logan, 1999) and this was also the most practical way of achieving reliability without increasing the number of overall trials.

Participants were motivated through verbal encouragement and rewards (stickers) for completing blocks of trials. If participants appeared to be slowing down, they were reminded to go as fast as possible. Sufficient understanding of the SST was demonstrated by responding correctly to at least 80% of go trials. One participant failed to meet these criteria and thus was excluded from the study.

RI was measured using the Stop Signal Reaction Time (SSRT) score, which estimates the speed of the stopping process and is most accurate when the SSD is set so that the probability of inhibiting a response, P(inhibit), is 0.5 (Ridderinkhof et al., 1999). It is computed by subtracting the average SSD from the mean reaction time averaged across the six blocks. Higher SSRT scores are indicative of greater difficulty in inhibiting responses.

Teacher-Rated Impulsivity Scale (TRIS). The TRIS (White et al., 1994) includes six items about children's behavioural impulsivity. Each child's classroom teacher completed the TRIS, indicating the degree to which he or she believed each item describes the child on a 3-point scale (0 = rarely; 1 = sometimes; 2 = always). Using a teacher rated measure is beneficial as teachers can provide a normative perspective of age-appropriate behaviours (Landau & McAninch, 1993). The scores for each item were combined to obtain the final TRIS score. Higher TRIS scores indicated that the child was higher in BI.

Disappointing Gift. In order to establish positive expectancies, children received an attractive gift (i.e., bubbles) at the end of the first session for completing the tasks. All children received the same gift and this gift was deemed desirable by a number of other children not involved in the study. The gifts were put in pink and blue gift boxes for the girls and boys respectively and were opened in the presence of the three experimenters and the other children. Following the administration of the PPVT at the second session, children received one of four disappointing gifts, which were rotated to control for the possibility that children would tell their friends about the first gift they mistakenly received. The disappointing gifts used were two old Lego farm animals, a small toy chicken figurine and a broken toy man. These gifts were disappointing because they were insubstantial, old and age-inappropriate. To ensure that they would elicit disappointment in participants, a number of other children not involved in the study were shown the gifts and the children considered the gifts to be undesirable.

Children were told that they were going to receive a present for all their hard work and effort. The experimenter presented children with a colored gift box and encouraged them to open it right away. The experimenter maintained a neutral expression and made a concerted effort to establish eye contact, without developing an interaction with the child. Once children had clearly finished reacting to the gift, the experimenter excused herself and left the room. A second experimenter then entered the room and asked the children what gift they received, and how they felt about getting it. If the children responded that they liked the unattractive gift a prompt was given: "Some children would be happy with this and some wouldn't. I want to know how you really feel?" Following children's responses, the experimenter pretended that the gift had been placed in the incorrect box and replaced the disappointing gift with an attractive one. To ensure that children who had not yet completed the second session were not informed about the disappointing gift by their classmates, children were asked not to tell their classmates about the mistake.

Tabel 1. The Hiding Emotion Scale used to determine disappointing gift global score

Score	Example behaviors
1	Child is unable / unwilling to inhibit their disappointment Child tells experimenter that he / she does not want / like the toy Child displays no positive behaviours
2	Child might express some disappointment Child displays minimal positive behaviours Child is indifferent to the gift
3	Childs displays both positive and negative behaviours Child makes attempt to inhibit their disappointment
4	Child produces expression that contradicts true feeling Child appears to like gift, but behaviour looks forced
5	Child produces expression that contradicts true feeling Child appears to really like the gift Child displays a high number of positive behaviours and little or no negative behaviours

Children's facial expressions and behaviours were recorded by a video camera. These were coded using a modified version of Saarni's (1992) behaviour coding system, which codes behaviour as positive, negative, social monitoring and tension. The first two categories include obvious indices of positive (e.g., relaxed broad smile with teeth showing) or negative affect (e.g., knit brows). Social monitoring behaviours (e.g., staring at experimenter) are indicative of attempts to control behaviour and are minimally positive in affect. Tension behaviours (e.g., nose wrinkle) are suggestive of uneasiness and stress (Davis, 1995). In addition to Saarni's (1992) system, children's behaviour was rated on a 1-5 scale, where a score of '1' was awarded when children were unable/unwilling to inhibit their disappointment and a score of '5' was given when children produced an expression that contradicted their true feeling (e.g., delight or happiness). Table 1 presents the criteria used to determine the rating (global score) that children received on this scale.

An independent rater was trained to code the disappointing gift measures. The second rater coded 20% of the sample, with inter-rater reliability being consistently high. Inter-rater reliability for each of the scales was as follows: positive, $r(10) = .92$ ($p < .01$); negative, $r(10) = .85$ ($p < .01$); social monitoring, $r(10) = .72$ ($p < .05$); tension, $r(10) = .84$ ($p < .01$); and global score, $r(10) = .69$ ($p < .05$).

3. Results
Preliminary analyses

Table 2 shows the descriptive statistics for the study variables. Two features of this table deserve mention. First, the distribution of TRIS scores was very skewed and, consequently, TRIS was recoded as a binary variable with children showing now signs of impulsivity coded '0' ($n = 21$) and children showing any signs of impulsivity coded '1' ($n = 29$). Second, the fourth hiding emotion story had to be dropped because a clear ambiguity in the story became apparent as children completed the task, resulting in a 0-3 scale for hiding emotion. In keeping with previous literature, children found the hiding emotion stories easier to understand when a negative emotion had been hidden (88% passing for story 2) rather than a positive emotion (22% passing for story 1 and 36% for story 3). Four children failed all three stories and seven children passed all three. Regarding the SST, the results of blocks 1 and 2 were omitted as these were practice blocks. There was a high proportion of correct responses on go trials ($M = .97$; $SD = .02$), indicating a small number of errors. In addition, the mean P(Inhibit) of 0.52 was close to the desired 0.5.

Concerning the disappointing gift paradigm, Table 2 suggests sufficient variability to detect individual differences. Children's responses to the like questions asked after receiving the disappointing gift suggested that they were disappointed with the unattractive gift.

Tabel 2. Means, standard deviations (SD), minimum and maximum scores on all tasks (N = 50)

Measure	Mean	SD	Minimum	Maximum
PPVT	130.5	20.07	81	166
Emotion understanding (EU)				
Belief-based emotion	2.2	1.02	0	4
ACES-faces	24.1	2.82	18	28
ACES-situations	5.6	1.26	3	8
Hiding Emotions	1.5	.84	0	3
Impulsivity				
TRIS	2.5	3.47	0	12
SSRT	409.8	108.11	237.1	712.5
Disappointing gift (emotion regulation)				
Positive affect	1.5	1.61	0	5
Negative affect	2.8	1.76	0	7
Social Monitoring	2.0	1.15	0	5
Tension	1.0	.86	0	3
Global Score	3.0	1.49	1	5

Overall, 40 (80%) children initially indicated that they liked the gift, and 30 (60%) maintained this position under questioning (prompting). The prompted findings were used in subsequent analyses. Table 3 shows relations amongst the dimensions of children's regulatory responses to the disappointing gift. It is encouraging to note the strong correspondence between the global score and the negative and positive dimensions.

Tabel 3. Correlations between measures on the disappointing gift task (N =50)

Dimensions	Positive	Negative	Social Monitoring	Tension
Negative	-.65**	--		
Social Monitoring	.20	-.29*	--	
Tension	-.16	.23	-.14	--
Global Score	.82**	-.69**	.27	-.10

** $p < .01$; * $p < .05$;

Background analyses

As expected, there was a significant relation between age and verbal ability, (r = .49, p < .01). Of the emotion understanding measures, only the ACES-situations were significantly correlated with age (r = .38, p < .01) and verbal ability (r = .44, p < .01). As expected, age was significantly negatively correlated with the SSRT (r = -.34, p < .05), suggesting that as children get older they become better at response inhibition, but the relation between age and the TRIS was not significant (r = -.14, ns), despite being in the same direction. Similarly, verbal ability was not significantly related to impulsivity measures.

Regarding gender, independent samples t-tests were used to compare scores between boys and girls on each of the measures. Boys received significantly higher scores on the TRIS, t(48) = 3.03, p < .01, but differences between girls and boys on the SST were not significant t(47) = 1.73, ns. Girls were significantly better at identifying emotional facial expressions, t(48) = -3.11, p < .01, but there were no other gender related differences on any of the other EU tasks.

There were no significant relations between emotion understanding domains. Whilst somewhat surprising, it was not altogether unexpected as these different tasks assess very distinct domains of emotion understanding. In fact the emotion understanding literature suggests poor concurrent reliability between emotion understanding domains, which are hierarchically organized (e.g., Pons et al., 2004), but good longitudinal stability in emotion understanding even between domains (e.g., Pons & Harris, 2005). There was a modest but significant relation between the TRIS and the SSRT, t(47) = -2.14, p < .05, but there were no systematic relations between emotion understanding and impulsivity measures.

Bivariate relations with disappointing gift task

Age, verbal ability and gender. Turning to the disappointing gift paradigm, and children's ER, there were only modest relations with age and verbal ability. Older children showed more positive behaviours and had higher global scores but these differences were only marginally significant (ps < .10). Higher verbal ability scores were associated with more negative behaviours, r = .29, p < .05, but there were no other indications that verbal abilities were related to children's ER behaviour or their global hiding emotion score. As with age, there was also a marginal relation between gender and global scores, t(48) = -1.96, p = .06, with girls more successfully hiding their feelings. There were no other relations with gender. Further analyses showed that age, verbal ability and gender were not related to children's tendency to maintain that they liked the disappointing gift (the like question).

Emotion understanding. Table 4 shows that, of the emotion understanding domains, only children's understanding of hiding emotions was related to performance on the disappointing gift task and, furthermore, this relation was only significant for the global rating of success in hiding emotion. There were no relations between children's emotion understanding and their response to the like question.

Tabel 4. Correlations between emotion understanding measures and disappointing gift measures. (N = 50)

Emotion task	Disappointing Gift Measures				
	Positive	Negative	Social Monitoring	Tension	Global
Belief-based	.09	.20	.15	.01	.02
ACES-faces	.08	-.14	-.09	-.02	.11
ACES-situations	.09	.15	-.22	-.11	-.03
Hiding emotion	.25[a]	-.12	-.01	.17	.33*

* $p < .05$; [a] $p < .1$

Impulsivity. Table 5 presents correlations between the two impulsivity measures and the disappointing gift measures. There was no significant impact of impulsivity on children's emotional expressions, their behaviour or their tendency to conceal their feelings. Examination of quadratic relations revealed the same pattern of findings. Similarly, there were no relations between children's impulsivity and their response to the like question.

Tabel 5. Correlations between impulsivity measures and disappointing gift measures

	N	Disappointing Gift Measures				
		Positive	Negative	Social Monitoring	Tension	Global
TRIS	50	.09	-.05	.02	-.04	.02
SSRT	49	.03	-.06	.02	-.07	-.04

Responses to the disappointing gift and the like question

When asked if they liked the disappointing gift, all children who received a global score of '5' (when given the disappointing gift) maintained that they did, even after the prompt was given (see Figure 2). To asses the relation between global scores for hiding emotion and children's answers to the like question, the global score was dichotomized into low (1-3; n = 27) and high groups (4-5; n = 23), so as to delineate between children who were successful at hiding their feelings and those who were not. A chi-square test confirmed that performance on the disappointing gift was strongly related to children's responses to the like question, $x^2(1) = 5.92$, $p < .05$; children who more successfully hid their feelings in the disappointing gift task were more likely, under questioning, to maintain that they liked the disappointing gift. This pattern of findings was reflected in the positive and negative affect scores for the disappointing gift, which are depicted in Figure 3. Children who said they liked the disappointing gift showed more positive ($p < .05$) and less negative ($p < .001$) affect.

Figure 2. Number of children saying they liked or disliked the disappointing gift (like question after prompt) by disappointing gift global score (N =50)

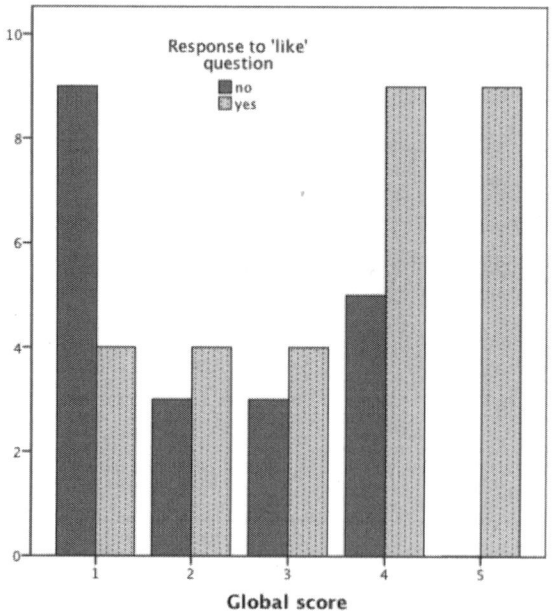

Figure 3. Mean scores for positive and negative affect in the disappointing gift task by children's response to the like question (N = 50)

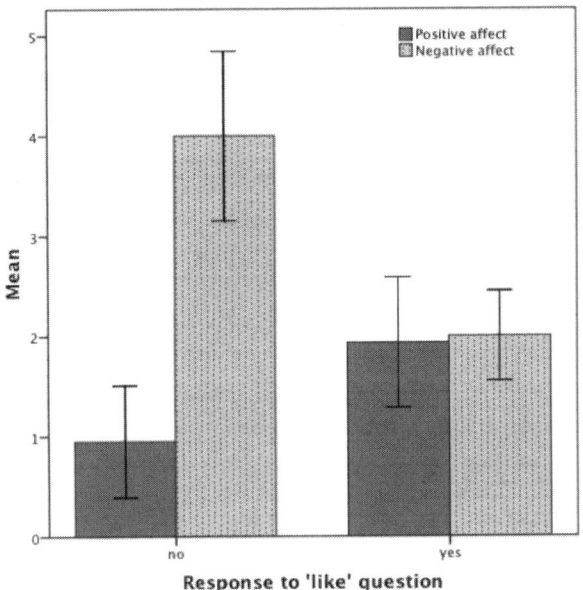

Predicting children's responses to the disappointing gift

The preliminary findings and bivariate analyses revealed relatively few relations between children's performance on the disappointing gift task and the other study variables. Therefore, we limit the subsequent regression analyses to those relations emerging the previous sections, but also taking into account children's age and gender.

Verbal ability and negative affect in the disappointing gift. To investigate the impact of children's verbal abilities on the expression of their negative affect in the disappointing gift task, a hierarchical regression analyses was built with age and gender (step 1), and verbal ability (step 2) as predictors of negative affect. At step 1, the model was not significant, $F(2,47) = .80$, ns, $R^2 = .02$. The addition of verbal ability at the second step made a significant contribution to the overall model, $\Delta F(1,46) = 8.73$, $p < .01$, $\Delta R^2 = .15$. The final model was significant, $F(3,46) = 3.52$, $p < .05$, $R^2 = .19$, with both age ($\beta = -.32$, $p < .05$) and verbal ability ($\beta = .45$, $p < .01$) making significant independent contributions to negative affect. Follow up analyses revealed no interaction between age and gender, or between age and verbal ability. Results indicated that older children tended to show less negative affect but, paradoxically, children with higher verbal ability scores tended to show more.

Emotion understanding and the disappointing gift. To investigate the impact of children's emotion understanding (hiding emotion) on their success in hiding their feelings (global score) in the disappointing gift task, a hierarchical regression analyses was built with age and gender (step 1), and hiding emotion (step 2) as predictors of the global score. At step 1, the model was significant, $F(2,47) = 3.27, p < .05, R^2 = .12$. The addition of hiding emotion at the second step made a marginally significant contribution to the overall model, $\Delta F(1,46) = 3.77, p = .06, \Delta R^2 = .07$. The final model was significant, $F(3,46) = 3.57, p < .05, R^2 = .19$, with none of the predictor variables making an independent contribution to the global score: Only hiding emotion (ß = .27, p = .06) approached a significant independent contribution. Follow up analyses revealed no interaction between age and gender. Results indicated considerable shared variance between age, gender and emotion understanding.

4. Discussion

The present study investigated sources of individual differences in children's tendency to conceal their emotions. Indeed, such individual differences were found: Some children made no attempt to hide the way they felt and others engaged in elaborate deceptions, smiling and pretending to like the clearly disappointing gift. There were still other children at neither extreme, refusing to reveal that they did not like the gift, yet not appearing overtly happy or grateful.

In keeping with previous studies, we found some indications that age and gender influence children's tendency to express how they feel but there were no strong or clear relations. The influence of age came through in relation to children's expression of negative affect and in their global scores. For both aspects of the disappointing gift paradigm, older children were more likely to behave in ways that were consistent with concealing their true feelings. Similarly, girls were more likely to try and conceal their feelings (global score) but the effect was modest and there was no independent contribution of gender to the global score. Such modest findings for gender and age sit comfortably with the existing literature, in which there have only been equivocal findings for these factors. With a larger sample it is likely that clearer influences of age and gender would emerge, but it is clear that, within this age-range, the child's age and gender are of relatively little significance in determining their response to receiving a disappointing gift.

Whereas most previous studies in this area have neglected to control for children's verbal abilities, we found a modest and paradoxical influence of verbal ability on children's performance in the disappointing gift paradigm. Specifically, children with higher levels of verbal ability were more likely to display negative affect and behaviours, and this remained true when age was controlled for. That is to say, more verbally able children were more likely to convey the negative impact of the disappointing gift. Given that the negative dimension of Saarni's (1992) scale includes negative verbal behaviours, it is likely that these children felt more able or compelled to verbally indicate their dissatisfaction. It is interesting to note, however, that verbal ability did not come through as a predictor of global scores or answers to the like question, so it is possible that, despite making the negative impact more known, verbally more competent children were able conceal their disappointment in other ways. Although this finding is provocative, so far as we know it is novel. Therefore, a replication of this finding is necessary before too much is read into it.

Concerning the role of children's impulsivity, neither behavioural impulsivity (BI) nor response inhibition (RI) had any impact on children's expression of affect, behaviour or success in concealing their feelings in the disappointing gift paradigm. Further, more impulsive children, in either sense, were not more likely to say that they disliked the gift. Thus, in contrast to the findings of Carlson and Wang (2007) we did not find a relation between impulse control and emotion regulation. It should be noted, however, that the children in the current sample were approximately three years older than in Carlson and Wang's study, which is likely to entail important differences that we discuss below.

Of the emotion understanding measures, only children's ability to understand hidden emotion predicted their behaviour in the disappointing gift paradigm, suggesting a high degree of specificity between emotion understanding and behaviour. The impact of such emotion understanding overlapped with age and gender, but still came through as the most potent predictor, of all study variables, of children's success at hiding their feelings when given a disappointing gift (global score).

Finally, and perhaps most interestingly, the extent to which children maintained their satisfaction at receiving the disappointing gift under questioning, was strongly related to their global scores and their expressions of negative and positive affect; such that verbal deception was strongly linked with more positive and less negative expression, and greater success in maintaining the deception. A plausible interpretation of these findings is that there is continuity between children's spontaneous behaviour upon receiving a disappointing gift and their more deliberate, continued deception under questioning. In conjunction with the other findings reported above, such continuity suggests that, at seven years of age, children's tendency to conceal their feelings is a relatively deliberate process. If it were otherwise, one would expect stronger links with impulsivity measures and chronological age, and one would not predict a paradoxical relation with verbal ability.

The interpretation that children's deceptive behaviours are relatively deliberate also holds true for the emotion understanding measures: The fact that children's global scores were only linked with their understanding of hiding emotions speaks against any interpretation that general improvements in emotion understanding result in more automatic deception. The specificity of the finding suggests, instead, that some children have domain specific knowledge about the importance of maintaining such social deceptions, and this knowledge is closely linked to their actions. Within the framework of the literature on the development of emotion understanding, it is entirely likely that certain families promote such understanding through their conversational/social interactions (de Rosnay & Hughes, 2006).

The current findings, therefore, suggest that the ways in which children regulated their emotions in response to a disappointing gift, at least, are likely to be open to socialization and, thus, intervention. Furthermore, these findings suggest that relations between emotion understanding and behaviour are likely to be quite context specific, so any intervention focusing on emotional comprehension or understanding may need to address specific situations facing children. Of course this interpretation needs to be qualified in light of the age of the sample, the fact that the sample was comprised of 'typical' children, and the limited measurement of emotion regulation.

Regarding age, it is likely, on the basis of the previous literature, that younger children also employ much more thoughtless or reflexive strategies in the disappointing gift paradigm, which could also be fashioned via socialization; such as rewarding deceptive behaviour and punishing or criticizing a failure to deceive in socially acceptable ways. So an operant pathway to socially deceptive behaviour remains entirely plausible despite the current findings. Regarding the composition of the sample, the variation seen in impulsivity may simply have been inadequate to detect meaningful individual differences, and clinical groups might yield very different insights. Finally, the disappointing gift paradigm creates a child-adult (hierarchical) deception context strongly influenced by cultural norms. While an intriguing paradigm, it may tell us little about children's emotion regulation in other contexts. This is a question for further research.

References

Achenbach, R. M., & Edelbrock, C. (1983). Manual for the child behaviour checklist and revised child behaviour profile. Burlington: T.M. Achenbach.

Alderson, R. M., Rapport, M. D., & Kofler, M. J. (2007). Attention-deficit/hyperactivity disorder and behavioural disinhibition: A meta-analytic review of the stop-signal paradigm. Journal of Abnormal Child Psychology, 35, 745-758.

Alderson, R. M., Rapport, M. D., Sarver, D. E., & Kofler, M. J. (2008). ADHD and behavioral inhibition: A re-examination of the stop-signal task. Journal of Abnormal Child Psychology, 36, 989-998.

American Psychiatric Association. (2000). Diagnostic and statistical manual of mental disorders: DSM-IV-TR. (4th ed., text revision). Washington, DC: Author.

Banerjee, M. (1997). Hidden emotions: Preschoolers' knowledge of appearance-reality and emotion display rules. Social Cognition, 15, 107-132.

Barkley, R. A. (1997). Behavioural inhibition, sustained attention, and executive functions: Constructing a unifying theory of ADHD. Psychological Bulletin, 121, 65-94.

Bell, M. A., & Wolfe, C. D. (2004). Emotion and cognition: An intricately bound developmental process. Child Development, 75, 366-370.

Berlin, L., & Bohlin, G. (2002). Response inhibition, hyperactivity and conduct problems. Journal of Clinical Child Psychology, 31, 242-251.

Bradmetz, J., & Schneider, R. (1999). Is Little Red Riding Hood afraid of her granmdmother? Cognitive vs. emotional response to a false belief. British Journal of Developmental Psychology, 17, 501-514.

Bridges, L. J., Denham, A., & Ganiban, J. M. (2004). Definitional issues in emotion regulation research. Child Development, 75, 340-345.

Byrne, J. M., DeWolfe, N. A., & Bawden, H. N. (1998). Assessment of attention-deficit hyperactivity disorder in preschoolers. Child Neuropsychology, 4, 49-66.

Carlson, S. M., & Moses, L. J. (2001). Individual differences in inhibitory control and children's theory of mind. Child Development, 72, 1032-1053.

Carlson, S. M., & Wang, T. S. (2007). Inhibitory control and emotion regulation in preschool children. Cognitive Development, 22, 489-510.

Cole, P. M. (1986). Children's spontaneous control of facial expression. Child Development, 57, 1309-1321.

Cole, P. M., Martin, S., E., & Dennis, T., A. (2004). Emotion regulation as a scientific construct: Methodological challenges and directions for child development research. Child Development, 75, 317-333.

Cole, P. M., Michel, M. K., & Teti, L. O. D. (1994). The development of emotion regulation and dysregulation: A clinical perspective. Monographs of the Society for Research in Child Development, 59, 73-100, 250-283.

Cole, P. M., Zahn-Waxler, C., & Smith, K. D. (1994). Expressive control during a disappointment: Variations related to preschoolers' behavior problems. Developmental Psychology, 30, 835-846.

Davis, T. L. (1995). Gender differences in masking negative emotions: Ability or motivation? Developmental Psychology, 31, 660-667.

de Luca, C. R., Wood, S. J., Anderson, V., Buchanan, J., Proffitt, T. M., Mahony, K., & Pantelis, C. (2003). Normative data from the cantab. I: Development of executive function over the lifespan. Journal of Clinical and Experimental Neuropsychology, 25, 242-254.

de Rosnay, M. & Hughes, C. (2006). Conversation and theory of mind: Do children talk their way to socio-cognitive understanding? British Journal of Developmental Psychology, 24(1), 7-37.

de Rosnay, M., Pons, F., Harris, P. L., & Morrell, J. M. (2004). A lag between understanding false belief and emotion attribution in young children: Relationships with linguistic ability and mothers' mental-state language. British Journal of Developmental Psychology, 22, 197-218.

Dunn, L. M., & Dunn, D. M. (2007). Peabody Picture Vocabulary Test (4th ed.). Bloomington, MN: Pearson Assessments.

Eisenberg, N., & Spinrad, T., L. (2004). Emotion-related regulation: Sharpening the definition. Child Development, 75, 334-339.

Elliott, D. S., Huizinga, D., & Ageton, S. S. (1985). Explaining delinquency and drug use. Beverly Hills: Sage Publications.

Friend, M., & Davis, T. L. (1993). The appearance-reality distinction: Children's understanding of the physical and affective domains. Developmental Psychology, 29, 907-914.

Gardner, D., Harris, P., Ohmoto, M., & Hamazaki, T. (1988). Japanese children's understanding of the distinction between real and apparent emotion. International Journal of Behavioral Development, 11, 203-218.

Gosselin, P., Warren, M., & Diotte, M. (2002). Motivation to hide emotion and children's understanding of the distinction between real and apparent emotions. The Journal of Genetic Psychology, 163, 479-495.

Geurts, H. M., Verte, S., Oosterlaan, J., Roeyers, H., & Sergeant, J. A. (2004). How specific are executive dysfunction deficits in attention deficit hyperactivity disorder and autism. Journal of Child Psychology and Psychiatry, 45, 836-854.

Gnepp, J., & Hess, D. L. (1986). Children's understanding of verbal and facial display rules. Developmental Psychology, 22, 103-108.

Gross, D., & Harris, P. L. (1988). False beliefs about emotion: Children's understanding of misleading emotional displays. International Journal of Behavioral Development, 11, 475-488.

Harnishfeger, K. K. (1995). The development of cognitive inhibition: Theories, definitions, and research evidence. In F. N. Dempstar, & C. J. Brainerd (Eds.). Interference and inhibition in cognition. San Diego: Academic Press.

Harris, P. L. (1989). Children and emotion: The development of psychological understanding. Cambridge, MA: Basil Blackwell.

Harris, P. L., Donnelly, K., Guz, G. R., & Pitt-Watson, R. (1986). Children's understanding of the distinction between real and apparent emotion. Child Development, 57, 895-909.

Harris, P. L., Johnson, C., Hutton, D., Andrews, G., & Cooke, T. (1989). Young children's theory of mind and emotion. Cognition and Emotion, 3, 379-400.

Hiatt, S. W., Campos, J. J., & Ernde, R. N. (1979). Facial patterning and infant emotional expression: Happiness, surprise and fear. Child Development, 50, 1020-1035.

Josephs, I. E. (1994). Display rule behavior and understanding in preschool children. Journal of Nonverbal Behavior, 18, 301-326.

Katz, L. F., & Gottman, J. M. (1994). Patterns of marital interaction and children's emotional development. In R. D. Parke & S. G. Kellam (Eds.), Exploring family relationships with other social contexts. Hillsdale, NJ: Erlbaum.

Landau, S., & McAninch, C. (1993). Young children with attention deficits. Young Children, 48, 49-58.

Liew, J., Eisenberg, N., & Reiser, M. (2004). Preschoolers' effortful control and negativeemotionality, immediate reactions to disappointment, and quality of social functioning. Journal of Experimental Child Psychology, 89, 298-319.

Livesey, D., Keen, J., Rouse, J., & White, F. (2006). The relationship between measures of executive function, motor performance and externalizing behaviour in 5- and 6-year-old Children. Human Movement Science, 25, 50-64.

Logan, G. D., & Cowan, W. B. (1984). On the ability to inhibit thought and action: A theory of an act of control. Psychological Review, 91, 295-327.

Logan, G. D., Schachar, R. J., & Tannock, R. (1997). Impulsivity and inhibitory control. Psychological Science, 8, 60-64.

Luengo, M. A., Carrillo-De-La-Pena, M. T., Otero, J. M., & Romero, E. (1994). A short-term longitudinal study of impulsivity and antisocial behaviour. Journal of Personality and Social Psychology, 66, 542-548.

Martin, C. S., Ealeywine, M., Blackson, T. C., Vanyukov, M. M., Moss, H. B., & Tarter, R. E. (1994). Aggressivity, inattention, hyperactivity, and impulsivity in boys at high and low risk for substance abuse. Journal of Abnormal Child Psychology, 22, 177-203.

McDowell, D. J., O'Neil, R., & Parke, R. D. (2000). Display rule application in a disappointing situation and children's emotional reactivity: Relations with social competence. Merrill - Palmer Quarterly, 46, 306-322.

Munden, A., & Arcelus, J. (1999). The ADHD handbook: A guide for parents and professional's on attention deficit/hyperactivity disorder. London: Jessica Kingsley Publishers.

Nigg, J. T. (1999). The ADHD response-inhibition deficit as measured by the stop task: Replication with DSM-IV combined type, extension, and qualification. Journal of Abnormal Child Psychology, 27, 393-402.

Oas, P. (1985). The psychological assessment of impulsivity: A review. Journal of Psychoeducational Assessment, 3, 141-156.

Oosterlaan, J., Logan, G. D., & Sergeant, J. A. (1998). Response inhibition in AD/HD, CD, comorbid AD/HD + CD, anxious, and control children: A meta-analysis of studies with the stop task. Journal of Child Psychology and Psychiatry, 39, 411-425.

Oosterlaan, J., & Sergeant, J. A. (1998). Response inhibition and response re-engagement in attention-deficit/hyperactivity disorder, disruptive, anxious and normal children. Behavioural Brain Research, 94, 33-43.

Olson, S. L. (1989). Assessment of impulsivity in preschoolers: Cross-measure convergences, longitudinal stability, and relevance to social competence. Journal of Clinical Child Psychology, 18, 176-183.

Pennington, B. F., & Ozonoff, S. (1996). Executive functions and developmental psychopathology. Journal of Child Psychology and Psychiatry, 37, 51-87.

Pons, F., Lawson, J., Harris, P. L., & de Rosnay, M. (2003). Individual differences in children's emotion understanding: Effects of age and language. Scandinavian Journal of Psychology, 44, 347-353.

Pons, F. & Harris, P. L. (2005). Longitudinal change and longitudinal stability of individual differences in children's emotion understanding. Cognition & Emotion, 19(8), 1158-1174.

Pons, F., Harris, P. L., & de Rosnay, M. (2004). Emotion comprehension between 3 and 11 years: Developmental periods and hierarchical organization. European Journal of Developmental Psychology, 1, 127-152.

Ridderinkhof, K. R., Bland, G. P. H., & Logan, G. D. (1999). A study of adaptive behaviour: Effects of age and irrelevant information on the ability to inhibit one's actions. Acta Psychologica, 101, 315-337.

Rieger, M., & Gauggel, S. (1999). Inhibitory after-effects in the stop signal paradigm. British Journal of Psychology, 90, 509-518.

Roberts, A. C., Robbins, T. W., & Weiskrantz, L. (1998). The prefrontal cortex: Executive and cognitive functions. Oxford: Oxford University Press.

Saarni, C. (1984). An observational study of children's attempts to monitor their expressive behavior. Child Development, 55, 1504-1513.

Saarni, C. (1992). Children's emotional-expressive behaviour as regulators of others happy and sad emotional states. In N. Eisenberg & R. A. Fabes (Eds.), Emotion and its regulation in early development: New directions for child development. San Francisco: Jossey-Bass.

Saarni, C. (1999). The development of emotional competence. New York, NY: Guilford Press.

Schachar, R. J., Chin, S., Logan, G. D., Ornstein, T. J., Crosbie, J., Ickowicz, A., et al. (2004). Evidence for an error monitoring deficit in attention deficit hyperactivity disorder. Journal of Abnormal Child Psychology, 32, 285-293.

Schultz, D., Trentacosta, C., Izard, C. E., Leaf, P., & Mostow, A. (2004). Children's emotion processing: The development of the assessment of children's emotion skills (ACES). Manuscript submitted for publication.

Sergeant, J. (2000). The cognitive-energetic model: An empirical approach to attention-deficit hyperactivity disorder. Neuroscience and Behavioural Reviews, 24, 7-12.

Sergeant, J. A., Geurts, H., & Oosterlaan, J. (2002). How specific is a deficit of executive functioning for attention-deficit/hyperactivity disorder? Behavioural Brain Research, 130, 3-28.

Sergeant, J., Oosterlaan, J., & Van der Meere, J. J. (1999). Information processing and energetic factors in attention deficit/hyperactivity disorder. In H. C. Quay & A. Hogan (Eds.). Handbook of disruptive behaviour disorders. New York: Plenum.

Tannock, R. (1998). Attention deficit hyperactivity disorder: Advances in cognitive neurobiological and genetic research. Journal of Child Psychology and Psychiatry, 39, 65-99.

Walcott, C. M., & Landau, S. (2004). The relation between disinhibition and emotion regulation in boys with attention deficit hyperactivity disorder. Journal of Clinical Child and Adolescent Psychology, 33, 772-782.

White, J. L., Moffott, T. E., Caspi, A., Bartusch, D. J., Needles, D. J., & Stouthamer-Loeber, M. (1994). Measuring impulsivity and examining its relationship to delinquency. Journal of Abnormal Psychology, 103, 192-205.

Zeman, J., Cassano, M., Perry-Parrish, C., & Stegall, S. (2006). Emotion regulation in children and adolescents. Journal of Developmental and Behavioral Pediatrics, 27, 155-168.

Chapter 4

Mental states, emotion and culture: A pragmatic proposal of the mentalistic understanding of culture[1]

Laura Quintanilla, Lina Arias and Encarnación Sarriá

The reader's eyes suddenly filled with tears,
and a tender voice whispered in his ear:
'Why are you crying
if everything in that book is a lie?'
And he responded:
'I know,
But what I feel is real'.
Ángel González

1. Introduction

One of the things we continue to view as a surprising peculiarity is the human capacity to bring about emotional experiences that do not merely depend on what happens in reality, but on what we suppose reality is and even on what we know that it is not. We apparently feel many things because of a strange and at times tenacious need for emotional tasting. Thus, we are able to experience the annoyance of a foolish act, the pleasure of reasoning something through, the bitterness of being disappointed, the satisfaction of achievement, the embarrassment of something inappropriate, the sadness which results from the idea that there will be a disaster, or the envy that follows when we perceive another is unworthy of possessing an object, and so on. Beyond our knowledge of the causes of such emotions is our understanding of the meaning attributed to events; for success, failure, misfortune,

---

[1] This chapter was supported by the Spanish Ministry of Science and Innovation (PSI2008-02174).

being worthy or inappropriate, are attributes based on social and cultural conventions. Further, people can also be aware that certain reasoning may be false but elegant, or that beliefs about the world, even one's own, may be misguided or biased. These facts result in the paradoxical observation by Angel Gonzalez's that, even though we may know it is not real, what we feel is real indeed.

This original human ability involves the existence of a relation between the emotion experienced as true and the meaning of the object to which it is connected. Based on this relation, we are able to recognize, attribute, control and predict others' emotions in such a way that is meaningful to the members of a community. In other words, this ability—and the mental states with which it is associated—is integral to our emotional understanding.

Knowledge of the relation between emotions and mental states is closely linked to theory of mind ability, which refers to understanding the relation between actions and their corresponding mental states. Just as the behaviors and actions displayed by an individual are closely related to his or her mental states, and we are able to understand such a relation, there is also an intrinsic relation between mental states and emotions. Understanding that someone else is experiencing an emotion is connected to the attributions that are made about his or her other mental states; including desires, beliefs, intentions, expectations, etc. Thus, understanding someone's emotion is also an interpretation of behavior; that is, the meaning that is attributed to action. Ultimately, of course, there is a complex network of subtle reasoning, inference, attribution, and action prediction processes in which mental and emotional states are interwoven. The interpretation of these states is produced in the context of, and for the purpose of, maintaining the interactions we have with others on a daily basis.

The aim of this chapter is twofold: first, to show that an understanding of the mind and emotions emerges in interactive and communicative contexts, where the meaning of action is born; and, second, to show that action has inter-cultural meanings. Regarding the second aim, the pragmatics of action generate similar meanings in different cultures but it is also needs to be recognized that different conceptions about what the mind is, and that which distinguishes it from what is real, may be very different between cultures.

2. The relation between mental states and action; or the meaning of behavior

A fundamental question in theory of mind research concerns the understanding of the relation between actions and mental states. In developmental psychology the question is usually, "When do children acquire an understanding of their own and other people's actions in light of the intentions, beliefs, desires and emotions of others?" (Baird & Astington, 2004, p. 37). This question contains a presupposition: intentions, beliefs and desires are concepts under which actions must be understood. Therefore, an action is not intelligible if we do not know which mental states are impelling it. In sum, the question we need to ask is when is it that children acquire the mental concepts to give actions meaning. This is, in short, an issue of meaning acquisition, as Derek Montgomery has noted (2005). That is, the meaning of action is acquired if it is understood in mentalist terms.

Another basic supposition of theory of mind scholars, which may have derived from certain philosophical traditions within the domain of semantics (Ogden & Richards, 1960), is the notion that meanings are closely related to referents; moreover, referents and objects are usually considered identical or similar. This explains why theory of mind scholars pose the difficulty that the acquisition of these concepts entails, as they neither have a referent or an object. Their surprise about the acquisition of these concepts is evident when it is stated that, "the peculiarity of mental states is that they are not observable, there is no perceptual access to these mental states (German & Leslie, 2001; Martí, 2003).

A mental state is not observable, certainly, we have no perceptual access to a belief, desire or intention, but neither is any concept observable, whether it refers to everyday objects, such as /table/, or more complex concepts, such as /number/, /social status/ or /rejection/, though in some cases we have experience with those objects that the culture has identified as /tables/ or /numbers/.

The idea usually held about concepts such as /table/ is that they are more visible than mental states. This idea results from the firm conviction that the concept /table/ is a representation of the object. Such a representation (or image) is similar to the object to which it refers and therefore the concept table is as accessible as the object itself (DeLoache & Sharon, 2002). However, mental states do not have a referent (or an observable object) in this sense, and therefore there is no perceptual access similar to what we might have for other concepts. Even when we may experience happiness, anger and sadness, or we may know, believe and desire things about the world, we do not necessarily access the mental and emotional concepts themselves.

Our staring point was the idea that we cannot allow ourselves to confuse objects or experiences with concepts or meanings. We posit that meanings, whether they refer to concepts or objects, are not the same as the objects or the experiences through which they are manifest. Concepts or words are abstractions we make of a multitude of single objects; they are a selective construction that reflects the essence of individuality. These abstractions or selective constructions are inserted within cultural networks. Therefore, meanings are closely related to cultural units that segment reality and allow us to interpret it[2]. Not all human groups interpret actions or experiences in the same manner; these phenomena do not have the same meaning for all because there is a conventional system of signs and meanings that not all cultures share, though certain inter-cultural signs and meanings may exist (Eco, 1968/1999; Racine, 2004).

What concepts and objects do have in common is that they are used in a particular community. We employ these concepts in communicative contexts to signify things about the world. Mental concepts are used to refer and give meaning to our behavior and that of others, but we also use them in interaction. It would not be possible to carry out any joint activity without understanding the goals and intentions or wishes of others. Under this premise, we think that the meaning of behavior, of actions or gestures, is acquired through use. Importantly, the use of mental and emotional states does not only refer to the linguistic use of these concepts. There is a non-linguistic use of mental and emotional states at the very heart of daily interaction. Communication exchanges do not only occur through linguistic and discursive forms, non-discursive information exchanges also take place and these also involve mental and emotional concepts (Sinha, 1999).

From a semiotic perspective, behavior, action, and gesture constitute signs that make possible the inferential function that goes with social interaction. This inferential function is characteristic of the activity of signs (Eco,

---

2 Eco (1963) establishes from semiotics that *cultural units* are segments that a culture defines from the reality continuum. Reality is considered to be continuous and the culture segments reality, separating into "discrete" units the continuous flow of experience. Thus, these cultural units act as interpreters that allow us to give meaning to these segments.

1984/1998). Just as we infer from a fever that there is a possible infection or illness, from an action or gesture, which are observable states, we infer mental and emotional attitudes. But unlike a fever which occurs naturally in the organism and without the intention of communicating or expressing the existence of illness, gestures, action and behaviors are regulated by social and cultural conventions and we very frequently use them with the intention of communicating to another something about the world. For example, emotional expressions are produced naturally (e.g., smiling, crying, moaning) but the production of such expressions is modulated by the culture. During the long period of upbringing, adults prescribe those behaviors that are adequate from those that are inadequate. Moreover, adults establish towards what object or situation it is adequate to express certain emotions. On the other hand, the culture regulates how behaviors are read and interpreted. As Averill (1980) has postulated, emotions are the products of a social construction for which meaning emerges in the pragmatics of social interaction[3]. In this sense, we understand culture not only as a way of understanding the world but also as an exercise of meanings through the community's actions.

This pragmatic view of mental and emotional comprehension may be better understood if we look at its origins in early infancy within the context of daily infant-parent interaction. Although our own studies do not center on these early developmental stages, focusing instead on children between three and five years of age, we consider the origin of interpersonal thought to be in everyday interaction. Within such interactions inter-subjectivity is developed, the first agreements about the world emerge and the use of pre-language symbolic systems in communicative contexts is initiated (Carpendale & Lewis, 2006; Hobson, 1998; Lewis & Carpendale, 2002; Rodríguez & Moro, 1998; Tomasello, 1992). This interactive and communicative setting is the privileged context to set up, evaluate and observe emotional and mental understanding.

---

3 Averill (1980) maintains the notion that to understand emotion a transitory social role is necessary, which gives way to the meaning that allows attributing an emotional label to behaviour. Knowledge of the social expectations of the cultural group to which one belongs is also required.

3. The pragmatic perspective

Bruner (1991) introduces an important perspective in relation to meaning acts with respect to language. He proposes that language is acquired through active use in interactive contexts. Thus, learning a language is equivalent to "doing things with words", as Austin (1975) suggests. Communicative intentions and different communication functions—imperatives, protodeclaratives —emerge before the child acquires language (Bates, Benigni, Bretherton, Camaioni, & Volterra, 1979); the meaning of what is said is understood before language is formally acquired. From this perspective, the acquisition of meanings (about the world) takes place in the negotiation we maintain through our interactions with others, in communicative acts.

Following this pragmatic view it would be reasonable to think that the meaning of action is constructed and acquired in the interaction itself. Action (or behavior), though not discursive, does have meaning and not all meaning is produced in terms of language. Although action may be translated into language and a discourse may be created, meaning based on action may also constitute a system that itself signifies what another has in mind.

Even if the linguistic terms communicating intention, belief and desire, or of certain emotional states, have not yet been acquired, there is empirical evidence which shows that children act as though knowing how to use intentions, desires and beliefs; indeed, they even know how to use and modulate some emotional expressions to gain benefits from others (Buss & Keil, 2004). This is not only prior to mastering the mental lexis but when the child has yet to acquire language per se. As Hoffman (1983) rightly points out, emotional expressions have instrumental purposes in children's social world; these uses generate the meaning of behavior intention, of mental and emotional experience.

The use of intention is expressed in infant-parent everyday interaction. Before participating in joint activities, babies are capable of sharing attentional states with an adult (Bretherton, 1991; Gómez, 2004; Gómez, Sarriá, Tamarit, Brioso, & León, 1995). At the end of the first year of life, infants are able to cooperate in certain actions with adults (Tomasello, Carpenter, Call, Behne, & Moll, in press; Tomasello & Rackozy, 2003). It could be said that children know how to put themselves in the intention of the other, which reveals that the prelude to understanding action with intentional meaning exists before language. Interactions that betray intentional understanding can be viewed as precursors of theory of mind, and their roots are linked to the origins of symbolic use. In this shared referentiality that results from inter-subjective encounters, emotion plays a fundamental role. Its function is to awaken the other's interest in relation to something; in Hobson's (1993) terms, to share an attitude towards something. From these exchanges we can understand and maybe explain the meaning acquisition process, particularly with respect to the meaning of interaction itself.

According to Bruner (1991), it is the active use of mental concepts in interaction contexts that promotes meaning. Recently, this pragmatic viewpoint has gained strength; some authors defend the importance of interaction as a privileged setting in which actions are given meaning and where the emergence of comprehension of the mind originates (Carpendale & Lewis, 2004; Dunn & Brophy, 2005; Harris, 2005; Hobson, 1998; Lewis & Carpendale, 2002; Montgomery, 2005; Nelson; 2005; Racine, 2004). Carpendale and Lewis's constructivist proposal maintains that physical and social knowledge are constructed simultaneously. The role of communicative interaction in this proposal is relevant because in such communication children discover different points of view about the world. Carpendale and Lewis state that children's knowledge about the world is not theoretical but practical, and it is constructed through the regularities discovered by interacting with others. Nelson (2005), who adopts a similar approach, argues that children's participation in their social environment depends on the communication expressed fundamentally through language. The young child's growing linguistic ability allows access to the mental world. Communication and theory of mind skills, in Nelson's conceptualization, maintain a two-way relation: the development of one is not possible without the other.

In general terms, the pragmatic proposal claims that it is in the interaction and communication process where meanings emerge, not only in their linguistic use but also in joint actions. The thesis on the pragmatics of mental knowledge has extensive empirical support. Part of this evidence comes from studies addressing children's understanding of the mind in natural contexts. Studies focusing on understanding behavior within the family group reveal that children between 18 months and three years of age progressively acquire knowledge about the expectations, desires and beliefs of others. They adjust this knowledge to the rules established in the family and they recognize and use mental states to ensure personal benefits or to benefit others (Dunn, 1988; Denham, 1998).

Children's play offers a context in which they share meaning because of their interactions, particularly situations that involve the assignment of roles and pretend suppositions (Park, 2001). Thus, in the dynamics of a shared pretense, children between three and five years of age are capable of interpreting the mental states of others, including knowledge and ignorance as well as desire and intention. Similarly, studies carried out in natural settings usually show that mentalistic, communicative, and behavioral abilities are evident at earlier ages than when they are examined in individual and experimental settings. Thus, it is possible that the pragmatic nature of mental and emotional knowledge makes children's abilities more visible when children have their own purposes in mind, rather than when they have to use this knowledge for the purpose of others; such as a researcher asking them to interpret or predict the behavior of another.

Further empirical evidence supporting the pragmatic nature of mental knowledge comes from studies evaluating the quality of parent-child interaction in the family setting. These studies support the notion that when an interaction is established in which the child is viewed as an agent with a mind, it promotes his or her subsequent understanding of mind and emotion (Meins, Fernyhough, Wainwright, Clark-Carter, DasGupta, Fradley, & Tuckey, 2003; Meins, Fernyhough, Johnson, & Lidestone, 2006). A family environment rich in sibling interactions also seems to support children's mental state understanding (Huges, Fujisawa, Ensor, Leche, & Marfleet, 2006; Jenkins & Astington, 1999; Perner, Ruffman, & Leekam, 1994). In such family settings, children's understanding of mind and emotion is fostered by certain kinds of communication and conversation (Dunn, Brown, Slomkowski, Tesla, & Youngblade, 1991; Harris, 2005; Hughes & de Rosnay, 2006; Slomkowski & Dunn, 1996). The idea that conversational interaction may help children understand mental and emotional states derives from studies with deaf children raised by hearing parents, which show that these children are delayed in some theory of mind tasks such as false belief understanding (Deleau, 1996; Peterson & Siegal, 2000; Figueras-Costa & Harris, 2001; Harris, de Rosnay, & Pons, 2005; Woolfe, Want, & Siegal, 2002). It is argued that deaf children raised by hearing parents have limited conversational experience and therefore also lack linguistic and extra-linguistic experience that is essential to understand a speaker's intent.

The meta-analysis undertaken by Wellman, Cross and Watson (2001) also reveals some interesting results in studies that use more structured and controlled evaluations of children's false belief understanding. Specifically, children's performance on false belief understanding tasks improves significantly when certain changes are introduced in the procedures; for example, the protagonist's explicit motive is made clear or the participant takes and active role in setting up the test situation. The impact of these changes (and others) points to the social nature of mentalistic comprehension, as Lewis and Carpendale (2002) maintain. At the same time, the impact of such interventions on children's false belief understanding highlights how the child's mentalistic conception is conditioned by its pragmatic nature: the child's reasoning about what an event or occurrence means to another person to some extent depends on the context, the role one has in it and the associated motivations, which have a causal role within the situation and for the mental and emotional reasoning of those involved.

Pragmatic reasoning about a character's action is made more obvious in situations where subjects (including children) actively participate in creating emotional and mental states. Children reveal more precocious mental state understanding in tasks that involve active behavioral participation than in situations where they are only spectators or observers of behavior; in the latter, the child's task consists in interpreting or predicting a behavior (in which they are not involved) at the researcher's request. When children participate in planning a strategy to create possible mental state in another it appears to support their ability to predict behavior based on that mental state (Bloom, 2004, Chandler, Fritz & Hala, 1989; Carpenter, Call, & Tomasello, 2003).

In summary, children's understanding of mind and emotion seems to depend to a certain extent on how mentalistic and emotional concepts are used in everyday interactions. Communication of mental concepts, both linguistic and non-linguistic, is part of the praxis. We use language to communicate mental states, but we also use actions, body expressions and gestures to transmit mental attitudes. Subjects as actors with their own purposes evaluate the situations in which interactions occur as containing relevant signs for understanding others.

4. The pragmatics of mental states in three- and four-year-old children's emotional comprehension

There has recently been growing interest in whether children who recognize, infer and attribute false beliefs are able to use such knowledge not only to predict actions but also to reason about emotions; that is, if children are able to evaluate the emotional meaning involved in having one or another belief with respect to a specific event.

The studies addressing this problem have employed classical false belief paradigms to assess emotional prediction ability; thus, a protagonist's false expectation about the content of some container or the identity of a protagonist (Little Red Riding Hood's grandmother or the wolf) needs to be taken into account to make a correct emotion attribution. The results show that four-year-old children can attribute false beliefs and belief-based action accurately but are not capable of using this mental state knowledge to predict emotion (Bradmetz & Schneider, 1999; 2004; de Rosnay, Pons, Harris, & Morrell 2004; Hadwin & Perner, 1991; Harris, Johnson, Hutton, Andrews, & Cooke, 1989). One attempt to explain this difference is based on the notion that children habitually conceive of actions as resulting from intentions (internal states); emotions, by contrast, are more often considered responses to changes in the external situation (de Rosnay, et al. 2004). For their part, Bradmetz & Schneider (2004) believe that children must understand emotion based on the belief about desire satisfaction, which is a process they consider developmentally more complex than predicting action based on the belief about reality.

To state that children understand emotions based on reality (i.e., resulting form a change in an external situation) more than on internal states requires one to suppose that reality is univocally conceived and is transparent; that is, reality is equally evaluated by all and therefore to conceive reality it is only necessary to present it as it is. However, there have been numerous empirical studies showing that children understand that the same situation may be evaluated differently depending on internal states such as desire (Flavell, Flavell, Green, & Moses, 1991; Rakoczy, Warneken, & Tomasello, 2007; Repacholi & Gopnik, 1997). We can also add that in pretend situations, where reality is only imagined, children can experience and attribute emotions in line with the imagined reality (Park, 2001). In our own work on how envy arises in naturalistic situations, we have found that there are conflicts between children for objects that objectively and a priori would not be considered desirable (e.g., a piece of plastic). The attraction for such an object resulted from its symbolic use or function attributed by one of the children; thus, a piece of plastic turned into a tool for building roads in the sand. In order to get the owner of the object to share it, play partners initially requested it politely, then they resorted to begging and patiently waiting. Eventually, play partners used threats and scorned the object and its owner. This produced in the children emotions typically linked to conflicts over possession, in addition to negotiation strategies concerning the desired object. Seen from this perspective, it would be reasonable to maintain that children experience emotions not by an association to an objective situation—the immediate external reality—but as a reality mediated by shared meanings.

Similarly, it is possible that conversational contexts are adequate contexts to assess what a reality means emotionally. Through language, we express the way we think about reality. In these situations, what is said, what is thought and the reality itself may or may not coincide, but in themselves they are also scenarios that generate emotions. Indeed, the role of conversation has been emphasized as an important influence on children's developing theory of mind ability (Huges, et al. 2006; Meins, et al., 2006); results showing that children who experience social and family contexts where conversation more often refers to internal states perform better on mental state understanding tasks.

In light of the pragmatic framework of mentalistic understanding sketched above we sought to further analyze the nature of the lag between understanding false belief and emotion prediction based on false belief. In keeping with our proposal, we adopted a conversational context as a means of acquiring information about a falsely held belief. A large sample ($N = 145$) of three- and four-year-old children witnessed a telephone conversation between two characters. In the story used, depicted as a film, Clara wants her father to bring her a racket. She goes to play at her friend's house and asks her brother, Jonas, to call her when their father returns. In one version of the story the father brings the racket and in the other he does not. Jonas calls Clara and misinforms her of the events, thereby creating a false belief in Clara. The film ends with Clara listening at the phone with her back to the camera. Children were asked: How does Clara feel after the phone call? Is she happy or sad? What does Clara think after the phone call? Does she think that her daddy has brought the racket or not? Thus, children had to predict an emotion based on the information transmitted to the listener together with the belief about the events (Arias, Quintanilla, & Sarriá, 2005). The results obtained in this study showed that the majority of three- and four-year-old children correctly predicted the emotion experienced by Clara on the basis of the information she has received (3 years, 60%; 4 years, 70%). However, in the belief questions, four-year-olds perform better (75%) than three-year-olds (50%). The degree of association between the two responses (emotion prediction and belief attribution) produced statistically significant results.

By using this conversational context it seems that access to the other's viewpoint and internal states is facilitated (Harris, 1996; 2005) and perhaps the executive component and working memory demands for inferring the belief is also reduced. By contrast, to undertake a belief attribution and emotion prediction, it is necessary to take into account both the fact that the information is counterfactual and the protagonist's desires in relation to the events. In our study, emotional prediction results obtained in a conversational context contrast with those obtained when employing the classic false belief paradigms described above. In this conversational context, the question about the emotional state in relation to the belief is much more appropriate than in the studies previously mentioned. That is, the question deals with the emotional consequence that results from information transmitted to the character. Contrast this with one of the tasks used by Bradmetz and Schneider (2004), in which the question regarding the emotional prediction based on the false belief is ambiguous: "[Maxi falsely believes his chocolates are in the cupboard.] When Maxi reaches the cupboard door, is he happy or not?" This question can give way to different kinds of responses: the child can focus on the false belief or s/he can anticipate what is going to happen subsequent to the door opening and thus reply according to anticipated reality rather than on the basis of Maxi's false belief. Indeed, the child could even believe that Maxi has no emotion because nothing has yet occurred that either satisfies or does not satisfies his desires. Moreover, in the question formulation it is not clear which is the desire about whose satisfaction one may have a false or true belief. It is possible, as Siegal and Beattie (1991) and Markman (1989) have pointed out, that questions made in experimental situations contradict some principles of conversational pragmatics proposed by Grice (1975).

From our point of view, emotional prediction requires knowing, without ambiguity, which is the desire about whose satisfaction one may have a false or true belief, not only about the belief and its relation with reality. On the other hand, given that emotions are characteristically discrete states, when someone is asked how he or she feels the response may be extensive or restricted depending on the information the speaker has in mind with respect to the other's situation. Therefore, if we intend to obtain a response about a discrete emotion, the question about someone's emotional state must be directed to a concrete situation relating the belief with the satisfaction of the desire. In the racket task, when subjects are asked about Clara's emotional state after receiving the information by telephone, there is no doubt that they are being asked about the impact that this information has on the expectations of satisfying the desire (i.e., to obtain the racket). This desire has been made manifest in the course of the film, during the characters' conversational interactions.

To assess the influence of children's active participation in a communicative interaction on emotional understanding, we designed a task in which participants were involved in planning and creating a false belief situation directed toward a peer. The strategy involved putting participants, together with the researcher, in a situation where they transmitted false information to a classmate. Participants were then asked about the emotional consequences of the information on the classmate. The situation was as follows. A researcher first asked two children to do a drawing to be used as part of a mural for the school, a typical activity for children in early childhood education. While the children were doing the drawing, the researcher told them that she had brought some sweets for them but had left them in a bag in another room. The researcher asked only one of the two children (the participant) to go with her to get the sweets but the child left behind was given a walkie-talkie so that he or she could be informed if the sweets were successfully retrieved. Once in the other room, the researcher produced two bags of sweets and told the participant that she only had two bags but she also wanted one for herself. So that she would not be left without sweets, the experimenter proposed, in a tone of complicity, that they trick the classmate by telling him or her over the walkie-talkie that they had not found the sweets. All the children accepted the agreement; they kept one bag and the researcher the other. Then, together with the participant, the researcher called the classmate and said: "We haven't found any sweets". (In actual fact the call was not received because the receiving walkie-talkie had been compromised so that the disappointing news could not actually be transmitted but this was unknown to the participant.) Having delivered the unfortunate news, the researcher asked the participant: "How does [X] feel now, after we have called him/her, sad or happy?" "Does he/she think that there are sweets or that there are not?" The results showed that performance on the emotional prediction improved when compared to previous studies, not only in four-year-old children (82% passed, 33 out of 40), but also in the three-year-old group (65% passed, 26 out of 40). Similarly, for the false belief question 82% (33 out of 40) of four-year-old children and 75% (30 out of 40) of three-year-olds indicated the correct response, differences between the two age groups were not significant.

Such findings are in line with those obtained in other studies in which children actively participate in planning and controlling a deceit directed to another (Bloom, 2004; Chandler, Fritz, & Hala, 1989). The strategic approach adopted in this study fully concurs with Carpendale and Lewis' (2006) arguments; mental knowledge is practical rather than theoretical, and it is in interactive contexts, which entail motivations or possible social benefits, where the efficient use of mental states is manifest. It is also in these contexts where it is possible for children to understand that such mental states produce emotional meanings.

In searching for an explanation of the disparity between our own results and those from other studies, we undertook a comparison of the procedures used to evaluate the child's ability to make emotion attributions based on false beliefs. We identified, as key elements, the task's conversational context and the active participation of the child in creating mental states. The conversational situation probably acts to release working memory from inferring mental state, both with respect to desire and belief. In previous studies involving emotion predictions within the context of classic false belief paradigms, the protagonist's belief acquisition occurs because of his or her absence from the scene and the lack of perceptual access to any changes. Thus, the participant must infer that such absence produces a false belief. Once the belief has been inferred, the participant needs to work out what emotion it produces in the character. This double work of inference [has not seen ® "believes Y", "wants X" ® must be sad] becomes easier in our study, which has the following form: [s/he has said Y ® "believes Y" "wants X" ® must be sad]. In the latter, the protagonist's belief is expressed in what is said in the conversation.

Furthermore, in the final study described above, the participant actively intervenes by transmitting verbal information that generates the other's (false) belief. This belief is evaluated in relation to desire satisfaction, which is the reason for the interactive situation, and allows the participant to make an emotional prediction in accordance with the protagonist's belief. Hence, the studies presented above together highlight the fact that that three- and four-year-old children know that false information about events can produce emotional states. The pragmatic nature of emotional and mental knowledge is manifested precisely in the use that children make of mental states, giving them an emotional meaning.

In summary, when we deal with the mental and emotional meaning of actions, contexts that favor meaning interpretation are precisely those in which meanings emerge: interaction, communication and conversation. In addition, these contexts possibly facilitate some components of executive functions demanded by emotional and mental reasoning. Interactive contexts emphasize how children use beliefs, desires and intentions to bestow emotional meaning. However, this analysis inevitably forces us to consider whether mental states that are basic to understanding actions are in fact culturally determined.

5. Pragmatic versus substantive mental knowledge in culture

There are different ways of dealing with mental knowledge in relation to culture. This is so because both mind and culture may be conceived in very open or restricted terms. In addition, mind and culture involve processes that are very closely linked. In this section, we shall refer to a distinction we have developed elsewhere (Quintanilla, 1999; Quintanilla & Sarriá, 2003, 2004; Rivière, 1991), between pragmatic mental knowledge found in everyday interactions in all cultures (e.g., basic reasoning to predict action) and the most substantive mental knowledge that culture conceives as mind. We shall also refer to their relation with the particular cosmovision on the distinction between the subjective and objective elements of a cultural group.

On the distinction between the subjective and objective, Piaget and Stern set out their opposing positions some time ago. Piaget (1933/1984) stated that egocentrism—the lack of distinction between subjective and objective elements—produced all known corollaries of the pre-operational stage: animism, realism, artificialism, magical thought, etc. Stern, for his part, argued that some children showed signs of understanding the subjective-objective distinction when they produced sentences such as, "I think he has a headache". According to Stern, such an utterance indicates that the child differentiates the perceived or apparent reality from the inferred reality. To this Piaget responded that it was necessary to avoid, "the sophism of the implicit, that one thing is the plane of action and another very different is the plane of reflection" (ibid, pp. 46).

In 1985, Wellman pondered a very interesting idea: in order to have a theory of mind it is necessary to distinguish between what is real and what is mental. His studies on the distinction that children make between the properties of what is real and mental showed that three-year-old children know that real things, physical objects, have specific properties such as public perceptual access. Such properties are absent in objects that have been imagined, thought, dreamt, etc. (Estes & Wellman, 1986). Within this empirical framework, Wellman put forth the notion that the distinction between what is real and mental precedes and underpins a theory of mind. However, Wellman himself knows that some cultures that maintain animist, realist or magic conceptions make a distinction between what is real and mental that has nothing to do with Western culture

Lillard (1998, 1999) reflects on the variety of ethnopsychologies and proposes that cultural differences should be taken into account even in the central concepts of folk psychology. The conception of a person in terms of the executor of acts is not shared in all cultures and the distinction between objective and subjective concepts also differs between cultures. For example, Lillard (1999) found differences in the ways urban and rural American children explained a character's actions. Whereas urban children explained behavior from a psychological point of view, rural children explained the same behaviors by drawing on situational features. Further, in some cultures the depiction of someone running towards a train would be explained in terms of the train's imminent departure, while in other cultures the explanation would be couched in terms of the person's desire to catch the train. These two explanations, according to Lillard, illustrate cultural differences that affect intentional understanding.

It is possible that both forms of reasoning are based on some implicit social suppositions: For example, trains leave at specific times and they do not usually wait for passengers; if you arrive with little time to get the train you will have to run to catch it. Such shared suppositions are part of culture, they are conventions that we share and use to explain behavior. To adhere to these suppositions would resonate with the first explanation, whereas the attribution of intentions to the subject would arguably render the explanation less certain; it is possible, for example, that the subject does not want to catch the train at all but is running to prolong his goodbyes to his departing girlfriend. For some reason there are cultures that avoid the less certain explanation and prefer situational accounts of behavior. What Lillard proposes is that the use we make of psychological or situational reasoning depends on the culture in which we are immersed. Our proposal is that both types of reasoning coexist perfectly in the daily life of any culture. Depending on the type of information we intend to transmit and our motivations for understanding and explaining the situation, we offer information based either on situations or on psychological motivations.

In order to present an example of the perfect coexistence of different types of reasoning within the same culture, we offer some ethnographic data collected during fieldwork in Tlacochahuaya (Mexico) where one of the current authors lived with the Zapotec community for a season (Quintanilla, 1999). Within the Zapotec culture, magic, realist and animist beliefs coexist with the most operative and pragmatic reasoning of mental explanations. At the end of the workday, Zapotec families usually sit round the hearth to tell and recall experiences. The stories are about the family members and are typically biographical. The events of these stories are generally explained with reference to magical conceptions. Practically every night during the research visit, the family talked about the effect witchery had on the behavior of the family members. Specifically, how the witch had taken Mr Morales—the head of the family—and had made him disappear for several days. The disappearance of Mr Morales took place after a tremendous drinking binge at a traditional wedding, which lasts several days and involves drinking great quantities of mescal. Dreams were routinely interpreted to predict future events and family members talked about how to protect themselves from friends when one had something new (an animal, object or even a new family member), so as to avoid, "being cast the evil eye". It was stated that Naguals—witches transformed into animals—could come upon someone on a path and cause him a tremendous shock. If the illness produced by the shock was not cured properly, patients could lose their soul; they would stop working, sleeping and eating until they looked like "living death".

At the conclusion of such evening tales, the family would say their goodnights and everyone went to sleep. On one of those nights of vivid and intense tales, everyone was awoken by the shouts of the mother of the family. She was agitated and cursed, the damage had been terrible, the water pump recently bought by her sons for irrigation had been broken and everything was destroyed. Everyone got up quickly and the sons called the constable, who said that nothing could be done in the dark of night and recommended that everyone wait until the next morning. The older sons of the family however spent the rest of the night going from the cultivated land to the house trying to find out what had happened. At dawn, the older sons did not stop formulating hypotheses and expressing doubts about who was responsible for the evening events, and speculating on their intentions: the sons suggested that the people form the local rural organization may have perpetrated the vandalism because they were cross that the family had purchased the water pump through their organization despite the fact that they were not members. It was also suggested that it could have been the people from the next village, with whom they had some debts. The sons concluded, "Whoever did this aren't professionals, they're novices because they've left things of value"; "They probably heard a dog barking and thought it was us, that we were going to watch the crops, and ran away because they left all those things here".

Importantly, there was no attempt by the elder sons to explain the evening's events by reference to magical constructs. The elder sons' explanations were couched in terms of the intentions and motivations of those responsible; who had wanted to cause them harm. But they also made hypotheses concerning the aggressors' skills, their intentions and the meaning of the act of aggression. In addition, they attributed a false belief to those responsible for the felony; that is, the villans must have heard some noise and suspected that it was the owners approaching, causing them to run away and leave behind some things of value. The family's conceptions about magic, animism or realism, which emerged every night, did not seem in any way dissonant with their reasoning about intentions, beliefs and motivations. Indeed, such apparent contradictions can be found in Western cultures as well.

From a pragmatic view of action as evidence of mental comprehension, we have proposed a differentiation between more substantive mental knowledge that makes us conceive the mind with certain properties (that makes it different from real objects) and more pragmatic mental knowledge that involves using mental states to reason about behavior. Our proposal is similar to the suggestion made by Piaget in response to Stern but we do not avoid the sophism of what is implicit, instead we use it as evidence that operational and pragmatic knowledge for everyday life differs from substantive knowledge about how we conceive the mental and the real world. In essence, our proposal suggests that uses of mental states appear in a plane of practical reasoning about action, while knowing the characteristics of mental states and their ontological properties would be in a more reflexive plane of reasoning. Knowledge of the latter kind would depend on the conception of the world, which categorizes experience and reality in specific ways and, therefore, is related to culture.

To clarify this distinction, consider the following analogy. Children know that water is drunk and they use it for drinking. It is not necessary that they know that one of the properties of water is its liquid state or that they can differentiate it from its gaseous state. We think knowledge of mental states is similar; we use them to predict and control the behavior of others and to understand ourselves but this efficient use of mental states does not necessarily involve the ontological distinction between the properties of mental states and real states, as Wellman (1985) and Lillard (1998) suggest. In sum, we needed to show empirically if this ontological distinction is at the conceptual base of a theory of mind or if, as we have hypothesized, these are two types of mentalistic knowledge differently related with culture. Re-defining Piaget's statement, we wish to establish whether in the plane of action we use certain mental knowledge that differs from that used in the reflexive plane.

6. A cultural comparison between Zapotec and Spanish children's understanding of false-belief and of the distinction between what is real and what is mental

In order to establish whether an ontological distinction between what is real and what is mental is necessary for a mentalistic comprehension of behavior, we compared children's performance on this distinction and their performance predicting actions that depend on false beliefs, with both first and second order recursion. Children were divided into two age groups, younger (4.6 years) and older (6.6 years), and they were from two different cultures, Zapotec and Spanish. If, following Wellman and Lillard's theses, the ontological distinction between what is real and what is mental differed in the two cultures, we expected that children would perform differently in the false belief task. If, however, the results of tasks that require an ontological distinction between what is real and mental are culturally differentiated but performance on the mentalistic reasoning tasks (i.e., false belief task) was similar, this would offer some confirmation of our view that there are two types of mentalistis knowledge: substantive and pragmatic.

We used two false belief tasks (first and second order) in which we asked about action prediction and belief attribution. In addition, we used six stories to assess the distinction between mental and physical properties, similar to the tasks designed by Wellman and Estes (1986). There were three stories asking about the perceptual access properties of mental states—inter- and intra-subjective—together with three additional stories concerning the perceptual access properties of real objects—inter- and intra-subjective. In these tasks each story had five questions; therefore, the maximum score for each story type, mental or physical, was 15 points.

Our results did not reveal any differences between Zapotec and Spanish children in the two false belief tasks for either of the mental state understanding questions: behavior prediction and belief attribution. There were also no differences between the two cultural groups with respect to how they characterized the properties of physical objects. However, we did find performance differences in tasks identifying the properties of mental states. The average scores for the four-year-old Zapotec group referring to perceptual access properties of mental entities were relatively low (4.4), and were statistically different from Spanish children's average scores (6.7). By six years of age, however, these differences were inverted. One causes for this difference is that six-year-old Spanish children responded affirmatively to questions about whether the protagonist could see what s/he thought, dreamt or remembered. It is interesting to note the metaphoric use of the verb to see in Western culture, which is used to mean understand, access an idea, and so on. It is also necessary to draw attention to the fact that six-year-old Western children already use such metaphoric meaning. This metaphoric notion of the mind as a container of images is deeply rooted in the Western world. In the Zapotecs' conception, however, the mind is a container of voices. Thought, according to a Zapotec child's explanations is, "like a voice one has inside and then comes out through the mouth". For Zapotecs, thought, and indeed the mind, has a connotation more closely linked to the voice, dialogue or conversation, than it is linked to mental images.

Our results indicate that children employ cultural knowledge to characterize the properties of mental states. Spanish (Western) children use the metaphor of thought as an image, while Zapotec children use the metaphor thought as a voice. On the other hand, and at the same time, mental states are used in both cultures to reason about action despite the fact that children's knowledge about the properties or characteristics of the mind is different in the respective cultures. What is remarkable about our results is the fact that four-year-old Zapotec children use false beliefs to correctly predict an action even though they do not reliably identify the ontological properties of mental entities. Our results also confirm that six-year-old children in the two cultures, despite manifest differences in their perception of the nature of mental states, perform very similarly in tasks involving inferences of second order recursion; second order false belief.

Certainly, the results concerning false belief performance obtained in our study are not in line with those reported by Vinden (1996) with the Quechua people from Peru but are consistent with those reported by Avis and Harris, (1991) and Callaghan et al. (2005), the latter evaluating children from various cultures between three and five years of age. Callaghan et al. propose that conversational experience is essential for theory of mind understanding and is a common element in all cultures: for deaf children raised by hearing parents, however, such conversational interaction is restricted and therefore likely to underpin their difficulties in understanding mind and emotion.

To summarize, our results from this cross-cultural study show that the use of these two essential mental constructs—belief and desire—in pragmatic reasoning of action can be characterized as inter-cultural knowledge. In other words, children reason efficiently about the possible action of others in terms of beliefs and desires even though the have clearly different conceptions about the properties of the mind. The latter, substantive mentalistic understanding, however, can clearly vary across different cultures.

One of the issues that remain to be solved is whether the meanings of actions, in terms of beliefs and desires, are also used inter-culturally to understand emotional consequences. For the moment, empirical evidence shows that the development of emotional comprehension does not have the same developmental structure in Western and non-Western children (Vinden's, 1999; Tennebaum, Visscher, Pons, & Harris, 2004). However, an aspect of these studies that needs to be highlighted is the difficulty of constructing assessment instruments that are cross-culturally valid; for example, the Test of Emotion Comprehension (Pons & Harris, 2000), which has been widely employed, uses comic strips as story telling support, and as a cue to elicit emotional reasoning. As the authors themselves point out (Tennenbaum et al., 2004), the use of this type of material in certain cultures is scarce. Such a method of presentation involves knowing how to interpret stories and emotional expressions presented as stylized visual images, which if not used frequently might be unfamiliar and thereby undermine the validity of the findings: the results obtained in evaluating emotional attribution may be due to the instrument rather than to the children's ability.

It is also necessary to know the meaning of emotional expressions—linguistic and non-linguistic—between cultures, and if emotions generate the same type of interaction strategies between cultural groups. That is, it is important to consider not only whether the linguistic emotional label is the same or differs in the various cultures, but whether the emotional experience has the same meaning. For example, Western Europeans would never think that diarrhea or problems getting to sleep are caused by receiving a shock. Nor would they go to the doctor to cure a shock because this emotional state is not considered to be an illness. Within Mesoamerican cultures however, which include the Zapotecs, it would not be unusual to consider a shock to be a cause illness, the symptoms of which can be treated by a doctor. In other words, interpreting behavior, as well controlling, predicting and recognizing it—in addition to supposing that mental and emotional states have a basic meaning—involves re-signifying behavior in wider contexts in order to understand its nature. All these issues need to be evaluated to address the problem of the acquisition of emotional meaning in the development of children from different cultures. For this purpose it is important to distinguish the pragmatic aspects of the emotion–action relation from the particular elements of different cultural conceptions.

In summary, from our perspective we can state that the meaning of action, in certain problems such as false belief, is basic to the functioning of any culture. It is possible to say that all human groups interpret behavior in and for our daily activity, and in turn behavior becomes the symptom of mental states. However, this mentalistic meaning of behavior coexists with different conceptions of the mind. The mind may be conceived as a voice or as a visual image, or as a computer. It is possible to think that certain mental processes, such as dreams, are related to destiny, as Zapotecs believe, or to conceive that certain emotional reactions, like a shock, are illnesses. But the truth is that the conception of how the mind functions and its properties, the metaphors we use to explain it, share this inter-cultural activity of signifying behavior in an intentional sense.

7. Conclusion

The development of the meaning of mental concepts is an issue that remains open. The question of when children acquire mental concepts to explain behavior, and how these concepts are acquired, are questions that still elude definite answers. Our intention has been to show that mentalistic meanings are constructed and emerge in interactive contexts.

Recent correlational studies suggest that the development of mentalistic comprehension is closely related with the interaction that takes place in communicative contexts. Conversation in particular is one of those interactions in which it is possible to make explicit how we conceive reality. Our experimental studies show that from three years of age children understand the emotional meaning of what is said in a conversation, whether it coincides or not with reality. In fact, when children are accomplices in a conversation where what is said does not adjust to reality they know what the emotional consequences of this are for their peers. When we study how the emotional and mental meanings of actions in conversational and interactive contexts are understood, children's abilities are more clearly revealed.

We have noted that the roots of using mental concepts are embedded in interaction with others. Although different cultures have different interaction patterns, it is not difficult to understand that all cultures require the concept of intention, desire or belief to understand others. This understanding is a pragmatic knowledge that places mental states in relation to behavior but this knowledge shares different cultural conceptions or diverse metaphors on how the mind functions.

References

Arias, L., Quintanilla, L., & Sarriá, E. (2005). Is there a lag between understanding false beliefs and emotions attributions in young children? Poster. XIIth European Conference on Developmental Psychology, La Laguna, Tenerife, Canary Islands.

Astington, J.W., & Jenkins, J. M. (1999). A longitudinal study of the relation between language and theory-of-mind development. Developmental Psychology, 35(5), 1311-1320.

Austin, J.L. (1975). How to do things with words. Cambridge: Harvard University Press.

Avis, J., & Harris, P.L. (1991). Belief-desire reasoning among Baka children: Evidence for a universal conception of mind. Child Development, 62, 460-467.

Averill, J. R. (1980). A constructivist view of emotion. In R. Plutchik and H. Kellerman (Eds.). Emotion: Theory, research and experience: Vol. I. Theories of emotion (pp. 305-339). New York: Academic Press. Reprinted in: Halberstadt, A. G., & Ellyson, S. L. (Eds.) (1990). Social psychology readings: A century of research (pp. 143-156). New York: McGraw-Hill.

Baird, J.A., & Astington, J.W. (2004). The role of Mental State understanding in the development of moral cognition and moral action. New directions for child and adolescent development, 103, 37-49.

Bates, E., Benigni, L., Bretherton, I., Camaioni, L., & Volterra, V. (1979). Cognition and communication from 9-13 months: correlational findings. In E. Bates

(Ed.). The emergence of symbols: cognition and communication in infancy. New York: Academic Press.

Bloom, M. (2004). Theory of mind and emotion. Perspectives in psychology, 3-8. Retrieved from http://bespin.stwing.upenn.edu/~upsych/Perspectives/2003/Bloom.pdf. May, 2005.

Bradmetz, J., & Schneider, R. (1999). Is Little Red Riding Hood afraid of her grandmother? British Journal of Developmental Psychology, 17(4), pp. 501-514.

Bradmetz J., & Schneider R. (2004). The role of the counterfactually satisfied desire in the lag between false-belief and false-emotion attributions in children aged 4-7. British Journal of Developmental Psychology, 22, (2), 185-196.

Bretherton, I. (1991). Intentional Communication and the Development of an Understanding Mind. In D. Frye & C. Moore (Eds). Children's Theories of Mind: Mental States and Social Understanding. Hove: LEA.

Bruner, J. (1991). Actos de significado. Más allá de la revolución cognitiva. Madrid: Alianza,

Buss, K., & Keil, E. (2004). Comparison of Sadness, Anger, and Fear Facial expressions when toddlers look at their mothers. Child Development, 75, 6, 1761-1773.

Callaghan, T., Rochat, P., Lillard, A., Claux, M.L., Odden, H., Itakura, S., Sombat Tapanya, S., & Singh, S. (2005). Synchrony in the Onset of Mental State Reasoning: Evidence From 5 Cultures. American Psychological Society, 16 (5), 378-384.

Carpendale, J. I. M., & Lewis, C. (2006). How Children Develop Social Understanding. Oxford: Blackwell.

Carpendale, J. E. M., & Lewis, C. (2004). Constructing an understanding of mind: The development of children's understanding of mind within social interaction. Behavioral and Brain Sciences, 27, 79-150.

Carpenter, M., Call, J., & Tomasello, M. (2003). A new false belief test for 36-month-old. British Journal of Developmental Psychology, 20, 393-420.

Chandler, M.J., Fritz, A.S., & Hala, S. (1989). Small-Scale Deceit: Deception as a marker of 2, 3- and 4-year olds' early theories of mind. Child Development, 60, 1263-1277.

Deleau, M. (1996). L'attribution d'états mentaux chez les enfants sourds et entendants: Une approche du role de l'expérience langagière sur une théorie de l'esprit. Bulletin de Psychologie, 5, 48–56.

DeLoache, J. S., & Sharon, T. (2002). Symbols and similarity: You can get too much of a good thing. Retrieved from www.faculty.virginia.edu/deloache/identical.subsep11.manuscript.doc. March, 2005.

Denham, S. (1988). Emotional Development in Young Children. New York: Guilford Press.

de Rosnay, M., Pons, F., Harris, P. L. & Morrell., J. M. B. (2004). A lag between understanding false belief and emotion attribution in young children: Relationships with linguistic ability and mothers' mental-state language. British Journal of Developmental Psychology, 22(2), 197-218.

Dunn, J. (1988). The beginnings of social understanding. Cambridge: Cambridge University Press.

Dunn, J., & Brophy, M. (2005). Communication, relationships, and individual differences in children's understanding of mind. In W. Astington & J. Baird (Eds). Why language matters for the theory of mind. New York: Oxford University Press.

Dunn, J., Brown, J., Slomkowski, C., Tesla, C., & Youngblade, L. (1991). Young children's understanding of other people's feelings and beliefs: Individual differences and their antecedents. Child Development, 62, 1352-1366.

Eco, U. (1968/1999). La estructura ausente. Barcelona: Lumen.

Eco, U. (1984/1998). Semiótica y filosofía del lenguaje. Barcelona: Lumen.

Estes, D., & Wellman, H.M. (1986). Early Understanding of Mental Entities: A reexamination of Childhood Realism. Child Development, 57, 4, 910-923.

Figueras-Costa, B., & Harris, P. H. (2001). Theory of Mind Development in Deaf Children: A Nonverbal Test of False-Belief Understanding. Journal of Deaf Studies and Deaf Education, 6, 2.

Flavell, J.H., Flavell, E.R., Green, F.L., & Moses, L.J. (1990). Young children's understanding of fact beliefs versus value beliefs. Child Development, 61, 915-928.

German, T.P., & Leslie, A.M. (2001). Children's inferences from knowing to pretending and believing. British Journal of Developmental Psychology, 19, 59–83.

Gómez, J. C. (2004). Apes, monkeys, children, and the growth of mind. Cambridge: Harvard University Press.

Gómez, J. C.; Sarriá, E.; Tamarit, J.; Brioso, A. y León, E. (1995). Los inicios de la comunicación: estudio comparado de niños y primates no humanos e implicaciones para el autismo. Madrid: Ministerio de Educación y Ciencia.

Grice, H.P. (1975/1991): "Lógica y conversación". En L.M. Valdés (Ed.). La

Búsqueda del Significado. Madrid: Tecnos.

Hadwin, J., & Perner, J. (1991). Pleased and surprised: Children's cognitive theory of emotion. British Journal of Developmental Psychology, 9, (2), 215-234.

Harris, P. L. (1996). Desires, beliefs, and language. In P. Carruthers and P.K. Smith (Eds), Theories of theories of mind (pp. 200-220). Cambridge: Cambridge University Press.

Harris, P. L. (2005). Conversation, Pretense, and Theory of Mind. In W. Astington & J. Baird (Eds). Why language matters for the theory of mind. New York: Oxford University Press.

Harris, P.L, de Rosnay, M., & Pons, F. (2005). Language and Children's Understanding of Mental States. Current Directions in Psychological Science, 14, (2) 69.

Harris, P. L., Johnson, C. N., Hutton, D., Andrews, G., & Cooke, T. (1989). Young children's theory-of-mind and emotion. Cognition and Emotion, 3, (4), 379-400.

Hobson, P. (1998). The intersubjective foundations of thought. In Stein Braten (Ed.) Intersubjective communication and emotion in early ontogeny. (pp. 237-297). Cambridge: Cambridge University Press.

Hobson, P. (1993). Autism and the development of mind. Hove, U.K.: Lawrence Erlbaum.

Hoffman, M. L, (1983). Affective and cognitive processes in moral internahzation. In E.T. Higgins, D. N. Ruble, & W.W. Hartup (Eds.), Social cognition and social development: a socio-cultural perspective. (pp. 236-274), Cambridge, MA: Cambridge University Press.

Hughes, C., & de Rosnay, M. (2006). Introduction to Special Issue: The role of conversations in children's social, emotional and cognitive development. British Journal of Developmental Psychology, 24, 1-6.

Hughes, C., Fujisawa, K., Ensor, R., Lecce, S., & Marfleet, R. (2006). Cooperation and Conversations about the Mind: A study of Individual differences in 2-Year-Olds and their Siblings. British Journal of Developmental Psychology, 24, 53-72.

Jenkins, J. M. & Astington, J.W. (1996). Cognitive factors and Family structure associated with the theory of mind development in young children. Developmental psychology, 32, 70-78

Lewis, C. & Carpendale, J. I. M. (2002). Social cognition. In P. K. Smith & C. Hart (Eds.). The handbook of social development. Blackwell.

Lillard, A. (1998). Ethnopsychologies: Cultural variations in theories of mind. Psychological Bulletin, 123, 3-32.

Lillard, A.S. (1999). Developing a cultural theory of mind: The CIAO approach. Current Directions in Psychological Science, 8, 57-61.

Nelson, K. (2005). Language Pathways into the Community of Minds. In J. W. Astington & J. Baird (Eds.) Why Language Matters to Theory of Mind. (pp. 26-49) Cambridge: Cambridge University Press.

Markman, E. (1989). Categorization and naming in children: Problems of induction. Cambridge, MA: MIT Press.

Meins, E., Fernyhough, C., Wainwright, R., Clark-Carter, D., Das Gupta, M., Fradley, E. & Tuckey, M. 2003. Pathways to understanding mind: Construct validity and predictive validity of maternal mind-mindedness. Child Development. 74, 1194-1211.

Meins, E., Fernyhough, C., Johnson, F. & Lidstone, J. (2006). Mind-mindedness in children: Individual differences in internal-state talk in middle childhood. British Journal of Developmental Psycholoyg. 24 (1), 181-196.

Martí, E. (2003). Representar el mundo externamente. La construcción infantil de los sistemas externos de representación. Madrid: A. Machado / Colección Aprendizaje.

Montgomery, D. (2005) The developmental origins of meaning for mental terms. In: J. W. Astington & J. Baird (Eds). Why language matters for the theory of mind. New York: Oxford University Press.

Ogden C. K. & Richards I. A. (1960). The meaning of meaning. A study of the influence of language upon thought and of the science of symbolism. Londres: Routledge & Kegan Paul.

Park, S. (2001). Theory of Mind Dynamics in Children's Play: A Qualitative Inquiry in a Preschool Classroom. PhD Disertation. Faculty of the Virginia Polytechnic Institute and State University. Blacksburg, Virginia. Retrieved from http://scholar.lib.vt.edu/theses/available/etd-12102001-173508/unrestricted/Soyeon_Park_ETD.pdf , March, 2005.

Peterson , C.C., & Siegal, M. (2000). Insights into Theory of Mind from deafness and autism. Mind & Language, 15, 123-145.

Piaget, J. (1933/1984). La representación del mundo en el niño. Madrid: Morata.

Perner, J., Ruffman, T., & Leekam, S.L. (1994). Theory of Mind is Contagious: You Catch it from Your Siblings. Child Development, 65 (4), 1228-1238.

Pons, F. & Harris, P. (2000). The Test of Emotion Comprehension – TEC.

Oxford: The University of Oxford.

Quintanilla, L. (1999). La Universalidad de la teoría de la mente y otras capacidades mentalistas: Un estudio evolutivo transcultural en niños zapotecos, españoles y regiomontanos. Unpublished dissertation. Facultad de Psicología. Universidad Nacional de Educación a Distancia.

Quintanilla, L., & Sarriá, E. (2003). Realismo, Animismo y Teoría de la Mente: características culturales y universales del conocimiento mental. Estudios de Psicología, 24 (3), 313-335

Quintanilla, L., & Sarriá, E. (2004). Realism and animism like metaphors of mental understanding" (Paper), 18th Biennial Meeting of ISSBD, Ghent, Belgium, 11-15 julio 2004.

Racine, T. P. (2004). Wittgenstein's internalistic logic and children's theories of mind. In J. I.M. Carpendale & U. Müller (Eds.). Social interaction and the development of knowledge. London: LEA.

Rakoczy, H., Warneken, F., & Tomasello, M. (2007). "This way!" "No! That way!"—3-year olds know that two people can have mutually incompatible desires. Cognitive Development, 22, 47-68.

Repacholi, B.M., & Gopnik A. (1997). Early reasoning about desires: evidence from 14- and 18-month-olds. Developmental Psychology, 33,(1), 12-21.

Rodríguez, C., & Moro, C. (1998). El uso convencional también hace permanentes a los objetos. Infancia y Aprendizaje, 84, 67-83.

Rivière, A. (1991). Objetos con mente. Madrid: Alianza Editorial.

Siegal, M. & Beattie, K. (1991). Where to look for children's knowledge of false beliefs. Cognition, 38, 1-12.

Slomkowski, C., & Dunn, J. (1996). Young children's understanding of other people's beliefs and feelings and their connected communication with friends. Developmental Psychology, 32(3) 442-47.

Tomasello, M. (1999). The cultural origins of human cognition. Harvard: Harvard University Press.

Sinha, C. (1999). Grounding, mapping and acts of meaning. In T. Janssen & G. Redeker (Eds.). Cognitive Linguistics: Foundations, Scope and Methodology. Berlin: Mouton de Gruyter.

Tenenbaum, H., Visscher, P., Pons, F., & Harris, P. (2004). Emotion understanding in Quechua children from an agro-pastoralist village. International Journal of Behavioral Development, 28 (5), 471-478.

Tomasello, M., Carpenter, M., Call, J., Behne, T., & Moll, H. (2005). Understanding and sharing intentions: The origins of cultural cognition. Behavioral and Brain Sciences, 28, 675 - 691.

Tomasello, M & Rakoczy, H. (2003). What Makes Human Cognition Unique? From Individual to Shared to Collective Intentionality. Mind and Language 18 (2):121-147.

Vinden, P. G. (1996). Junin Quechua Children's Understanding of Mind. Child Development, 67, 1707–1716.

Vinden, P. G. (1999). Children's understanding of mind and emotion: A multi-culture study. Cognition and Emotion, 13 (1), 19–48.

Wellman, H. M. (1990). The child's theory of mind. Cambridge, M.A.: MIT press/Bradford Books

Wellman, H.M., Cross D., & Watson, J. (2001). A meta-analysis of theory of mind development: The truth about false belief. Child Development, 72, 655-684.

Woolfe, T., Want, S.C., & Siegal, M. (2002). Signposts to Development: Theory of Mind in Deaf Children. Child Development, 73 (3), 768-778.

Study of the evolution of children's social representations of emotions at ages five and six

Chapter 5

Marie-France Daniel, Emmanuelle Auriac and Lee Londei

1. Introduction

To situate the context of our research and the objective pursued, we consider two fields. Firstly, the field related to emotions is covered as studied by psychologists, and then as addressed by philosophers. Secondly, we briefly define what we mean by social representations (SR), and why studying them is of interest with regard to the evolution of pupils' verbal-conceptual abilities.

Emotions

A historical overview of the theories (see Christophe, 1998) reveals the absence of a consensus among theoreticians in defining emotion (among others: Frijda, 1993), showing that emotion is a vague notion that is not easily definable (Alvarado & Jameson, 2002; Dantzer, 2002).

With regard to psychologists' perspectives, first there were the peripheral theories, those of James, of Lange and of Cannon (end of the 19th century), that essentially linked emotional states to physical perceptions. Then Schachter and Singer (mid 20th century) proposed a cognitive-psychological theory of emotions. This theory is situated at the junction of physiological and cognitive theories of emotion. It includes physiological manifestations and their cognitive interpretation. Later, cognitive theories appear with Arnold (mid 20th century), who maintains that the brain is not the place of simple reflexes, but that it is very active in decoding emotional stimuli. Arnold appeals to the concept of the memory of previous emotional experiences and to the evaluation of possible consequences. Next, the relational theory of emotions appears in the 1970s with Lazarus, who introduces the individual's interaction with his environment as a decisive factor in emotion. Emotion would therefore be influenced by the standards, rules and social characteristics of the environment, although the fundamental process behind the determination of emotion remains an internal cognitive process (Lazarus et al., 1970). The same goes for Averill (1980, 1982), who views emotions as social constructions managed by social rules and behavioural expectations, which in turn influence the individual's emotional experience. Thus, emotions participate in the construction of a person's social identity (also see Sarbin, 1989).

In the tradition of the socio-constructivist allegiance, more contemporary psychologists actualise in their works the demonstration of what was already present in Lev Vygotski's (1932) thesis: emotion does not belong to the physiological universe but it is a complete and complex phenomenon. Studies then showed the importance of taking into consideration communication phenomena (Cosnier, 1994), and recent works integrate the emotional lexicon study component to discourse analysis (Gombert, 2003, Bannour, 2005). Moreover, others have largely demonstrated the need to further studies of the social representations of emotions, emotion being first and foremost a social phenomenon (Dumouchel, 1995, in Christophe, 1998) of an interpersonal type – which helped to make progress on the question of the social division of emotions (Rimé, 1989, Rimé et al., 1998, Rimé, 2005). Thus, these works highlight that evoking certain emotions is linked to the context in which the emotions are voiced; some of them are more easily verbalised in an environment of isolation – fear and sadness –, compared to others that are better shared by confiding in others, in a dyad (Cosnier, 1994). Finally, it should be noted that the field of study that concerns emotional phenomena currently pertains to the childhood sector that is referred to as normal (Nadel, 2003a, 2003b; Perron & Gosselin, 2004) or pathological as is the case with trisomy 21 (Pochon, Brun & Mellier, 2006) or to cases of depression (Hammen & Rudolph, 1996; Marien & Bell, 2004; Murray et al., 2001). Studies that focus on the production, or the comprehension of emotions (Harris, 2000), are often placed in relationship with those that focus on the progressive edification of a theory of mind (Boucher et al., 2006; Gauthier & Bradmetz, 2005; Pons & Doudin, 2001; Pons & Harris, 2001, 2003; Pons et al., 2003, 2005; Thommen & Rimbert, 2005 for a review), also known as comprehension of a « false-belief ». In this vein, we will place our work at the key age of five to six-year-olds, age at which pupils have sufficient verbal tools but, paradoxically, still show verbo-conceptual difficulties. This supposes the need for exploratory or experimental studies (Gouin-Décarie et al., 2005) that take into consideration the diversity of individual modalities of representations (see hereafter), accompanied by the possibility of actualising them verbally with young children/pupils.

To complete our overview, we will add points of view that pertain to philosophy; this discipline is likely to draw attention to the ethical aspect of emotions, which we feel is interrelated to the social aspect put forward by psychology. Most philosophers consider that emotions stem from the irrational: emotions are passions that are in opposition to reason and that must be fought (Plato); they are physiological manifestations that are inferior to reason (Descartes, Hume, Malebranche, etc.); emotions are responses linked to instincts, to physiological feelings (James), to muddled perceptions (Leibniz), even to pathologies (Kant). Nevertheless, some philosophers have positively valued the role of emotions over the centuries by associating them with cognition. Thus, according to Aristotle, judgment plays a crucial role in emotions. Seneca and other Stoics maintain that emotions are judgments, ways of perceiving and understanding the world – although these judgments are often irrational. Several years later, Spinoza took up the Stoics thesis, maintaining that emotions are thoughts, and as such represent judgments that can be improved through education. In this day and age, several philosophers (of whom the leaders are Marta Nussbaum and Robert Solomon) maintain that emotion cannot exist without perception or belief (i.e.: anger implies the belief that something has been deliberately done against me). To that effect, emotion is a judgment – a prescriptive judgment regarding a situation (Solomon, 2003). Here, judgment is understood in the Kantian sense of "practical judgment". In other words, constituent elements of the experience are pre-reflexive rather than associated with a deliberate and well thought-out interpretation. To this effect, Solomon (1989, 2004) explains – and this establishes a link to Averill's socio-constructivist perspective – that emotions are "constructions" of the mind. In addition, since the individual is part and parcel of his culture and the social standards that underlie it, emotions are described as "social constructions". More provocatively, some philosophers maintain that since social standards underlie ethical principle and values, emotions indirectly result in "ethical judgments" (Nussbaum, 1992, 2004) for which each individual is responsible (Solomon, 2003). The individual, who is able to verbalize, becomes responsible for his emotions inasmuch as he acquires the ability to control and change them (Solomon, 2003). To these authors, an emotion is a dynamic system that interconnects judgments, beliefs and intentions; it is a complex and organized (by the culture) structure of judgments the constituent elements of which reflect a way of perceiving, of acting and of being[1].

As with Averill, Nussbaum and Solomon, we consider that emotions: a) are constructions of the mind; b) are understood in reference to the socio-cultural context in which they occur ; c) are ethical judgments because they express a manner of being in the world ; d) can be transformed by education; and e) are each individual's responsibility.

Social Representations (SR)

In this text we analyze children's SR of emotions. According to the socio-constructivist perspective, which we share, SR correspond to the opinions, beliefs and attitudes attached to an object or a situation. In other words, SR constitute a view of the world developed by social agents, allowing them to decode the expectations and presumptions of other members (Abric, 1994). In other words, representation guides and determines practice, while practice creates or transforms representation. This is the process which must be studied as soon as children begin school, since emotions imply individual as well as social stakes. Individual stakes are situated on cognitive and emotional levels, among others, in that refining a child's SR of emotions provides him with a better understanding of the ins and outs of actions (his own and those of peers) and, consequently, a better understanding of the world and of the meaning of existence, as well as better control over his life (see Pons et al., 2005). The stakes are also social, since the refinement of children's SR of emotions is likely to affect their aggressive or cooperative pro-social behaviours and the classroom climate.

Research Objective

The objective of our research is related to the following question: If emotions are judgments, ways of perceiving and comprehending the world, how do children develop their representations of emotions? In this text, the questions we look into are: What are the representations that kindergarten children have of eight emotions, some of which are considered "basic" and others "secondary" (e.g. more complex)? Do these representations evolve between

---

[1] That an emotion is a system of judgments does not imply that every judgment is an emotion.

the beginning and the end of the kindergarten year, that is, between age five and age six? Finally, what is the children's representation of the role played by others in their emotions? We have chosen to study emotions commonly found in the (psychological and philosophical) literature (happiness, fear, anger and sadness), to which we have added more complex emotions (surprise, disgust, pride and guilt) (see Solomon, 2002).

2. Method of analysis

Our general methodology combines an interview at the beginning and at the end of the year (to test the evolution of SR) and the use of an approach that is influenced by the Grounded Theory (to analyze and suggest elements to model the SR construction process). The Grounded Theory (Chamaz, 2005) consists in bringing to light elements that are likely to lead to a better understanding of the process studied (here, related to the children's SR of emotions), from data collected in the field (children's words). This methodology implies a categorization and a conceptualization of the data collected, with the intention of suggesting theoretical avenues for understanding the SR construction process between the beginning and the end of the kindergarten year).

Use of the Grounded Theory requires sample diversity so that a maximum of information emerges from the analysis (Laperrière, 1997). Therefore, our sample consisted of 10 preschool classes, four of them in Ontario, four in Quebec and two in France. Individual interviews were conducted with nine children in each classroom, for a total study population of 90 pupils. To ensure representativeness in each class, instructions were given to each teacher asking them to choose three children that were strong academically, three that were average and three that were weak. The number of boys and girls was taken into consideration to balance the groups. The interviews consisted of word associations with the eight emotions selected for study (for example, Surprise: "What does surprise mean to you?") The children's answers were tape-recorded and then transcribed in full.

To analyze the children's answers, we used a grid that reflects a possible model of the construction process of five and six-year-old children's SR of emotions. This model emerged from a previous study (Daniel et al., 2006) and is characterized by three main steps (or categories), about which we were able to hypothesize that they would be organized hierarchically: 1) non-representation or absence of a name for the emotion, 2) self-centered or concrete representation of the emotion, 3) socializing representation of the emotion that suggests the interpersonal dimension is taken into account (see also Auriac & Daniel, 2006). Each of these three categories is composed of constituent elements (or criteria) that are not organized hierarchically (see Table 1) and that emerged during analysis of the transcripts.

Table 1. SR of Emotions: Three Categories and their Constituent Elements based on the Inductor Word "Happiness"

Category 1: Unnamed Representation

Constituent Elements	Description and Examples
A	Unknown inductor word (i.e.: I don't know).
B	Definition unrelated to the inductor word (i.e.: spending the day, bandage).
C	Repetition of the inductor word (i.e.: happiness is happiness).

Category 2: Self-centered or Concrete Representation of the Emotion

Constituent Elements	Description and Examples
A	Emotional state or verbalized feeling (i.e.: feeling pleased, feeling calm).
B	Evocation of sensory experiences (i.e.: eating chocolate cake).
C	Evocation of manifestations (i.e.: smiling).
D	Evocation of a causal event (i.e.: when it's your birthday).

Category 3: Socializing Representation of the Emotion

Constituent Elements	Description and Examples
A	Explicit intervention of others as actors (i.e.: when someone likes you).
B	Social aspect: moral duty or obligation that is learned and integrated (i.e.: you must share with your friends).
C	Description of an interpersonal relationship that reflects reciprocity (i.e.: having fun with others).

Grid adapted from Daniel et al. 2006.

Two coders used the elements of this grid to code the transcripts. Discussions between the two coders and a third person, who had not participated in the coding, took place when the coders felt that the children's answers were ambiguous. When differences of opinions were manifested (less than 10% of cases) a discussion continued until a consensus was reached.

3. Results

For all of the participants, six of the eight emotions that were targeted generated answers oriented toward self-centered SR, both at age five (beginning of the school year) and at age six (end of the school year). When considering all eight emotions, the children evolved insofar as the number of non-represented SR (category 1) decreased during the year in favour of a representation that was either self-centered (category 2) or, but in a lesser percentage, socializing (category 3). The following Table synthesizes the results obtained.

Table 2. *Evolution of children's SR (in percentages linked to each category) between the pre-test (October) and the post-test (May) for the eight emotions tested*

Emotion	Non-represented (1)		Self-centered (2)		Socializing (3)	
	October	May	October	May	October	May
Fear	38.4	21.2	59.5	74.4	5.6	4.2
Happiness	38.8	27.2	50	51	11.1	21.5
Anger	45.5	36.6	47.7	46.1	6.6	17.5
Sadness	37.7	27.1	54.4	52.1	7.7	20.6
Surprise	34.8	16.8	59.5	78.6	5.6	4.49
Disgust	66.2	54.9	33.7	45	0	0
Guilt	98.9	98.9	1.1	1.1	0	0
Pride	79.7	59.3	17.9	36.2	2.2	4.3

With regard to Table 2, we note that almost each emotion follows its own evolution. Some emotions are under-represented (guilt, pride). Others could possibly be grouped together (i.e.: fear, sadness and surprise) in that they may provide access to a level of self-centered representation that favours experience. However, in actual fact, it should be noted that, at the end of the year, one-fifth of the pupils reached a socializing representation only with regard to sadness.

The four basic emotions (Fear, Happiness, Sadness and Anger): Validation and novelty

With regard to fear, a sizeable number of five-year-old pupils are not able to verbalize a representation ("I don't know.") – this phenomenon continues to affect 21.2% of six-year-old pupils. More than half (59.5%) of five-year-olds and three-quarters (74.4%) of six-year-olds share a representation that is of a self-centered type. For example, in response to the question "What does fear mean to you?", the verbalizations were the following: "When I am alone in the dark."; "It reminds me of when I have nightmares." However, predominantly, imaginary causes were mentioned: "Monsters", "Ghosts", and "Witches". A minority of pupils (approximately 1 in 20), both at age five and at age six, without any evolution, may offer a representation of the socializing type (that is, including another in one's representation) : "Afraid because he's a big boy." Thus, as previously highlighted, these results confirm that a majority of kindergarten children associate fear with imaginary beings, probably influenced by social (i.e. children's books) and family culture (Auriac & Daniel, 2006). The social dimension of others is not constructed in these situations.

Regarding happiness we find that, at age five, pupils find it hard to offer a verbalized representation (almost 40%) even though we know that this emotion is widely recognized as early as age three, when children decode facial expressions (Brun, 2002). The transition to age six augurs a progression, but still almost one-third of the class (27.7%) cannot offer a verbalization in answer to the question "What does happiness mean to you?" Nevertheless, for half the pupils, happiness is verbalized in relation to experiences from their personal points of view. This rate does not evolve between age five and age six. Representations and verbalizations are of the following kind: "Party because there are lots of fun things there", or "We laugh". Some pupils, 1 in 10 at age five (11%), then 2 in 10 at age six (21.5%) are able to formulate a line of thought that includes others as explicit actors in the situation they bring up: "Of my friends that are nice to me", "We make friends", "Sharing a toy".

Anger is an emotion that, according to previous studies, is better verbalized in dyads or in small groups (see Cosnier, 1994). In our interviews, almost half the five-year-old pupils (45.5%), and more than one-third at age six (36.6%) do not actualize any verbalization of anger. Expressions that illustrate representation of a self-centered type are: "Punches", "Mean words", "Fighting". Some representations are brought up in relation to an emotional state or a feeling: "It's when you're angry". Among pupils' verbalizations that reached a socializing type of representation, there are some explanatory mini-scenarios: "Because sometimes when kids do dumb things, adults might get angry". We note that anger is represented as a spontaneous reaction to a situation rather than as a desire to hurt others. The anger of others is also represented mainly as a consequence of behaviour. This may bear similarities to a structured representation of anger as "cause of action" easily observable in everyday life where, from the age of four, children are able to identify with an angry person (Gouin-Décarie et al., 2005).

Regarding sadness, a developmental profile that is almost identical to that of happiness emerged from the data collection. The same result, that one-third of the pupils persist in not verbalizing a representation, is brought to light, although one pupil in 10 progresses between age five and age six (from 37,7% to 27,1%). More than half the pupils (54,4% of five-year-olds and 52,1% of six-year-olds) exhibit a self-centered representation, among others things conveying observable manifestations ("Eyes that are crying"), or the elaboration of logical scenarios ("I was trying to push my couch and I hurt my foot"). However, two in 10 pupils at age six (20.6%) – in comparison to less than one in 10 pupils at age five (7.7%) – are capable of representing others as explicit actors that cause sadness, although that sadness is experienced from one's own point of view: "Sad because a boy or a girl steals the ball", or "If someone hits you, you feel sad, you hurt". Here, the data collected illustrates a progressive transfer from our step 2 to our step 3 that is, the children's representation gradually integrates the role of others into the scenario while maintaining a focus on one's own feelings. We also note the verbalized connection between violent actions ("Hitting") and the evocation of sadness, these violent actions being just as likely to cause anger. In this sense, at the conceptual level, sadness appears as an ambiguous (over-generalized) emotion that presupposes bias in its representation.

In conclusion, with regard to the evolution of representations that are considered "basic", pupils actualized a progressive transfer from one step to another, abandoning step 1 for an actualization of the following steps, even though in step 3, progress is sometimes at its start – which validates previously-observed tendencies (Auriac & Daniel, 2006; Daniel et al., 2006).

Four additional emotions are tested: Surprise, Disgust, Guilt and Pride

Among these four emotions, only surprise and pride manifest a progression (reaching step 3) between age five and age six.

One-third of five-year-old pupils have no representation of surprise. However, less than two in 10 (16.8%) continue this non-verbalization ("I don't know") at six years old. Most of them progress toward SR of a self-centered type (step 2). Diversity of answers dominates in this category: "Surprise when something happens to us and we don't know about it", or "A gift… well you mustn't show it to anybody". The context of a surprise is referred to by taking into account some event in that context. The characteristic of a self-centered type is less present than in the basic emotions, since the context of the gift is referred to. This conveys a representation of the situation in its entirety, without reference to an explicit personal intervention. Nonetheless, some children explicitly integrate actors into these scenes, thus: "Surprise because Mom gives me presents at my birthday." (step 3).

With regard to disgust, the majority of pupils (66.2% at age five and 54.9% at age six) are situated at step 1; in other words, they verbalize nothing (absence of related verbalization). However, some pupils actualize answers that correspond to the construction of SR of a self-centered type: "Poop", "It makes me think of something I don't like." There is a lot of confusion between the word "disgust" and the word "sewer", due to their similarity in French (dégoût and égout); this creates a bias in our data collection. SR of the following type "Sewers are really gross" were recorded in category 2.

With regard to pride, many answers (79.7% at age five and 59.3% at age six) are situated at step 1 of non-representation. Here again, lack of vocabulary dominates as an impediment. Nonetheless, 17.9% of five-year-old pupils and 36.2% of six-year-old pupils offer structured SR: "Like when you make a beautiful castle and you're proud of making it", or "The day I won a medal because I like medals". Some pupils actualize the role that others actively play in this type of feeling (step 3): "Because if you think really well, your friend is proud", or "Giving stickers away and sharing with someone". Verbalizations of a socializing type illustrate a form of integrated morality. A slight but actual improvement of the rate concerning step 3 (2.2% to 4.3%, namely a doubling) was noted in relation to pride.

With regard to guilt, it was clearly apparent that virtually all of the children had no representation of it – which does not mean they had never experienced guilt. Nevertheless, in some six years old children, when the SR becomes more structured, the emotion is placed into a context: "When I was at home I did some dumb things".

4. Validation of our interpretation grid

In each step of our interpretation grid, elements of confirmation appear with regard to our previous study (Daniel et al., 2006).

Step 1: absence of verbalized representation.

Being unable to verbalize a representation concerning an emotion seems to be an essential first step in the construction process. Non-verbalization implies either that the child does not know the inductor word, either that he knows it but refuses to share his experience with the interviewer, or that he has not yet acquired experiential elements related to it. The literature indicates that what is felt about oneself, as it concerns a form of attention at the moment emotions occur, is not necessarily "consciously" oriented (see Damasio, 1999; Lewis, 1989). Furthermore, not knowing the word is not a sign of absence of meaning for the individual (see Pons et al., 2003). Meaning depends on many factors that can be linked to emotional situations as a whole, or to the manner in which these situations were perceived then reconstructed in the child's personal history, or to the value (positive or negative) attached to it by those around him, etc. (Damasio, 1999; Emde et al., 2003; Strepparava, 2005). Being able to represent an emotion to the point of knowing how to verbalize it in a meaningful way is a challenge for any individual. Bringing to light the fact that a majority of five and six-year-old children have SR concerning happiness, anger, sadness, fear and surprise, whereas most do not in relation to disgust, guilt and pride, not only provides information about the development of SR in children, but also provides a look into the very complexity of the verbal-conceptual process that accompanies any construction.

Step 2: access to a verbalized representation of a self-centered type.

Pupils from our sample group became increasingly capable, between ages five and six, of talking about their experiences by means of what they feel in connection to the emotion named; this means that they are able to pay attention to their inner selves. The fact that this attention is verbalized around certain elements, such as the description of facial expressions or of concrete situations that often evoke material or physical causes, shows that the emotional phenomenon is first apprehended by uncovering one of the elements, without addressing the complexity of the phenomenon as a whole. It can be inferred that in this step, several of the children's emotions assumed the form (and meaning) of a simple "personal story" (Nussbaum, 2000, 2004) that they are able to reconstruct in a coherent manner. This construction process through verbalization implies the progressive development of a form of detailed explanation, which serves to construct personal identity, such as a prescriptive judgment of situations. Most of the children we questioned were situated at this step with regard to their SR of emotions, with the exception of guilt.

Step 3: access to a verbalized representation of a socializing type.

The ability to access a SR that situates the interpersonal and reciprocal nature of the actors (self/others) as an explanatory link in the situation experienced brings to light the child's ability to add elements to his personal story that originate from the social context of the experience. We consider, in light of the actual tendencies for six of the emotions targeted, that this ability constitutes a true step 3, since at the end of the year the differences between the pre-test and the post-test for all of the emotions except fear and surprise widened. The fact that the SR of happiness, anger, and sadness actualize, between ages five and six, a leap to this last step 3 (on average one in five pupils is likely to provide a socializing explanation of these emotions), seems to confirm that the socializing explanation gradually settles in, but also that certain emotions are more likely to be conducive to this settling in at ages five and six. Particularly for these three emotions (happiness, sadness and anger), the pupil becomes aware of the fact that his peers exert an influence over the development and the progress of his emotions, and vice versa. The other person is not simply accidental; the other person takes on an explanatory type of meaning for one's own feelings. It is during this step that emotion integrates the dimension of prescriptive judgment of a moral nature (i.e.: "Happiness is when I share with others.") that we can relate either to the development of morality (Nussbaum, 2004, 2005), or to the development of a finer awareness of others, which opens the way to an increased complexity of thought and judgment (Daniel et al., 2006; Daniel et al., 2006b). Since open-mindedness to others presupposes (and leads to) the discovery of uncertainty, reaching the third step means accepting being challenged by others and modifying one's judgment if necessary.

5. Discussion and Conclusion

The relevance of studying the construction process of children's SR of eight emotions was situated in our pragmatist and socio-constructivist perspective, considering that being neither innate nor universal, emotions are constructions of the mind. The verbalizations of young pupils, such as those collected and analyzed according to our grid, confirm based on the variety of answers received that the pupils' representations of emotions are influenced by underlying social and moral norms (see Averill, 1980; Nussbaum, 2004, 2005), and that language as a social carrier plays a central role in the emotional development of individuals (i.e. the difficulties that children encounter regarding guilt and disgust).

The results of this study tend to validate the hypothesis of a three-step hierarchy (Daniel et al., 2006) in the process of constructing the SR of emotions. The three steps appear to follow one another; the progress from non-representation to a self-centered representation and then to a socializing representation occurs between the ages of five and six years. We suggest that the hierarchy between step 1 and the two subsequent steps appears to be non-reversible: our results provided no indication to support the existence of a collective regression from established self-centered or socializing SR (steps 2 and 3) to an erroneous type of SR (step 1). Finally, the age of the five and six-year-olds proved to be an appropriate period of life for the development of representations. The perspective is to eventually develop a form of modeling for the evolution of SR among pupils.

Children's SR of emotions are gradually constructed, presupposing an initial settling-in of a practical judgment, namely a pre-reflexive intention linked to a simple personal story. Then, when the emotions concern a representation of their selves linked with the environment, this can be characterized as a "bidirectional environmental interaction" (see Neisser, 1992). Finally, when the construction of SR becomes more complex, the child's SR of emotions continues in parallel to the development of a theory of the mind that gradually includes others in their thought processes. This generates a form of refinement of the awareness of self, through the emergence of awareness of others in one's representations, and it is actualizable between the ages of five and six years. This reflective social relationship situates the child in an intersubjectivity that we refer to as being active.

The fact that in our study the SR of happiness, sadness and anger are most impregnated with the awareness of others leads us to consider these emotions as potential targets for development, of interest to teachers. If pupils aged five and six are able to increase the complexity of the manner in which they approach the emotional phenomenon in its social dimension by explicitly and concretely verbalizing the role of others, it is significant. More generally, developing the ability to use an exact vocabulary associated with emotions, and to verbally share these emotions with others, might be considered a factor of progression that fosters every person's access to complex representation of their own emotional experiences, beginning at the age of five or six years. The development of a global feeling of self-efficiency, crucial to success in school (Saarni, 1999), could be fostered by developing the feeling of emotional self-efficiency.

References

Abric, J.-C. (1994). Pratiques sociales et représentations, Paris: PUF.

Alvaredo, N., & Jameson, K.-A., (2002). Varieties of Anger: The Relation Between Emotion Terms and Components of Anger Expressions. Motivation and Emotion, 26(2). 153-182.

Auriac, E., & Daniel, M.-F., (2006). La pratique de dialogue philosophique comme espace de construction, transformation, confrontation des valeurs et des croyances. In. A.-R. Mousa (ed). Education, religion, laïcité. Des concepts aux pratiques : enjeux d'hier et d'aujourd'hui. (pp. 331-362). Louvain La Neuve: Editions de l'AFEC.

Averill, J. R. (1980). A constructivist view of emotion. In R. Plutchik and H. Kellerman (eds.), Emotion. Theory, Research and Experience, Vol. 1, (pp. 305-339) New York: Academic Press.

Averill, J. R. (1982). Anger and Aggression: An essay on Emotion. New York: Springer.

Bannour, R. (2005). EMOTAIX : Un outil d'analyse du lexique émotionnel employé par des rédacteurs plus ou moins appréhensifs en situation d'écriture expressive. Communication affichée au Congrés National de la Société française de Psychologie, Nancy, France : septembre.

Boucher, J., Pons, F., Lind, S., Williams, D. (2006). Temporal cognition in children with autistic spectrum disorders: Tests of diachronic thinking. Journal of Autism Development Disorders, Electronic version.

Charmaz, K. (2005). Grounded Theory in the 21st Century: Applications for Advancing Social Justice Studies. In N. Denzin & Y. Lincoln (eds.). The Sage Handbook of Qualitative Research (pp. 507-537). Third Edition. London: SAGE Publications.

Christophe, V. (1998). Les émotions, tour d'horizon des principales théories. Paris: Presses Universitaires du Septentrion.

Cosnier, J. (1994). Psychologie des émotions et des sentiments, Paris, Éditions Retz.

Damasio, A. R. (1994). Descartes' Error: Emotion, Reason and the Human Brain, New York, Putnam.

Damasio, A. R. (1999). The Feeling of what Happens. Body and Emotion in the Making of Consciousness. New York: Harcourt Brace.

Daniel, M.-F., Auriac, E., Garnier, C., Quesnel, M., Schleifer, M. (2006). A study of children's representations of four basic emotions. In F. Pons, M.-F. Daniel, L. Lafortune, P.-A. Doudin, O. Albanese (eds.). Toward emotional competencies. Aalborg, Denmark: Les Presses de l'Université d'Aalborg.

Daniel, M.-F., Doudin, P.-A., Pons, F. (2006b). Children's social representations of violence. Epistemology and moral development. Journal of Peace Education, 3(2) 209-234.

Dantzer, R. (2002). Les émotions. Paris: Presses universitaires de France. Collection Que sais-je ?

Emde, R., Wolf, D., Oppenheim, D. (2003). Revealing the Inner Worlds of Young Children. Oxford: Oxford University Press.

Frijda, N. H. (1993). Les théories des émotions: un bilan, In B. Rimé and K. R. Scherer (eds.), Les émotions (pp. 21-72), Neuchâtel, Delachaux et Niestlé.

Gauthier, G. & Bradmetz, J. (2005). Le développement de la comprehension des fausses croyances chez l'enfant de 5 à 8 ans. Enfance, 4, 353-368.

Gombert, A. (2003). Effet d'une couleur gaie ou triste sur l'usage du lexique émotionnel par des enfants de 11 ans lors de la redaction d'un récit. In J-M. Colletta & A. Tcherkassof, Les emotions. Cognition, langage et développement. (pp. 235- 247). Sprimont : Mardaga.

Gouin-Décarie, T., Quintal, G., Ricard, M., Deneault, J. & Morin, P.-L. (2005). La compréhension précoce de l'émotion comme cause de l'action. Enfance, 4, 383-402.

Harris, P. (2000). Understanding emotion. In M. Lewis & J.M. Haviland-Jones (Eds.), Handbook of emotions (2nd edition) (pp. 281-292). New York: Guilford Press.

Hammen & Rudolph, K.D. (1996). Childhood depression. In E.J. Mash & R.A. Barkley (Eds.) Child psychopathology (pp. 153-195). New York: Guilford Press.

Laperrière, A. (1997). La théorisation ancrée: Démarche analytique et comparaison avec d'autres approches apparentées, In. J. Poupart, J.-P. Deslauriers,

L. H. Groulx, A. Laperrière, R. Mayer and A. Pires (eds.), La recherche qualitative: Enjeux épistémologiques et méthodologiques (pp. 309-346), Boucherville, Gaëtan Morin Éditeur.

Lazarus, R. S., Averill, J. R., Opton, O. M. (1970). Toward a cognitive theory of emotions, In M. B. Arnold (ed.), Feelings and emotions (pp. 207-232), New York, Academic Press.

Lewis, M. (1989). What do we mean when we say emotional development? In L. Cirillo, B. Kaplan, S. Wapner (eds.) Emotions in ideal human development (pp. 53-77). New Jersey: Lawrence Erlbaum Associates Publishers.

Marien, W.E. & Bell, D.J. (2004). Anxiety and depression-related thoughts in children: Development and evaluation of a cognition measure. Journal of Clinical Child and Adolescent Psychology, 33, 717-730.

Murry, L., Woolgar, M., Cooper, P. & Hipwell, A. (2001). Cognitive vulnerability to depression in 5-year-old children of depressed mothers. Journal of Child Psychology and Psychiatry, 42, 891-899.

Nadel, J. (2003a). Le développement émotionnel : régulations et dysfonctionnements. In M. Kail & M. Fayol (Dir.), Les sciences cognitives et l'école. (pp.55-89). Paris : Presses Universitaires de France.

Nadel, J. (2003b). Le futur des émotions : un nécessaire tressage des données normatives et psychopédagogiques. Enfance, 1, 23-32.

Neisser, U. (1992). The development of consciousness and the acquisition of skill. In F. Kessel, P. Cole, D. Johnson (eds.). Self and consciousness: Multiple perspectives (pp. 1-18). Hillsdale, N.J.: Erlbaum.

Nussbaum, M. (1992). Emotions as judgments of value. The Yale Journal of Criticism, 5 (2), 201-212.

Nussbaum, M. (2000). Emotions and social norms. In L. Nucci, G. Saxe, E. Turiel (eds.). Culture, Thought and Development (pp. 41-63). Mahwah, N.J.: Lawrence Erlbaum Associates Publishers.

Nussbaum, M. (2001). Upheavals of Thought. The Intelligence of Emotions. Cambridge: Cambridge University Press.

Nussbaum, M. (2004). Emotions as judgments of value and importance. In R. Solomon (ed.) Thinking about feeling: Contemporary philosophers on emotions (pp. 183-199). New York: Oxford University Press.

Nussbaum, M. (2005). Emotions and the Origins of Morality. In W. Edelstein & G. Nunner-Winkler (eds.) Morality in Context (pp. 61-119). Amsterdam: Elsevier.

Perron, M. & Gosselin, P. (2004). Le développement de l évocation des émotions. Enfance(56), 133-147.

Pochon, R., Brun, P. & Mellier, D. (2006). Développement de la reconnaissance des émotions chez l'enfant avec trisomie 21. Psychologie française (51)4, 381-390.

Pons, F. & Doudin, P.A. (2001). La conscience : de Piaget aux sciences cognitives contemporaines. Intellectica, 3, 125-143.

Pons, F., Doudin, P.A., Martin, D., Lafortune, L. Harris, P. (2004). Psychogenèse de la conscience et pensée réflexive (p.14-37). In R. Pallascio, M.-F. Daniel et L. Lafortune. Pensée et réflexivité. Théories et pratiques. Québec: Presses de l'Université du Québec.

Pons, F. & Harris, P. (2001). Piaget's conception of consciousness : An examination of two hypotheses. Human Development, 44, 220-227.

Pons, F. & Harris, P. (2003). Theory of Mind Test – TMT. Cambridge: Harvard University.

Pons, F., Doudin, P.-A., Harris, P., de Rosnay, M. (2005). "La compréhension des émotions. Entre affect et intellect." In L. Lafortune, M.-F. Daniel, P.-A. Doudin, F. Pons and O. Albanese (eds.) Pédagogie et psychologie des émotions. Vers une compétence émotionnelle. Quebec City, PUQ, p. 179-202.

Pons, F., Lawson, J., Harris, P. de Rosnay, M. (2003). Individual differences in children's emotion understanding: Effects of age and language, Scandinavian Journal of Psychology, 44(4), p. 345-351.

Rimé, B. (1989). Le partage social des émotions. In B. Rimé & K. Scherer. Textes de base en psychologie. : Les émotions.. (pp. 271- 303). Neufchâtel et Paris : Delachaux et Niestlé.

Rimé, B. (2005). Le partage social des émotions. Préface de Serge Moscovici. Paris: Presses Universitaires de France.

Rimé, B., Finkenauer, C., Luminet, O., Zech, E., & Philippot, P. (1998). Social sharing of emotion: New evidence and new questions. In W. Stroebe W. et alii (Eds.). European review of social Psychology, 9, 145-189. Chichester, UK: John Wiley & Sons Ltd.

Saarni, C. (1999). The Development of Emotional Competence. N.Y.: The Guilford Press.

Sarbin, T. (1989). Emotions as situated actions. In L. Cirillo, B. Kaplan, S. Wapner (eds.) Emotions in ideal human development (pp. 77-101). New Jersey: Lawrence Erlbaum Associates Publishers.

Solomon, R. (1989). Emotions, philosophy, and the self. In L. Cirillo, B. Kaplan, S. Wapner (eds.) Emotions in ideal human development (pp. 135-151).

New Jersey: Lawrence Erlbaum Associates Publishers.

Solomon, R. (2002). Back to Basics: On the very idea of "Basic Emotions". Journal for the Theory of Social Behavior, 32 (2), 115-144.

Solomon, R. (2003). Not Passion's Slave. Emotions and Choice. Oxford: Oxford University Press.

Solomon, R. (2004). Emotions, thoughts and feelings: Emotions as engagements with the world. In R. Solomon (ed.), Thinking about feeling: Contemporary philosophers on emotions (pp. 76-88). New York: Oxford University Press.

Strepparava, M.-G. (2005). Cognition des émotions et psychopathologie. In L. Lafortune, M.-F. Daniel, P.-A. Doudin, F. Pons, O. Albanese (eds.). Pédagogie et psychologie des émotions. Vers la compétence émotionnelle (pp. 207-243). Quebec City: Les Presses de l'université du Québec à Montréal.

Thommen, E., & Rimbert, G. (2005). L'enfant et les connaissances sur autrui . Paris : Belin Sup.

Vygotski, L. (2003). Conscience, inconscient, émotions. Paris : La dispute/ Snédit.

Chapter 6

Emotion and emotion regulation in typical and atypical development: implications for affect education

Hedy Stegge and Mark Meerum Terwogt

1. Introduction

Although the practice of psychology has always recognized the importance of emotions for children's adaptive functioning, it is only recently that prevention and intervention programs have started to incorporate components explicitly aimed at the training of emotional skills. Specifically, these programs seek to enhance children's understanding of emotion as well as their emotion regulation abilities. Examples are Kendall's (1990) "Coping Cat" program for children with anxiety disorders, Stark and Kendall's (1996) "Taking Action" protocol for children with depressive symptoms, Lochman and Welsh's (2002, 2004) "Coping Power" program for children with behaviour problems, as well as Kusché and Greenberg's (1994) preventive PATHS curriculum for regular and special education classes. As our knowledge about the relation between emotion and (mal)adaptive functioning rapidly increases, programs aimed at the reduction of problem behavior and/or the improvement of children's social skills are likely to increase their focus on emotion even further in the near future. In this chapter, it will be argued that the development of these programs and the training of professionals in charge of their implementation may benefit from scientific advances in the field of emotion. In particular, the integration of knowledge about the nature of the emotion process and children's developing emotional skills into more general notions of children's socioemotional functioning is expected to improve the effective application of these programs.

In this chapter, we will first discuss the features of the emotion system, the relation between emotion and cognition, and the relevance of emotional awareness and emotional understanding. Next, a short overview of some of the major highlights in the process of learning about emotion is provided:

children's developing emotion concepts, their understanding of the (cognitive) antecedents of emotion, and their knowledge of (cognitive) strategies of emotion regulation. I will then make an attempt to bridge the divide between typical and atypical development by discussing the case of depression as an example of emotional development gone awry. Specifically, I will discuss depressed children's sensitivity to particular modes of appraisal and their limited emotion regulation skills. Finally, an attempt will be made to translate emotion theory and the developmental findings into principles that should guide the development of prevention and intervention techniques aimed at the improvement of children's emotional competence.

2. Core features of the emotion process

Contemporary theories of emotion highlight their potential adaptive value. Emotions signal the relevance of events to personal concerns and prepare the individual to take action so as to ensure the satisfaction and protection of these concerns (Frijda, 1986). In order to serve its adaptive function, the emotion system needs to be able to quickly detect relevant changes in the person-environment relationship and to generate responses that are optimally suited to tackle the situation at hand. Levenson (1999) eloquently describes these basic characteristics of the emotion process in his two-system design of human emotion. The emotional core system is a kind of radar and response facility that provides quick, standard solutions to a limited number of prototypical life problems. By synchronizing the activity of different response systems (physiology, perception, motor behaviour, expression, and also higher cognitive processes), the core systems enables us to escape a danger, adapt to a loss, or fight an attack. However, the basic action programs of the core system do not always serve our best interests, and fine-tuning to situational demands is required when multiple, potentially conflicting goals (within the self, or between the self and others) are at stake. Therefore, humans are endowed with a cognitive control system that acts on the activity of the core system in two ways. In antecedent-focused regulation, cognitive activity aims at changing the input of the system. In response-focused regulation, the actual output of the system is influenced (Gross & Thompson, in press). I may feel the urge to verbally assault the person who has just offended me by his critical remarks, but regulatory activity may prevent me from doing so. A reappraisal of the situation (the person was not being offensive at all but rather trying to help me to avoid a similar mistake in the future) changes the input of the system, and thereby diminishes my anger and the accompanying urge to attack. It might also be that I keep thinking the person was being offensive while at the same time realizing that a verbal assault would harm our relationship. I may then try to calm down first in order to be able to discuss the event more reasonably, thereby influencing the output of the system.

The activity of the emotional core system concerns mainly unconscious primary appraisal processes. However, the activation of the basic emotion program along with its corresponding action tendencies usually results in the experience of an emotion, and elicits secondary appraisal processes. Secondary appraisal is often conscious and functions to facilitate voluntary controlled action. In a recent paper, Lambie and Marcel (2002) have argued that emotional experiences may occur at different levels of awareness. First order phenomenological experience merely refers to an intuitive grasp of "what the feeling is like". Second order awareness, in contrast, is more reflective and refers to thoughts about the experience and the identification of the subjective feeling state as a specific emotion (e.g. anger, sadness, shame, and so on). This cognitive process concerns a focus on how we feel, why we feel the way we feel, and what we can do about it. It is second order emotional awareness that is particularly relevant for the strategic employment of regulatory activity.

Emotion and cognition

Two distinctive perspectives on the relation between cognition and emotion have figured prominently in the literature. Appraisal theories (e.g. Frijda, 1986; Lazarus, 1991; 1999; Ellsworth & Scherer, 2003) have emphasized the role of cognition in the activation of an emotion: the quality and intensity of an emotion is not determined by objective parameters but rather by one's subjective interpretation of reality. Similarly, traditional cognitive approaches to psychopathology (e.g. Beck, 1976) assume that dysfunctional cognitions (i.e. a biased interpretation of reality) are responsible for the maladaptive emotional responses seen in anxiety or depression. Evolutionary theories of emotion, on the other hand, emphasize the primacy of emotion, and argue that the functional design features of basic emotion programs are responsible for cognitive biases (Cosmides & Tooby, 2000). A specific emotion stimulates an analysis of the world in terms of concepts relevant to the problem that needs to be solved. When the fear program is activated, for example, it is useful to approach the environment in terms of categories related to safety. When one is angry, on the other hand, inferences about responsibility, blame and punishment are evoked. Given the function and nature of different emotions, certain biased are thus to be expected. However, the two-level architecture of the emotion system also allows for the redirection of basic emotion programs through cognitive activity. Emotional biases can be countered by strategic reasoning, and emotional responses can be tailored to specific situational demands as a result of a careful analysis of the problem and its possible solutions.

In recent accounts, the close bi-directional relationship between emotion and cognition has increasingly been acknowledged (Lazarus, 1999; Scherer, 2003). Cognition activity is evident in all phases of the emotion process, and can be seen as a stimulus or a response depending on where one begins one's entry into the ongoing emotional experience. This decision is arbitrary. In the remainder of this chapter, therefore, a focus on cognition or emotion as being primary in models of typical and atypical development is only taken for conceptual and analytical purposes. Meanwhile, the reader should bear in mind the fugue-like nature of emotion and cognition. (Lewis & Michalson, 1983; Mineka, Rafaeli & Yovel, 2003).

Emotional awareness and emotion knowledge

As has already been argued, emotions are considered to be basically adaptive. They alert the individual to relevant situations and motivate him or her to take action on those situations. Emotional competence involves the skill of taking full advantage of the potentials of the emotion system (Parrott, 2001). Key components are the ability to adequately process emotion-laden information, to reflectively regulate emotions, and to access and generate emotional experiences to inform adaptation (Mayer & Salovey, 1997; Salovey, Mayer & Caruso, 2002). These skills are dependent to a considerable extent on the human capacity for emotional awareness. The incorporation of emotional information into conscious thought allows for the explanation and prediction of behavior and stimulates strategic emotion-based action (Meerum Terwogt & Olthof, 1989; Stegge & Meerum Terwogt, in press). I may choose to avoid or approach certain situations because of their anticipated emotional consequences. Similarly, I may decide whether or not I will express certain emotional responses based on their anticipated effects. The capacity to put emotions to purposeful use thus depends critically on the person's understanding of emotion. As Saarni (1999), has argued, emotional competence entails the ability to "respond emotionally, yet simultaneously and strategically apply knowledge about emotions in interpersonal exchanges."

Emotional awareness involves the processing of information related to internal stimuli. As cognitive and language abilities mature, children develop an progressively more sophisticated conceptual framework for their own and others' affective experiences. They build up a coherent body of knowledge of relevant appraisal processes, subjective feeling states and emotional responses. Whenever they encounter an emotional episode, this knowledge base is activated and functions as an internal working model for the further processing of information. The quality of this secondary appraisal process is dependent on the nature and complexity of the child's conceptual framework. More differentiated and integrated knowledge helps the child to adequately elaborate on the available emotional information and use it in the service of adaptive behavior (Arsenio & Lemerise, 2004; Lane & Pollerman, 2002; Lemerise & Arsenio, 2000). Specifically, the ability to sort experiences into (blends of) discrete emotion categories draws the child's attention to useful strategies for dealing with the prevailing event (Niedenthal, Dalle & Rohman, 2002).

3. The development of emotional understanding

In the developmental literature, numerous knowledge components have been studied (Denham, 1998; Denham & Kochanoff, 2002; Harris, 1989; Pons & Harris, in 2005; Saarni, 1999; Meerum Terwogt & Stegge, 2001). Here, we mainly focus on the development of children's understanding of the relation between cognition and emotion, as it becomes evident in their understanding of the causes of emotion and their reasoning about the usefulness of different emotion regulation strategies.

Children's knowledge of the cognitive antecedents of emotion

At the age of 2 or 3, children already start to talk about emotions. They report on their own feelings as well as those of others. These references are not limited to current emotional states, but concern past and future feelings as well (Harris, 2000). Simple emotion words (happy, sad, mad) are used in a causal way: "grandma mad, I wrote on wall" (Bretherton & Beegly, 1982). The spontaneous utterances of these young children thus seem to demonstrate an early understanding of the link between situation and emotion. Empirical studies have shown that in subsequent years, children's knowledge about the causes of emotion increases rapidly and is characterized by a number of significant improvements. First, the capacity for belief-desire reasoning helps the child to acknowledge that emotions are the result of someone's subjective appraisal of an emotion-eliciting event (Harris, 2000). Second, the ability to form increasingly complex mental representations contributes to the ability to engage in more sophisticated appraisal processes, resulting in an understanding of multiple and complex emotions, as well as atypical responses based on personal characteristics.

Desires and beliefs

At the age of 3 or 4, children already show an understanding of the external causes of a number of basic emotions. They know, for example, that getting a present results in happiness, that the death of a pet causes sadness, that the wilful destruction of your favourite toy by your little brother elicits anger toward the perpetrator, and that being alone in the dark produces fear (Barden, Zelko, Duncan & Masters, 1980; Harris, 1989). However, although prototypical elicitors of common emotions can readily be identified, it is important to note that there is not a one-to-one correspondence between situation and emotion. The same situation can evoke different feelings in different people depending on their varying subjective appraisals of the event. Children thus need to go beyond a simple script-based approach in order to be able to correctly explain and predict a protagonist's emotional response. As Harris (2000) has argued, they need to acknowledge that an emotion starts with "an event that is inherently psychological, namely a person appraising a situation" (p. 285).

From the early 1980s, researchers have extensively studied children's acquisition of knowledge about the mental world and their development as naïve psychologists. Research within this flourishing tradition, that has become known as the study of the "Child Theory of Mind", shows that even very young children use the hypothetical construct of a "mental state" to make sense of people actions (Onishi & Baillargeon, 2005). The same fundamental notion helps children understand why people can experience different emotions in response to one and the same situation: they hold different desires and/or beliefs.

Empirical studies have shown that at the age of 3, children start to com-

may feel relieved because he expected failure, whereas Alex may be disappointed because he expected a much better result. To correctly predict Mike and Alex' emotional reactions, children need to consider the actual result, the counterfactual outcome, and the relation between the two: a positive emotion (relief) is experienced if an actual outcome is better than expected, a negative emotion (disappointment) is elicited in situations where the actual outcome is worse than expected. In a study among children between 5 and 9 years of age, we found that young children predicted the same emotion for two story characters who were exposed to the same outcome but had different expectations. When asked to justify their answer, these children referred only to the actual outcome and ignored previous expectations. Older children, in contrast, referred to the actual outcome as it differed from what was expected, and predicted the story actors to feel different (Stegge, Meerum Terwogt, Begeer & Lunenburg, in prep.).

Children's understanding of cognitive strategies of emotion regulation

In the course of development, children learn to respond to emotion-eliciting events in a strategic way. They gain proficiency in emotion regulation: the ability to turn the action tendencies elicited by the emotional core system into adaptive responses tailored to specific situational demands and long term personal and social goals. Although being angry or fearful, children may now choose not to show their emotion based on their knowledge of dissemblance (the fact that inner feelings and outer expression do not need to coincide) and cultural display rules. A person who only did the best (s)he could may be hurt if you become overtly angry at him or her for making a mistake. And if you show your fear of diving in front of all your classmates, they may laugh at you and call you a coward. Between the ages of 4 and 10, children's understanding's understanding of strategies to hide emotions and the circumstances in which they need to do so increases rapidly (Banerjee, 1997; Gross & Harris, 1988; Saarni, 1999).

Emotion regulation not only involves the adjustment of overt emotional behaviours when needed, but also the ability to change inner feeling states. Children need to learn to deal with their emotional experiences, and knowledge of effective emotion regulation strategies may assist them in reaching this goal (Meerum Terwogt & Olthof, 1989; Stegge & Meerum Terwogt, in press). Empirical studies have shown that 4-year-olds are already able to sug-

because your dog was involved in an accident, but happy since he seems to be recover from his wounds quite well (Harter & Whitesell, 1989). Children now have access to "representational mappings" (Saarni, 1999). They are able to consider multiple perspectives on the situation that are at odds with one another at the same time.

Children's growing understanding of mixed emotions reflects their capacity to integrate multiple appraisal-components into complex mental representations. Various elements of emotion-eliciting situations also need to be integrated in the case of complex emotions like guilt, shame, pride, relief, or disappointment. In the literature, different characteristics of complex emotions are emphasized. In terms of the complexity of the appraisal process involved, these emotions are labelled attribution-dependent (Thompson, 1989) or counterfactual (Guttentag & Ferrell, 2004) emotions as opposed to outcome-dependent emotions like happiness or sadness.

As has already been argued, young children are already able to analyze the appraisal process in terms of the relation between a protagonist desire and the expected (i.e. belief-based) outcome. However, in order to be able to understand complex emotions, the child has to engage in a more sophisticated appraisal process in which the factors that caused the outcome are appreciated as well. Thompson (1989) has provided empirical evidence for a developmental transition from outcome-dependent to attribution-dependent emotional inferences. Whereas second-graders mostly predicted emotions based on the outcome in achievement and moral situations, fifth graders and adults provided mainly attribution-dependent inferences. Similarly, research on the so-called "happy victimizer" phenomenon has shown that whereas young children argue that a protagonist who gets something (s)he wants by committing a moral transgression will feel happy, older children predict him or her to feel sad or report a mixture of positive and negative emotions (Nunner-Winkler & Sodian, 1988; Arsenio & Lover, 1995).

A somewhat different approach to the cognitive abilities needed for an adequate understanding of complex emotions is taken in the literature on counterfactuals. Counterfactual emotions also require children to integrate different mental representations into their judgements. Both the actual outcome of the situation and an alternative outcome reflecting previous expectations need to be considered (Guttentag & Farrell, 2004). Depending on previous expectations, people can experience relief or disappointment in response to the same outcome. If Mike and Alex just pass their tests, Mike

for example, that although 5- and 6-year-old children may realize that additional knowledge about a protagonist is called for, it is only at a somewhat later age that they are actually capable of asking the right questions to get the information needed. In addition, between the ages of 5 and 8, children become skilled at using cultural stereotypes like a protagonist's age or sex to judge an emotional event. They are now able to infer an actor's goals or desires from a general knowledge base about preferences in specific social groups. However, in many cases cultural stereotypes do not suffice either and personalized inferences about a protagonist's likely appraisals are needed. Between the ages of 8 and 12, children learn to integrate information based on the actor's previous experiences or personality traits into their emotion explanations or predictions (Gnepp, 1989). They now realize, for example, that someone might be afraid even of a cute little dog, because it is a generally fearful person or because of previous bad experiences with dogs. This development signifies children's understanding of the mind as an interpretative device (Carpendale & Chandler, 1996). Whereas 6-year-old children realize that people may hold different beliefs because they have had access to different information, 8-year-olds realize that people may attach distinctive personal meanings to one and the same object or event.

Children not only learn to appreciate that different people may experience different emotions because of diverging appraisals, but also that the same process may take place within individuals. Most emotion-eliciting events allow for different perspectives depending on the person's focus of attention and the context used for interpretation, and this may result in the experience of different emotions simultaneously. When asked open-ended questions about their own or a protagonist's responses to an emotion-eliciting event, 5-year-olds usually report only one emotion. They seem to stop analyzing the situation as soon as a reasonable emotional response is identified (Harris, 1989). As they grow older, children come to analyze the situation more extensively, and spontaneously acknowledge the possibility of mixed feelings. At the age of 7, they realize that different feelings of the same valence can coexist: you can feel both sad and mad if your little brother destroys the drawing you just finished with great effort. Sadness in this case is triggered by a focus on the ruined drawing, whereas anger is elicited by a focus on your little brother's responsibility for the negative outcome. And still somewhat later, at about 11 years of age, children also understand that feelings of opposite value can be elicited in one and they same situation: you feel sad

bine desire-outcome information to explain or predict a protagonist's emotional response (Stein & Levine, 1989). Getting what you want or avoiding something that you don't want results in a positive emotion, whereas not being able to get something you do want or getting something you don't want elicits a negative emotion. Michelle will be happy when given orange juice if that's what she likes to drink, whereas Eric will be sad if he doesn't like juice and prefers coke instead. However, it is only some years later that this simple desire-based concept of emotion is replaced by a more complex adult like belief-desire conceptualisation. At about the age of 6, children start to realize that it is not so much the actual fulfilment of the protagonist's desire but rather his or her expectations regarding fulfilment that will determine the emotional response. If John likes coke and thinks there is coke in his mug, he will be happy, even if his belief is false because someone secretly replaced his favourite drink by something he doesn't like at all (Harris, Johnson, Hutton, Andrews & Cooke, 1989).

Cognitive elaborations of the appraisal process

As children's cognitive capacities increase, they are able to analyse the appraisal process into greater causal depth. This allows for a more sophisticated understanding of its subjective nature. Specifically, children knowledge develops to include 1) the use of personal information to explain or predict atypical emotional reactions, 2) the acknowledgement of simultaneous emotions, and 3) an understanding of complex emotions that require attribution-dependent or counterfactual inferences.

Although young children already realize that emotional responses are dependent on subjective appraisal-components like desires and beliefs, they still have a long way to go before being able to apply this principle adequately in most of the situations they encounter in daily life. In the laboratory, relevant information is explicitly provided, and usually care is taken to provide children with typical situations: a child that prefers juice to coke or the other way round. However, in daily life, children may encounter atypical beliefs or desires, or they may have to actively search for the information needed to come up with a correct explanation for or prediction of someone's feelings.

Empirical work has shown that between the ages of 6 to 12, children learn to integrate personal information into their analysis of the appraisal process and develop strategies to acquire or infer relevant information that is not explicitly provided. A study by Gould (reported in Gnepp, 1989) has shown,

gest useful regulation options when asked how a negative emotion can be changed. They argue that in order to feel better, you can engage in active problem-solving (try to fix a broken toy), leave an emotional situation (just walk away from the kids who are teasing you), engage in other activities (do something fun), or ask a parent or teacher for help. Between the ages of 4 and 6, children clearly understand that situational or behavioural changes may be helpful in alleviating a negative feeling state. However, at this age they hardly ever spontaneously suggest that emotions can be changed through mental activity as well. Ten-year-old children, in contrast, have extended their knowledge base of effective emotion regulation strategies to include different types of cognitive strategies involving the use of selective attention or cognitive reappraisals (see Brenner & Salovey, 1997; Denham, 1998; Harris, 1989; Saarni, 1999 for reviews).

The general developmental shift toward an emphasis on cognitive strategies of emotion regulation has been firmly established. Somewhat surprisingly, however, only very limited attention has been paid to the development of children's understanding of specific cognitive manipulations. In the next section, we will argue that two different levels of understanding can be distinguished in children's reasoning about the use of cognition for emotional change.

Automatic thoughts and multiple meanings

Cognitive emotion regulation strategies aim at altering the input of the emotion system. Two broad classes of strategies can be distinguished: changes of attentional focus and cognitive reappraisals. In the former case, the person emphasizes a different aspect of the situation or concentrates on something else altogether. In the latter case, the person changes his or her subjective interpretation of the incoming information. In a large scale interview study (Meerum Terwogt & Stegge, 1998; Stegge et al., 2004), we studied children aged 4, 6, 10 and 15 and were able to show that their understanding of specific cognitive strategies of emotion regulation reflects a changing view of the relation between cognition and emotion. These changes become evident in both children's understanding of the role of attentional focus and their understanding of cognitive reappraisals.

Even 4-year-olds understand that the intensity of a negative emotion decreases if one stops thinking about the emotion eliciting event. At the age of 6, they also realize that a change in attentional focus is the mechanism responsible for the positive effect of distracting activity: doing something fun when feeling sad helps you to forget about the cause of your sadness. Similarly, children aged 4 to 6 acknowledge that thinking about the sad event increases your negative feeling state. However, at this young age, children only have a limited awareness of mental activity as an ongoing "stream of consciousness". They do not realize that thoughts automatically trigger one another, that people therefore often have unwanted thoughts, and it is hard to get rid of these thoughts (Flavell et al., 1998). Between the ages of 5 and 13, children's understanding of cognitive cueing gradually increases, and by the age of 10, children realize that mental avoidance or distraction may not always work: although you are busy doing something else, unwanted thoughts about the event may pop up. These cognitive advances have important consequences for strategic attempts at emotion regulation. As children understand that memories of emotional events may be triggered by a broad variety of cues, care can be taken to avoid or confront certain people, situations or stimuli depending on the their regulatory aims. Moreover, as children come to realize that often thoughts automatically trigger one another, they may realize that simply trying to forget about an emotional event often will not work (especially in the long run) and they may realize that something more is needed: the event needs to be interpreted in a different way in order to find a more lasting emotional solution.

As emotional information can be interpreted in a variety of ways, emotional change can be accomplished through different cognitive manipulations. Even 4- to 6-year-olds are of the opinion that a negative feeling state is changed for the better if you "replace" a negative thought by a positive one: "my classmates didn't want to play with me, but I'm sure next time they will", or "my car is broken, but I'm sure my dad will be able to repair it". Similarly, they appreciate the introduction of a new, more positive perspective on the situation: "You may feel sad because your friend is going to move, but you feel better as soon as you realize that now you can plan to stay over at each others place during the holidays". Young children's understanding of reappraisals is limited, however, in that they are tied to one cognitive representation of reality. The cognitive reappraisals in the examples just given seem to reflect a kind of wishful thinking in which a "new reality" that replaces the old, unfavourable situation is simply accepted. Contrary to 10-year-olds, children aged 4 to 6 do not seem to understand that different perspectives on one and the same situations can strategically be taken in order to influence one's feeling state. When asked, for example what would happen to a protagonist's feelings who had just seen his precious toy car ruined if (s)he would think "well, I didn't like the car that much anyway", or "well, my brother didn't do it on purpose", they quite often denied that such an alternative perspective on reality was possible: "but he did like the car", "but his brother did do it on purpose". Apparently, these children have not yet adopted a conception of the mind as an interpretative device, and do not seem to appreciate the co-existence of different perspectives that can be strategically adopted for mood improvement.

Based on these findings, we concluded that young children seem to assume a one-to-one relationship between cognition and emotion: sad feelings are triggered by sad thoughts, and in order to change your sadness you have to avoid negative thoughts and/or should replace them by more positive ones. Older children, in contrast, are no longer tied to a "same valence" perspective on the relation between cognition and emotion and acknowledge that different perspectives on reality are possible at the same time: sad feelings may be triggered by sad thoughts in response to affectively neutral or even positive cues, and a different perspective on reality can always be taken and thus actively be sought.

4. Atypical development: the case of depression

In the course of development, emotion and cognition become increasingly connected to form cognitive-affective structures (Izard, 2002; Izard & Ackerman, 2000). Generally, these emotion schemas are functional in that they highlight salient features of the environment and help the child to adequately deal with emotion-eliciting situations based on previous experiences. However, emotions can also become linked to faulty cognitions and form rigid affect-cognition structures that serve the child maladaptively (Ferguson & Stegge, 1995; Ferguson, Stegge, Miller & Olson, 1999). In atypical development, adaptive functioning is compromised as a result of biased appraisal processes, the inadequate allocation of priorities among multiple existing goals, and/or the selection of inappropriate emotional responses. In this section, we will discuss examples of maladaptive emotion-cognition linkages as they appear in children with depressive symptoms.

Although depression is characterized by different classes of symptoms (motivational, somatic, cognitive), it is primarily an affective disorder. Its core feature is sad or depressed affect (APA, 1994), combined with a lack of positive feelings, and frequently with (self-directed) anger or hostility. In keeping with an increasing focus on the role of emotion in biased cognitive processing, recent accounts have argued that depressive symptoms result from a failure to regulate negative emotions (Power & Dalgleish, 1997; Teasdale, 1996; Teasdale et al., 1995). Specifically, depressed people are hypothesized to suffer from inadequate input and output regulation.

Appraisal biases

Cognitive schemata capture generic features of experiences and represent high level, implicit knowledge about the self in relation to the world. Individual differences in the content of these mental models result not so much from differences in experience as such, but mainly from differences in the information people extract from their experiences. Affect plays a major organizing role in this appraisal process. In the course of development, emotion-related schematic models are formed in which the relevant features of situations eliciting a specific emotion or combination of emotions are represented. Depressed affect can become associated, for example, with situations concerning loss, social rejection or achievement failures and perceptions of the self as being entirely worthless, unlovable or incompetent, and unable to change the situation now or in the future. Importantly, the information encoded may concern specific evaluations (I failed as this task; my teacher justifiably criticized my work), but also direct sensory feedback (the person's facial expression, posture or bodily reactions). As a result, a depressogenic cognitive scheme may be triggered by a wide range of environmental cues including, for example, subtle facial expressions indicative of social rejection (e.g. an expression of contempt). Information concerning this new experience subsequently feeds back into the existing mental model, so that a self-perpetuating negative processing configuration is created (Teasdale et al., 1995).

In line with theoretical predictions and findings obtained in studies with adults, empirical work in children has shown that depressive symptoms are associated with negative cognitions about the self, the world and the future (Hammen & Rudolph, 1996), and center around themes of loss and failure (Marien & Bell, 2004). These cognitive schemata bias the online processing of information, especially under conditions of negative affect. Studies employing a vignette methodology have shown, for example, that children high on depressive symptoms process the information provided in negative emotion-eliciting events in a more negative way (Garber, Braafladt & Weiss, 1995; Quiggle, Garber, Panak & Dodge, 1992). Using a similar approach, we have shown that these children perceive rejection experiences as more emotionally distressing and are inclined to respond with catastrophizing thoughts about the event (Reijntjes, Stegge, Meerum Terwogt & Hurkens, submitted; see Garber, Weiss & Shanly, 1993, for similar findings in adolescents).

Further support for the activation of negative cognitive schemata in emotion-eliciting events has been obtained experimental studies. Murray, Woolgar, Cooper and Hipwell (2001) have shown that a cognitively vulnerable group of 5-year-olds (i.e. children of depressed mothers) demonstrated negative self-related cognitions when sad affect was induced by means of an ecologically valid experimental manipulation in the laboratory (i.e. children lost a familiar card game). In the context of winning, no such cognitive bias became evident. Studies with somewhat older children (8 to 12-year-olds; Taylor & Ingram, 1999) and adolescents (Kelvin, Goodyer, Teasdale & Brechin, 1999) have also shown evidence of negative self-referencing only when a negative mood was experienced.

According to recent information processing accounts (Lemerise & Arsenio, 2000), the activation of negative self-schemata will influence the way in which children deal with an emotion-eliciting event. A creative study by Hilsman and Garber (1995) offers some support for this line of thought. Using a prospective design, these researchers have shown that a depressogenic attributional style (i.e. a tendency to ascribe negative outcomes to negative, global characteristics of the self) and low perceived academic control predicted negative affect 6 days after 10- to 12-year-old children had been confronted with a stressful event (i.e. receiving a low grade). The intensity of the stressor, in contrast, only predicted immediate negative emotional responses. Apparently, prolonged negative feelings are due not so much to the degree of induced stress as such, but to the child's cognitive style. Presumably, the confrontation with a negative emotional event results in the activation of negative emotion-cognition schemata in the vulnerable group who may then engage in dysfunctional coping responses (i.e. rumination).

Emotion regulation strategies

Although conceptually depression has been associated with emotion regulation problems, empirical studies demonstrating this relation have generally be lacking. Using a vignette approach, Garber and colleagues (1995) have shown that children scoring high on depressive symptoms were less likely to report the use of problem-focused strategies in response to hypothetical emotionally distressing events. In addition, the "depressed" group was less inclined to endorse cognitive strategies of emotion regulation. Moreover, both types of strategies were evaluated as being less effective in producing mood improvement. Very similar findings were obtained with a small clinic referred depressed sample (Garber et al., 1991).

In our own work, we sought to extend these findings by studying the relation between depressive symptoms and specific (cognitive) emotion regulation strategies in more detail. Specifically, we focused on children's anticipated use of attentional deployment strategies and cognitive reappraisals in response to hypothetical achievement failures and social rejection experiences. In two studies among children aged 10 to 13 (Reijntjes et al., in press, submitted)., it was shown that those high on depressive symptoms were less likely to endorse active problem solving strategies or behavioural distraction and more likely to report passivity In addition, these children were less likely to endorse positive reappraisals, and more likely to report rumination. In response to social rejection a relationship between depressive symptoms and cognitive disengament was found ("I don't really care anyway", "I might just as well play with someone else"). Probably, this reflects depressed children's tendency to avoid the risk of additional rejection.

Importantly, we were able to show very similar emotion regulation difficulties in depressed children's responses to an actual peer rejection experience, that proved to be highly effective in eliciting negative affect (Reijntjes, Stegge, Meerum Terwogt, Kamphuis & Telch, submitted). Children aged 9 to 13 were led to believe that were playing an on-line computer game (Survivor) along with five other players (in fact, these were computerized confederated). Players were voting each other in or out the game on the basis of personal information they (supposedly) provided about themselves (e.g. strengths and weaknesses in different domains, hobbies, physical appearance). Participants were told that the game's objective was to survive each voting round and become the only remaining player. In the rejection condition, the child was voted out of the game by the other players in the first round, in the control condition a co-player was voted out. After children had rated their current feelings, they were warned that there would be a short delay due to a technical problem. During this 5 minute waiting period several alternative activities were available representing distinct emotion regulation strategies: active distraction (listening to music or reading comic books), behavioural approach (inspecting the content of folders providing information on previous alleged winners or losers of the game), or passive behavior (just sit and wait). Children higher in depressive symptoms were more likely to stay passive, which may reflect the learned helplessness attitude characteristic of depression. In addition, these children were more reluctant to engage in approach behaviour. They spent less time reviewing information on previous players of the game, and when asked whether they wanted to know the reasons for being voted out, they were less willing to receive that information. Differences between children high and low in depression were only found in the rejection condition, suggesting that they concern responses to an emotional stressor (i.e. social rejection) rather than behavioural differences reflective of depression in general.

Taken together, the empirical evidence for the relation between depressive symptoms and different emotion regulation strategies, although limited, shows a rather consistent picture. Across methodologies, it has been demonstrated that children high on depressive symptoms endorse emotion regulation strategies that most likely will not be very helpful in improving their negative feeling state (i.e. staying passive), may intensify it (i.e. rumination), or not prove to be very effective in the long run (i.e. disengagement from a stressful peer interaction). In contrast, they seem to refrain from strategies that have been shown to be effective in dealing with emotional problems (i.e. behavioural distraction, positive reappraisals or active problem solving) at least in older samples (Compas et al., 2001; Gross & John, 2002).

5. Implications for affect education

During the course of development, important connections are established between emotion and cognition. Children build up an emotion knowledge base that can be used in the service of adaptive emotional responding. In this section, we will first discuss the essentials of a functional emotion theory. It will be argued that children need to develop a two-level emotion theory, in which emotion is acknowledged both as an autonomous, regulatory process and as a to-be-regulated phenomenon. We will then turn to the case of atypical development and discuss how intervention programs that aim to target dysfunctional cognition-emotion relationships may benefit from recent scientific advances in our knowledge of the core features of the emotion process, children's developing understanding of emotion, and specific emotion-related appraisal and regulation biases.

The development of a two-level theory of emotion

As has already been argued, adaptive functioning requires a delicate balance between the emotional core system and the cognitive control system. In order to serve its adaptive function, the emotion system needs to be given free reign to some extent, so that relevant signals will be picked up and responded to. At the same time, regulatory activity is needed to adapt the often crude and stereotypical responses of the core system (attacking, fleeing) to situational and personal demands. Although in some situations, either the autonomous or the regulatory component of the process may be dominant, in many emotional situations both features will be prevalent to some extent. In order to be able to adequately use emotions in the service of adaptive functioning, then, an adequate emotion theory requires two knowledge levels: 1) an understanding of the characteristics of the emotional core program, including the features of specific emotions, and 2) knowledge of the potential usefulness of regulation strategies that may influence the different components of an emotional experience.

In order to be able to acquire knowledge of specific emotions, children need extensive practice in a supporting social context. Conversation about emotion takes an important place in their learning process (Dunn, Brown & Beardsall, 1991). Through relevant emotional experiences and the opportunity to discuss them with knowledgeable, empathic others, children start to develop an understanding of the intrinsic relations between different components of emotional core programs at a relatively young age. They learn to associate different basic emotions with prototypical eliciting events, characteristic emotional expressions and behaviours (Harris, 1989; Saarni, 1999). This type of knowledge is important in that it helps children to identify specific feeling states in themselves and others based on one or several distinctive components of the emotion process.

In their interactions with others, children not only learn that emotions are associated with common elicitors, bodily reactions, facial expressions or behaviours, but also that there need not be a one-to-one correspondence between these different elements of the emotion process. Lisa may be sad, but hide her sadness behind a smile; Peter may be angry, but not become aggressive; Mark may at first be very sad because he lost his favorite toy, but less distressed some moments later, although the actual situation has not changed. Children come to understand that regulatory activity may impact on one or several components of the emotion program. They acquire knowledge of emotion as a to-be-regulated phenomenon.

At first, children are dependent on the social environment to a great extent for the identification and/or regulation of emotions. Caretakers help children to structure their emotional experiences, to put their feelings into words, and to regulate emotional distress. With age, children become more and more self-reliant as a result of accumulating experiences and cognitive advances. They come to acknowledge the subjective nature of emotion, perceive the mind as an active, interpretative device and learn to form complex cognitive representations. These cognitive abilities allow for the integration of personal information into the appraisal process and the acknowledgement of complex (mixtures of) emotions in the self and others. As a result, the child is able to engage in an increasingly sophisticated emotion identification process. Moreover, these cognitive advances stimulate proficiency in emotion regulation as well. As children come to understand that emotion-eliciting events are multi-faceted and that diverging perspectives on the same situation are (almost) always possible, they acknowledge the usefulness of (complex) cognitive reappraisals and –more importantly- understand that a change in perspective can be actively sought.

Although a conceptualisation of emotion as a to-be-regulated phenomenon is crucial in the emotionally competent child's emotion theory, it is important to note that the possibilities of the conscious control system should not be exaggerated. First, emotions may be elicited by non-conscious processes that require only minimal cognition. They may result from a "quick and dirty" evaluation of simple perceptual features taking place at a preconscious level of awareness. LeDoux (1996) has called this the "low route" to emotion activation. Both natural triggers and signals that are learned through the mechanism of classical conditioning may turn on the emotion system in this way. Fear, for example, may automatically be elicited by an environmental cue, such as an angry voice or face, without the person knowing the reason for the experienced arousal (Öhman, 1999). Although our cognitive system is usually quite able to deal with the important task of identifying the causes of emotions, it is important to realize that there are limitations. The existence of a "low route" to emotion implies that in some cases, something more than mere introspection and/or reflection on the current situation is needed to understand why we feel the way we feel.

Second, it is important that the child realizes that emotions have a phenomenological truth: to be angry of afraid is to perceive the world in a certain way (Lambie & Marcel, 2002). A prevailing emotion determines, at least to some extent, which thoughts, images and memories come to mind. Anger stimulates a world-focused view, evokes thoughts about the responsibility and blameworthiness of others and elicits a tendency to aggress. Similarly, sadness stimulates a more inward focus, in which the person reflects on loss or failure in order to be able to evaluate priorities given to important goals (Power, 1999). Because of their adaptive function, emotions obey to certain laws: given my anger or sadness, it is logical that I'm inclined to think a, b or c, and I would like to do x or y (Frijda, 1988). Knowledge of these autonomous features of the emotion process may help children to better understand their own reactions and those of others: he yelled at me not so much because of what I did, but because he was already irritated; she didn't mean to hurt me, I overreacted because I was already in a depressed mood.

Knowledge of the intrinsic relations between different components of the emotion process stimulates emotional awareness: the own emotions and those of others not only become understandable, but also predictable, at least to some extent. The child learns to recognize when an emotional problem occurs. A view on emotion as a to-be-regulated phenomenon subsequently sets the stage for the strategic employment of regulatory activity. Useful regulation options are, at least partly, dependent on the child's cognitive abilities. Children who operate within a one-to-one correspondence model of the relation between cognition and emotion will be willing to try avoiding options (distraction, mental avoidance). Children who have developed a genuine conception of the mind as an interpretative device, in contrast, may also be responsive to the use of cognitive reappraisals.

The adequate coaching of emotion not only requires a sensitivity to the child's developmental level, but also to individual differences in children's naïve theories of emotion. As has been argued already, emotional problems are characterized by dysfunctional emotion-cognition linkages. Children high in depressive symptoms were shown to be prone to appraisal biases, especially in the case of prevailing negative emotions. In addition, empirical evidence was discussed suggesting a limited and biased coping repertoire. In the next paragraph, we will discuss how programs aimed at the correction of these children's cognitive biases and the development of a more extensive coping repertoire may benefit from the findings on typical and atypical development discussed previously.

Correcting biased emotional responding

Children high in depressive symptoms demonstrate characteristics patterns of appraisal: they are inclined to attribute failure to internal, global, enduring features of the self, tend to elaborate on negative self-referencing material, and are likely to catastrophize. Cognitive-behavioural interventions aim to correct these errors of evaluation, either by tackling the interpretation of specific events or by changing the core beliefs underlying the online interpretation process (Kendall, 1998). Traditionally, cognitive behaviour therapy assumes that dysfunctional emotional responses can be changed by changing the dysfunctional cognitions they are based on. As emotions take on a more prominent place in theoretical models guiding cognitive therapy (Teasdale, 1996) the effect of emotion on cognitive processing is increasingly acknowledged. In more recent models, it is argued that vulnerability to depression results from the negative thinking patterns that become activated in a negative mood (Ingram et al., 1998; Teasdale et al., 1995, 2002). From this perspective, the main problem to be tackled concerns the escalation of a mildly negative feeling state to more enduring dysphoric states.

The activation of depressogenic cognitions under negative mood conditions mainly concerns the automatic processing of information and results in a vicious circle in which cognition and emotion mutually influence each other. In order to break the circle, children with elevated levels of depression need to learn to switch from automatic processing to strategic or controlled processing. One way of reaching this goal is to increase the child's emotional awareness. In depression, emotional awareness is typically limited. The presence of negative affect triggers a stream of self-devaluative thoughts and feelings of helplessness and hopelessness. The autonomous nature of the emotion process is emphasized: I feel horrible and there is nothing I can do about it.

In order to be able to redirect the activity of the emotional core program and stimulate corrective action, depressed children need to learn to identify their negative feelings in an early stage. Specifically, they need to become aware of their feelings as specific emotions that can be examined and acted upon (Teasdale, 1996). At a meta-cognitive level, they have to develop a conception of emotion as a to-be-regulated phenomenon. Two basic skills therefore take a central place in intervention programs: the identification of emotion and the development of adequate strategies of emotion regulation. The identification of emotion helps the depressed children realize when a worsening of mood is imminent and regulatory activity is called for. The development of a coping repertoire provides them with the tools necessary to actually be able to exert control.

Although it has been suggested in the literature that depressed children primarily suffer from a lack of adequate emotion regulation skills rather than from deficits in the basic understanding of emotion (Southam-Gerow & Kendall, 2000), recent findings suggest otherwise. A longitudinal study (Fine, Izard, Mostow, Trantacosta & Ackerman, 2003) has shown that internalizing problems at age 11 were predicted by children's lack of ability in the recognitions of emotions at the age of 7. In addition, a study with adolescents suffering from internalizing problems has shown that these youth display poor emotion language specificity (O'Kearney & Dadds, 2005). First, they were shown to represent negative emotions in situational terms (e.g. feeling abandoned, alone, let down). Moreover, when being presented with an actual emotional challenge (having to give a talk and receiving feedback from other children), they used less specific emotion terms when asked to described their feelings, and also proved to be hypercognizant about the event (e.g. I feel full of doubt). A nonproblem control group, in contrast, was shown to focus more closely on the immediate affective responses. The results of studies like this are relevant for the development of tailored affect education approaches, in that they suggest that programs for depressed youth should focus on the development of a more purely affective or experiential language for specific emotions. Contrary to global affective states, specific emotions are typically associated with causal objects and plans of action. The accessibility of this information during the emotion process should facilitates attempts at emotion regulation. And indeed, research in adults has shown the expected relation between emotion differentiation and the regulation of negative affect (Feldman Barrett, Gross, Christensen & Benvenuto, 2001).

As studies in developmental psychology have convincingly shown that the development of emotion knowledge profits from discussions about emotion in the family (Hughes & Dunn, 1998), it might be expected that affect education programs can effectively remediate depressed children's deficits in this respect. For an answer to the question of how to stimulate the development of a conceptual organization of emotion in children, the empirical findings discussed previously may be useful. First, we know that some emotion concepts (those of basic emotions like happiness, sadness, anger or fear) are easier to understand than others (complex attribution dependent emotions like guilt or shame, or counterfactual feelings like disappointment or relief). Second, we know that children's understanding of ambivalence develops through certain stages. For example, children come to understand the simultaneity of same valence emotions (sadness and anger) before they understand that emotions of opposite valence (happiness and sadness) can be experienced at the same time. Finally, the ability to use personal characteristics in the appraisal process develops as children acquire a conception of the mind as an interpretative device. This allows for a better understanding of individual differences and also for an insight into the own emotional make-up. A child may realize, for example, that (s)he easily becomes frightened or sad compared to other kids, or that certain emotions and certain cognitions are strongly intertwined. In our opinion, then, lessons on emotion identification should stimulate 1) the development of a wide range of specific emotion concepts, 2) the understanding of emotional ambivalence, and 3) the understanding of individual differences in the tendency to respond with certain emotions rather than others. A careful assessment of the child's emotion identification skills in each of the three relevant domains helps the therapist to determine the next logical step in development. And as the child's emotional awareness increases, (s)he will be better able to decide when control is needed, so that emotions can be put to adaptive use.

The next important issue concerns the question of how to control. As has already been mentioned, empirical research has provided evidence for a changing perspective on emotion with age. Young children emphasize the intrinsic relation between cognition and emotion and consider the confrontation with any negative element to be the starting point of an associative chain of negative events. In order to remediate a negative feelings state, then, these children suggest avoidance or distraction: you should stop thinking about what has happened and do something fun instead. In this phase, children's understanding of cognitive reappraisals is also limited. As they have not yet access to representational mappings, they do not realize that conflicting perspectives on one and the same situation are possible.

From a developmental perspective some regulation strategies thus seem to make higher demands on children's capabilities than others. Especially the beneficial effects of those strategies that strongly rely on the representational nature of mental processes and/or require the endurance of at least some amount of negative affect are difficult to appreciate. Depressed children seem to experience emotion regulation difficulties that are to some extent quite similar to those of young children. Like young children, they prefer avoiding options, and do not seem to acknowledge the positive effects of cognitive reappraisals. In addition, these children suffer from relatively strong associations between different components of the emotion process, due to the activation of dysfunctional cognitive schemata under conditions of negative affect. It is not very surprising then, that these children are inclined to avoid confronting strategies (i.e. active problem solving or cognitive engagement strategies that require the acknowledgement of negative elements in the situation). Knowledge of both typical development and the specific emotion regulation problems of depressed children may be used to determine the optimal sequencing of different steps in the affect education program for individual children. The therapist should start with relatively easy strategies before turning to the more demanding ones. On a behavioural level, children may learn to use distraction or simple problem solving strategies, as these are among the most frequently used successful strategies in typical development (Sandstrom, 2004). On a cognitive level, some principles should guide the introduction of cognitive reappraisals. Developmental findings suggest that it is relatively easy to agree to a changed evaluation of the situation when new information has come available, whereas it is much harder to accept that the same information allows for different interpretations (Carpendale & Chandler, 1996). We would suggest, then, that at first the therapist should direct the child's attention to elements in the stimulus situation that have not been considered yet, before suggesting a radically different interpretation of exactly the same information. Especially in the case of emotionally biased information processing, it will probably be hard to correct the child's interpretations without putting forward new proof. Preferable, the new information is unambiguously positive, since developmental findings have shown that reappraisals are interpreted, at first, from what we called a "same valence perspective" on the usefulness of different cognitive manipulations. Moreover, this approach will fit in with depressed children's tendency to avoid the confrontation with negative information. As depressed children's competences increase, the therapist may subsequently turn to more demanding options that also require the child the endure a certain amount of negative affect.

Finally, we would like to reemphasize that the use of cognition in establishing emotional change should not be exaggerated. Emotions may be triggered automatically and nonconsciously through the thalamaoamygdala pathway (LeDoux, 1996). Empirical evidence has shown that in these cases, the emotion program usually runs its own course and is relatively impenetrable to cognition (Öhman & Wiens, 2003). Emotional problems established through these subcortical pathways are the result of associative learning mechanisms and an intervention that is strictly cognitive in nature is problaby not very effective in changing them. Corrective emotional experiences are needed based on direct behavioural exposure. The child needs to get the opportunity to profit from new experiences so that existing stimulus-thought-emotion sequences become dissociated and more functional structures can develop (Izard, 2002; Power & Dalgleish, 1997). Effective emotion-centered prevention or intervention programs need to distinguish these different emotion activation processes so that individual differences in emotional responding can be better understood and more adequately remediated.

References

Arsenio, W.F. & Lemerise, E.A. (2004). Aggression and moral development: Integrating social information processing and moral domain models. Child Development, 75, 987-1002.

Arsenio, W.F. & Lover, A. (1995). Children's conceptions of sociomoral affect: Happy victimizers, mixed emotions and other expectancies. In M. Killen & d. Hart (Eds.), Morality in everyday life: Developmental perspectives. (pp. 87-128). Cambridge: Cambridge University Press.

Banerjee, M. (1997). Hidden emotions: Preschoolers' knowledge of appearance-reality and emotion display rules. Social Development, 15, 107-132.

Barden, R.C., Zelko, F., Duncan, S.W. & Masters, J.C. (1980). Children's consensual knowledge about the experiential determinants of emotion. Journal of Personality and Social Psychology, 39, 968-976.

Beck, A.T. (1976). Cognitive therapy and the emotional disorders. New York: Meridian.

Brenner, E.M. & Salovey, P. (1997). Emotion regulation during childhood: Developmental, interpersonal and individual considerations. In P. Salovey & D.J. Sluyter (Eds.), Emotional development and emotional intelligence. New York: Basic Books.

Bretherton, I. & Beegly, M. (1982). Talking about internal states of mind: The acquisition of an explicit theory of mind. Developmental Psychology,

18, 906-921.

Carpendale, J.I. & Chandler, M.J. (1996). On the distinction between false belief understanding and subscribing to an interpretative theory of mind. Child Development, 67, 1686-1706.

Compas, B.E., Connor-Smith, J.K., Salzman, H., Harding Thomsen, A. & Wadsworth, M.E. (2001). Coping with stress during childhood and adolescence: Problems, progress, and potential in theory and research. Psychological Bulletin, 127, 87-127.

Cosmides, L. & Tooby, J. (2000). Evolutionary psychology and the emotions. In M. Lewis & J.M. Haviland-Jones (Eds.), Handbook of emotions (2nd ed.). (pp. 91-115). New York: Guilford Press.

Denham, S.A. (1998). Emotional development in young children. New York: The Guilford Press.

Denham, S.A. & Kochanoff, A. (2002). Why is she crying: Children's understanding of emotion from preschool to preadolescence. In L. Feldman Barrett & P. Salovey (Eds.), The wisdom in feeling: Psychological processes in emotional intelligence. (pp. 239-270). New York: Guilford Press.

Dunn, J., Brown, J. & Beardsall, L. (1991). Family talk about feeling states and children's later understanding of others' emotions. Developmental Psychology, 27, 448-455.

Ellsworth, P.C. & Scherer, K.R. (2003). Appraisal processes in emotion. In R.J. Davidson, K.R. Scherer & H.H. Goldsmith (Eds.), Handbook of affective sciences. (pp. 572-595). Oxford: Oxford University Press.

Feldman Barrett, L., Gross, J., Christensen, T.C. & Benvenuto, M. (2001). Knowing what you're feeling and knowing what to do about it: Mapping the relation between emotion differentiation and emotion regulation. Cognition and Emotion, 15, 713-724.

Ferguson, T.J. & Stegge, H. (1995). Emotional states and traits in children: The case of guilt and shame. In J.P. Tangney & K.W. Fischer (Eds.), Self-conscious emotions. (pp. 174-197). New York: Guilford Press.

Ferguson, T.J., Stegge, H., Miller, E.R. & Olsen, M.E. (1999). Guilt, shame and symptoms in children. Developmental Psychology, 35, 347-357.

Fine, S.E., Izard, C.E., Mostov, A.J., Trentacosta, C.J. & Ackerman, B.P. (2003). First grade emotion knowledge as a predictor of fifth grade self-reported internalizing behaviors in children from economically disadvantaged families. Development and Psychopathology, 15, 331-342.

Flavell, J.H., Green, F.L., Flavell, E. (1998). The mind has a mind of its own:

Developing knowledge about mental uncontrollability. Cognitive Development, 13, 127-138.

Frijda (1986) The emotions. Cambridge: Cambridge University Press.

Frijda, N.H. (1988). The laws of emotion. American Psychologist, 43, 349-358.

Garber, J., Braafladt,, N & Zeman, J. (1991). The regulation of sad affect: An information processing perspective. In J. Garber & K. Dodge (Eds.), The development of emotion regulation and dysregulation. (pp. 208-240). New York: Cambridge University Press.

Garber, J., Braafladt, N. & Weiss, B. (1995). Affect regulation in depressed and nondepressed children and young adolescents. Development and Psychopathology, 7, 93-115.

Garber, J., Weiss, B., & Shanly, N. (1993). Cognitions, depressive symptoms, and development in adolescents. Journal of Abnormal Psychology, 102, 47-57.

Gnepp, J. (1989). Children's use of personal information to understand other people's feelings. In C. Saarni & P.L. Harris (Eds.), Children's understanding of emotion. (pp. 151-180). New York: Cambridge University Press.

Gross, D. & Harris, P.L. (1988). False beliefs about emotions Children´s understanding of misleading emotional displays. International Journal of Behavioural Development, 11, 475 488.

Gross, J.J. & John, J. (2002). Wise emotion regulation. In L. Feldman Barrett & P. Salovey (Eds.), The wisdom of feelings: Psychological processes in emotional intelligence. (pp. 297-318). New York: Guilford Press

Gross, J. & Thompson, R.A. (in press). Emotion regulation: Conceptual foundations. In J. Gross & R. Thompson (Eds.), Handbook of emotion regulation. New York: Guilford Press.

Guttentag, R. & Farrell, J. (2004) Reality compared with its alternatives: Age differences in judgments of regret and relief. Developmental Psychology, 40, 764-775.

Hammen & Rudolph, K.D. (1996). Childhood depression. In E.J. Mash & R.A. Barkley (Eds.), Child psychopathology. (pp 153-195). New York: Guilford Press.

Harris, P.L. (1989) Children and emotion: The development of psychological understanding. Oxford: Blackwell.

Harris, P.L. (2000). Understanding emotion. In M. Lewis & J.M. Haviland-Jones (Eds.), Handbook of emotions (2nd ed.). (pp. 281-292. New York: Guilford Press.

Harris, P.L. Johnson, C.N., Hutton, D., Andrews, G. & Cooke, T. (1989). Young children's theory of mind and emotion. Cognition and Emotion, 3, 379-400.

Harter, S. & Whitesell, N.R. (1989). Developmental changes in children's understanding of single, multiple and blended emotion concepts. In C. Saarni & P.L. Harris (Eds.), Children's understanding of emotion. (pp. 81-116). New York: Cambridge University Press.

Hilsman, R. & Garber, J. (1995). A test of the cognitive diathesis-stress model of depression in children: Academic stressors, attributional style, perceived competence, and control. Journal of Personality and Social Psychology, 69, 370-380.

Hughes, C. & Dunn, J. (1998). Understanding mind and emotion: Longitudinal associations with mental-state talk between young friends. Developmental Psychology, 34, 1026-1037.

Ingram, R.E., Miranda, J. & Segal., Z.V. (1998). Cognitive vulnerability to depression. New York: Guilford Press.

Izard, C.E,. (2002). Translating emotion theory and research in preventive interventions. Psychological Bulletin, 128, 796-824.

Izard, C.E. & Ackerman, B.P. (2000). Motivational, organizational and regulatory functions of discrete emotions. In M. Lewis & J.M. Haviland-Jones (Eds.), Handbook of emotions (2nd ed.). (pp. 253-322). New York: Guilford Press.

Kelvin, R.G., Goodyer, I.M., Teasdale J.D., & Brechin, D. (1999). Latent negative self-schema and high emotionality in well adolescents at risk for psychopathology. Journal of Child Psychology and Psychiatry, 40, 959-968.

Kendall, P.C. (1990). Coping Cat Workbook. Philadelphia: Temple University.

Kendall, P.C. (1998). Empirically supported psychological therapies. Journal of Consulting and Clinical Psychology, 66, 3-6.

Kusché, C.A. & Greenberg, L.S. (1994). The PATHS curriculum: Promoting alternative thinking strategies. Seattle, WA: Developmental Research and Programs.

Lambie, J.A. & Marcel, A.J. (2002) Consciousness and the varieties of emotional experience: A theoretical framework. Psychological Review, 109, 219-259.

Lane, R.D. & Pollerman, .Z. (2002). Complexity of emotion representations. In: Feldman Barrett & P. Salovey (Eds.), The wisdom in feeling: Psychological Processes in Emotional Intelligence. (pp. 271-293). New York: The Guilford

Press.

Lazarus, R.S. (1991). Emotion and adaptation. New York: Oxford University Press.

Lazarus, R.S. (1999). The cognition-emotion debate: A bit of history. In T. Dalgleish & M. Power (Eds.), Handbook of cognition and emotion. (pp. 3-19). New York: Wiley.

LeDoux (1996). The emotional brain. London: Weidenfeld & Nicolson

Lemerise, E.A. & Arsenio, W.F. (2000). An integrated model of emotion processes and cognition in social information processing. Child Development, 71, 107-118.

Levenson, R.W. (1999). The intrapersonal functions of emotion. Cognition and Emotion, 13, 481-504.

Lewis, M. & Michalson, L. (1983). Children's emotions and moods: Developmental theory and measurement. New York: Plenum.

Lochman, J. & Wells, K. (2002). Contextual social-cognitive mediators and child outcome: A test of the theoretical model in the Coping Power Program. Development and Psychopathology, 14, 971-993.

Lochman, J. & Wells, K. (2004). The Coping Power Program for preadolescent aggressive boys and their parents: Outcome effects at the 1-year follow up. Journal of Consulting and Clinical Psychology, 72, 571-578.

Marien, W.E. & Bell, D.J. (2004). Anxiety and depression-related thoughts in children: Development and evaluation of a cognition measure. Journal of Clinical Child and Adolescent Psychychology, 33, 717-730

Mayer, J.D. & Salovey, P. (1997). What is emotional intelligence? In P. Salovey & D. Sluyter (Eds.), Emotional development and emotional intelligence: Implications for educators. (pp. 3-31). New York: Basic Books.

Meerum Terwogt, M. & Olthof, T. (1989). Awareness and self-regulation of emotion in young children. In C. Saarni & P.L. Harris (Eds.), Children's understanding of emotion. (pp. 209-239). New York: Cambridge University Press.

Meerum Terwogt, M. & Stegge, H. (1995). Children's understanding of the strategic control of negative emotions. In J.A. Russell (Ed.), Everyday conceptions of emotion. NATO ASI Series. (pp. 373-390). Dordrecht: Kluwer.

Meerum Terwogt, M. & Stegge, H. (2001). The development of emotional intelligence. In I.M. Goodyer (Ed.), The depressed child and adolescent, second edition. (pp. 24-45). Cambridge: Cambridge University Press.

Mineka, S., Rafaeli, E. & Yovel, I. (2003). Cognitive biases in emotional disorders: Information processing and social-cognitive perspectives. In R.J. Davidson, K.R. Scherer & H.H. Goldsmith (Eds.), Handbook of affective sciences. (pp. 976-1009). Oxford: Oxford University Press.

Murray, L., Woolgar, M., Cooper, P. & Hipwell, A. (2001). Cognitive vulnerability to depression in 5-year-old children of depressed mothers. Journal of Child Psychology and Psychiatry, 42, 891-899.

Niedenthal, P.M., Dalle, N. & Rohman, A. (2002). Emotional response categorization as emotionally intelligent behavior. In L. Feldman Barrett & P. Salovey (Eds.), The wisdom in feeling: Psychological processes in emotional intelligence. (pp. 167-190). New York: Guilford Press.

Nunner-Winkler, G. & Sodian, B. (1988). Children's understanding of moral emotions. Child Development, 59, 1323-1338.

Öhman, A. (1999). Distinguishing unconscious from conscious emotional processes: Methodological considerations and theoretical implications. In T. Dalgleish & M. Power (Eds.), Handbook of cognition and emotion. (pp. 321-352). New York: Wiley.

Öhman, A. & Wiens, S. (2003). On the automaticity of autonomic responses in emotion: An evolutionary perspective. In In R.J. Davidson, K.R. Scherer & H.H. Goldsmith (Eds.), Handbook of affective sciences. (pp. 256-1275). Oxford: Oxford University Press.

O'Kearney, R. & Dadds, M.R. (2005). Language for emotions in adolescents with externalizing and internalizing disorders. Development and Psychopathology, 17, 529-548.

Onishi, K.H. & Baillargeon, R. (2005) Do 15-month-old infants understand false beliefs? Science, 308, 255-258.

Parrott, W.G. (2001). Implications of dysfunctional emotions for understanding how emotions function. Review of General Psychology, 5, 180-186.

Pons, F., & Harris, P. (2005). Longitudinal change and longitudinal stability of individual differences in children's emotion understanding. Cognition and Emotion, 19(8), 1158-1174.

Power, M.J. (1999). Sadness and its disorders. In T. Dalgleish & M. Power (Eds.), Handbook of cognition and emotion. (pp. 497-519). New York: Wiley.

Power, M.J. & Dalgleish, T. (1997). Cognition and Emotion: From order to disorder. Hove: Psychology Press.

Quiggle, N.L., Garber, J., Panak, W.F. & Dodge, K.A. (1992). Social information processing in aggressive and depressed children. Child Development, 63, 1305-1320.

Reijntjes, A.H.A., Stegge, H., Meerum Terwogt, M. & Hurkens, E. (submitted).

Emotion regulation and depressive symptoms in pre-adolescent children.

Reijntjes, A.H.A., Stegge, H., Meerum Terwogt, M. (in press). Children's coping with peer rejection: The role of depressive symptoms, social competence and gender. Infant and Child Development,

Reijntjes, A.H.A., Stegge, H., Meerum Terwogt, M., Kamphuis, J. & Telch, M. (submitted). Children's responses to an in vivo peer rejection experience: the moderating influence of depression.

Saarni, C. (1999). The development of emotional competence. New York: The Guilford Press.

Salovey, P., Mayer, J.D. & Caruso, D. (2002). The positive psychology of emotional intelligence. In C.R. Snyder & S.J. Lopez (Eds.), The handbook of positive psychology. New York: Oxford University Press.

Sandstrom, M. (2004). Pitfalls of the peer world: How children cope with common rejection experiences. Journal of Abnormal Child Psychology, 32, 67-81.

Scherer, K.R. (2003). Introduction: Cognitive components of emotion. In R.J. Davidson, K.R. Scherer & H.H. Goldsmith (Eds.), Handbook of affective sciences. (pp. 563-571). Oxford: Oxford University Press.

Southam-Gerow, M.A. & Kendall, P.C. (2000). Emotion regulation and understanding: Implications for child psychopathology and therapy. Clinical Psychology review, 22, 189-222.

Stark, K. & Kendall, P.C. (1996). Treating depressed children: Therapist manual for 'taking action'. Ardmore: Workbook Publishing.

Stegge, H. & Meerum Terwogt, M. (in press). Children's reasoning about emotion and emotion regulation. To be published in J. Gross & R. Thompson (Eds.), Handbook of emotion regulation. New York: Guilford Press.

Stegge, H., Meerum Terwogt, M., Begeer, S. & Lunenburg, P. (in prep). Children's understanding of counterfactual emotions.

Stegge, H., Meerum Terwogt, M., Reijntjes, A.H.A. & Van Tijen, N. (2004). Children's conception of the emotion process: consequences for emotion regulation. In I. Nyklicek, L. Temoshok & A. Vingerhoets (Eds.), Emotional expression and health: Advances in theory, assessment and clinical applications. (pp. 240-254). New York: Brunner-Routledge.

Stein, N.L. & Levine, L.J. (1989). The causal organization of emotion knowledge: A developmental study. Cognition and Emotion, 3, 343-378.

Taylor, L. & Ingram, R.E. (1999). Cognitive reactivity and depressotypic information processing in children of depressed mothers. Journal of Abnormal

Psychology, 108, 202-210.

Teasdale, J.D. (1996). Clinically relevant theory: Integrating clinical insight with cognitive science. In P.M. Salkovskis. Frontiers of cognitive therapy. New York: Guildford Press.

Teasdale, J.D., Segal, Z. & Williams, M.G. (1995). How does cognitive therapy prevent depressive relapse and why should attentional control (mindfulness) training help? Behaviour Research and Therapy, 33, 25-39.

Teasdale, J.D., Moore, R.G., Hayhurst, H., Pope, M., Williams, S. & Segal, Z.V. (2002). Metacognitive awareness and prevention of relapse in depression: Empirical ecidence. Journal of Consulting and Clinical Psychology, 70, 275-287.

Thompson, R.A. (1989). Causal attributions and children's emotional understanding. In C. Saarni & P.L. Harris (Eds.), Children's understanding of emotion. (pp. 117-150). New York: Cambridge University Press.

Chapter 7

Emotional experiences at elementary school: Theoretical and pragmatic issues

Frédérique Cuisinier, Céline Clavel, Marc de Rosnay and Francisco Pons

1. Introduction

The emotions, for a long time cast out of the scientific field, today represent a very productive and diversified field of research, and research on emotions in the school context is currently experiencing significant developments. The objective of this chapter is to present the main trends of emotion research in the school context. In the first part, we briefly present two significant concepts corresponding to two approaches to the study of affectivity, which can be considered either globally in terms of affects and moods, or in terms of emotions. In the second part, we will see how these concepts are studied in the school context. Lastly, we present a study on the emotional experience of elementary school children before introducing a discussion on the possible continuation of such research.

2. Current approaches of emotions

Several approaches to the study of affectivity are distinguished according to the privileged level of analysis and temporal perspective under consideration. The first approach conceives the affects as durable, overarching phenomena, such as personality and mood, while the second approach concerns emotions, conceived as transitory and fleeting phenomena.

Studies on personality and mood

The aim of research on personality and mood is to identify relatively stable tendencies to feel affects of the same valence (pleasant versus unpleasant). The concepts of positive affectivity (a tendency to feel pleasant affects), negative affectivity (a tendency to feel unpleasant or painful affects), and subjective well-being (a prevalence of positive affectivity) result from this approach (Diener & Lucas, 2000, Tellegen, Watson, & Clark, 1999). Many studies relate the effect of emotional state (e.g., good, bad or neutral mood; positive or negative affectivity; personality's traits like anxiety) on various aspects of behavior (e.g., problem resolution, social judgment, consumption behaviors, etc). The findings of these studies are complex and, more specifically, they are characterized by an absence of symmetry between the negative and positive affects. Nevertheless, some conclusions can be made. The positive affects mostly have facilitator effects, like the increase of creativity, altruistic behaviors or purchase behaviors (Isen, 2001). In contrast, the negative affects mostly have an inhibitory effect (Isen 1984). Research with children leads to comparable results, although such research is less common. Green and Noice (1988) observe facilitator effects of positive mood in a task of creativity (i.e., problem resolution and a verbal task) with children at approximately nine years of age. Keenan (2002) notes that, in the very young child (i.e., nine months) poorer performance in a task of object search associated with greater negative affect. These works reveal that the emotional state of the child, like the adult, affects performance. However, this work concerns an over-arching and diffuse state. Other studies focus on the emotions likely to arise in a given situation.

Emotions

The emotions are mostly described as phenomena of relatively short duration but, sometimes, strong intensity. Emotions alone represent several fields of research that are relatively distinct but also complementary; such as investigations focusing on emotional expressions (face or voice) or emotional experience (subjective feelings). The first group of studies follows Darwin's assumptions concerning the adaptive role of the emotional expressions resulting from evolution. While Ekman's work, which directly addressed Darwin's evolutionary theory, established the universality of the expected interpretation of the emotional expressions, the expression of emotions has also been shown to vary according to context and culture (Keltner & Ekman, 2000). Each culture builds up its own rules of expression, either supporting expressiveness per se or dissimulation according to cases. This situation leads to uncertainty about the links between the internally felt experience of an emotion and the expression made visible to others.

The emotional experience: A complex process

The nature of emotional experience has given rise to many studies (Frijda, 1987). Nevertheless, there is currently a strong consensus concerning several significant properties of the emotions. One characteristic of emotion is the simultaneous association of a physical feeling (e.g., modification of the heart rhythm, muscular tonus, sudation etc), mental representations (e.g. the subjective psychological experience of an emotion such as happy, sad, angry, scared, surprised, disgust, etc.), and a specific behavioral answer (e.g. escape, attack, smile, scream, etc.). Despite the fact that the importance attached to each of these aspects of emotional experience and assumptions about their place in the course of such experience vary according to author, emotions are usually conceived in dynamic terms. They are not reduced to isolated phenomena, instead being connected with complex processes that integrate a multiplicity of components (particularly cognitive) and generate other processes. Frijda (1987) proposes the emotional processes should be represented in term of sequences of the treatment of information, where several sequences are focused on the detection of the relevance and the hedonic valence of the situation, and the individual's possible adjustments to face it. The emotion defines itself, according to Frijda, as an analysis by the individual of the event's valence (pleasant-unpleasant), an interaction between this valence and the potential (or actual) consequences, and as the modification of the preparation state for action. This complex expression indicates the nature of the relation between the individual and his environment at the current time: does he wish to maintain or intensify his experience, to withdraw himself from or stop the situation, or to modify the type of transaction by developing, for example, agonistic behaviors (behaviors of opposition or aggressiveness)? The modification of the preparation state for action derives quantitatively from an activation (i.e., physiological awakening), and qualitatively from a particular action tendency (i.e., behavior orientation). This action readiness tendency can then manifest, or not, as obvious behavioral answers, which might be observable (e.g., facial expressions, escape behavior, burst of laughter, etc) or discrete cognitive responses (e.g., thoughts, recollections, representations).

According to Scherer (1984, 1992), the evaluations of the various aspects of an emotional situation would successively be developed in the following invariable order: novelty, intrinsic valence, meaning with regard to the goals and needs of the individual, possibility of facing (coping) and compatibility with the cultural and internal standards (concept of oneself). This sequence, which is constantly operative and therefore very rapid, is likely to be expressed in the increasingly significant muscular activation of the face that progresses with the evaluation of dimensions of the situation. In this way, for example, a new stimulus involves an opening of the eyes, then a closing of the face if it is evaluated as unpleasant, a contraction of the face if it is in contradiction with the individual's goals, and so on.

Theories such as Frijda's and Scherer's underline the dynamic character of the emotion and the role of the evaluation of the situation for the individual. Such theories to some extent concern a modeling of subjectivity.

The development of the emotions: Intricacy of cognitive, emotional and social factors

The literature on emotions in childhood suggests a development related to cognitive and emotional factors. This literature underlines the socialized character of the emotions and the active contribution of the environment. Two significant findings emerge from research. On the one hand, a great disparity between preschool children in their level of emotion comprehension level is observed (i.e., individual differences) and, on the other hand, there is a progressive development of children's competence in understanding emotion. Individual differences in emotion comprehension are observable very early. Dunn, Brown and Beardsall (1991) showed that, from three years of age, the number of words referring to emotion varies profoundly between children, ranging from 25 references per hour to none. Further, Pons and Harris (2005) established that these individual differences observed early in the childhood remain marked in spite of school attendance. In fact, various empirical contributions show that individual differences in emotion understanding are relatively stable between three and 12 years of age. Research has not yet clarified the factors that explain these differences but various factors appear to be of importance: specific characteristics of the child, such as linguistic competence, and social and family characteristics.

Furthermore, it appears that the understanding of emotions is built around several components with increasing level of complexity. The child acquires them progressively during his development and there is evidence to suggest that there are nine components of emotion understanding organized in three groups (Pons & Harris, 2005). The first group gathers simple components calling upon external dimensions of emotions. The task facing the child is to recognize basic emotions from facial expression and to understand the causal role of situations and memories in the emergence of emotions. Smiley and Huttenlocher (1989) showed that, from two years of age, when one presents children with two images, they can discriminate expressions of joy from other emotions. Similarly, from four years of age, children acquire a lexicon to describe emotions expressed on a face. However, Thommen, Châtelain and Rimbert (2004) moderate these findings, underlining the observation that the spontaneous use of verbal emotional description remains rare up to eight years of age. Further, Wellman, Harris, Banerjee and Sinclair (1995) indicate that from three years of age children integrate the idea that no situation is a priori pleasant or unpleasant, but that the emotional reaction of an individual depends on the adequacy of the fit between his goals and the actual situation. Nevertheless, despite the fact that young children do show some awareness of subjectivity and mental life, this early period of emotion comprehension is marked by a focus on the ostensive manifestations of emotional experience.

The second group of emotion components relates to mental aspects of the emotions. It concerns understanding false beliefs and the role of (conflicting) desires in the emergence of the emotions, as well as the ability to distinguish expressed emotions from those that are felt. Wellman et al. (1995) show that from about five or six years of age children gradually represent to themselves the factors likely to influence the emotional experiment. Thus, the child starts to consider the beliefs of individuals as part of their formulation of an emotional response. Finally the third group of components combines emotion dimensions which call upon a setting in perspective. For the child, it is a question of recognizing the existence of mixed emotions, to understand that it is possible to control emotional states and, finally, to conceive of the moral emotions. The acquisition of these components occurs between seven and 12 years of age.

The findings outlined above therefore aim to show that emotional competences develop gradually during childhood, that they result from an understanding based on the situations, as well as the intentions, expectations and beliefs of the individual. This framework suggests the development of specific cognitive-emotional competences, which are in their turn likely to influence the cognitive and social development of the child. The psychology of the emotions in the realm of education largely refers to these approaches. Thus, in the following section, we present some examples of studies on the emotions conceived in term of such processes.

3. Emotions at school

School constitutes a favorable environment to study emotions both in terms of qualias and intensity. Two research traditions may be identified: the first is centered on wellbeing and the second on emotions.

An approach centered on wellbeing

Research on the well-being of the pupil explores the well documented construct of subjective well-being for the adult (Diener & Lucas, 2000). Subjective well-being is organized around three criteria: high positive affectivity, weak negative affectivity and perceived quality of life. Well-being is a crucial construct, not merely from perspective of the assumption of responsibility for depressive disorders in adolescence, for example, but also from the point of view of prevention (Huebner, Shannon & Smith, 2004). Taking the mid-teenage period as their starting point, Huebner and McCullough (2001) studied relations between the perceived quality of life at school, positive and negative daily events, major life events (both positive and negative), and the feeling of self-efficiency. Amongst 15-year-olds, results showed that school satisfaction was not only related to the existence of pleasant events (daily and major) but also to the feeling of auto-effectiveness. A more focused analysis exploring the causal direction of these relations showed than the environmental variables better predicted school satisfaction than did the feeling of auto-effectiveness. In this study, however, the events of life only marginally concerned school life. By contrast, in a major national study involving nearly 100,000 Finnish pupils between 14 and 16 years of age, Konu, Lintonen and Ville (2002) directly explored the contribution of school in the subjective wellbeing of pupils. Despite significant variability between pupils, this study revealed a strong effect for school. According to the authors, the effect of school can be explained by the existence of impressive homogeneity within Finnish schools, which affect pupils' wellbeing in a relatively uniform manner.

Opdenakker and Van Damme (2000) have also attempt to clarify the relation between the pupils' well-being and the school setting. This study falls under a longitudinal seven-year program initiated in 1997 and was designed to evaluate the impact of school in several learning domains. They assessed the well-being of pupils on eight dimensions: total well-being at school, social integration in class, interest for learning activities, motivation to learn, attitude displayed regarding work at home, attention in class, and school self-esteem.

These pupil data were then connected with the characteristics of schools (teaching practices, teaching staff co-operation in relation to teaching methods and pupil counseling, attention to pupil differences and development, orderly learning environment). Two significant insights emerged from this study. On the one hand, the effect of the school proves to be more significant for pupil academic performance (mathematics and mother language) than wellbeing. On the other hand, this effect on well-being seems to be mediated by the co-operation between teachers variable. The authors also note an interaction between two other variables; pupils' initial motivation (assessed at time of entry to secondary school) and orderly learning environment. The learning organization is beneficial in terms of well-being only for the strongly motivated pupils. In contrast, it is unfavorable to the well-being of poorly motivated pupils. In sum, these findings suggest that the pupils' point of view—their expectations for themselves as pupils as well as their feeling of being able to address themselves to the demands of the school—affects their sense of wellbeing.

Engels, Aelterman, Van Petegem and Schepens (2004) also investigated significant aspects of pupil's life circumstances and environment that contribute to wellbeing. This research addresses a Flemish government request that considers how the wellbeing of pupils functions as an indicator of the operation of schools and classes. The purpose of this study was to evaluate wellbeing state (which presumably related to a local context) and to identify dimensions of school life that according to the pupils themselves contribute to wellbeing. To address these issues, the authors prepared a questionnaire, the structure of which was evaluated with a sample of 2054 pupils (from 26 schools across all six years of secondary education). Their findings showed that total wellbeing scores are strongly determined by the perception and the satisfaction of the pupils with respect to the level of the class and the school. These significant poles of satisfaction related to school building (e.g., architecture, maintenance), atmosphere, friendship network, degree of participation in the class, active working methods, and diversification of the media. The wellbeing thus results from the integration of judgments on multiple facets of the school environment, but the question of the direction of causal relations remains open.

In a further study of well-being in high school, Gumora and Arsenio (2002) explored relations between emotional regulation, emotionality, affects relating to school and academic performance in pupils between the sixth and eighth grade; from 11 to 14 years of age. School performance was evaluated using a total index of Mathematics and English, and standardized tests of knowledge. Pupils also answered a questionnaire concerning their feeling of school competence (Academic Competency Scale). Affects were identified on the basis of (i) self-evaluation of negative affectivity relating to the school (Negative Academic Affect Scale), (ii) global negative affectivity (Self-Reported Negative Mood), (iii) emotional regulation (Emotion Regulation scale), and (iv) teacher evaluation of pupil affect (Positive Affect and Negative Affect Scale). This study revealed very interesting relations between negative affectivity towards school (NAAS), global negative affectivity (Negative Mood), feelings of competence and academic performance. While global academic performance was correlated with teacher evaluations of pupil affect ($r = .36$ for positive affectivity, $p < .001$), there was a stronger connection between the feeling of academic competence and the two measurements of negative affectivity from the pupil ($r = -.51$ for negative affectivity towards school and $-.44$ with global negative affectivity). Emotional regulation was weakly correlated ($r = .17$) with academic performance (tests of knowledge), but more robustly correlated with feelings of competence ($r = .28$) and negative affectivity towards school ($r = -.23$). This pattern of correlations evokes an intricate picture of the pupil's emotional experience, feelings of competence and learning. It is our view that this intricate picture needs further scrutiny because of the connections between the tendency to feel negative affects, negative affectivity towards school and school performance. Such findings raise the question of the contribution of emotional experience in the development of the feeling of both emotional and academic competence.

Emotions and learning at school

A major analysis of the literature between 1974 and 2000 concerning emotions and learning shows that studies have primarily investigated anxiety (Pekrun, Goetz & Titz, 2002). However conversations with secondary school and younger students reveal a diverse repertoire of emotions are evoked in connection with schooling, with the exception of disgust. Pekrun et al. (2002) propose the expression "academic emotions" to delineate emotions directly related to school activities, learning and knowledge, and success (classroom instruction). These authors devised the Academic Emotions Questionnaire (AEQ) to study relations between academic emotions and various aspects of school behaviors, such as performance, adjustment, and coping strategies.

The AEQ includes three sub-scales according to context: learning, work in class, and evaluation. On the basis of AEQ responses by university students, three clusters were formed according to the antecedents of the emotion: (1) Joy, hope and pride were the result of positive events; (2) Anxiety, shame and despair followed negative events associated with a feeling of lack of control and anger, and boredom followed unpleasant events associated with a feeling of high control; (3) Relief alone constituted a cluster by itself, and was defined as occurring at the end of an unpleasant event that has ceased. Importantly, these emotional experiences varied as a function of pedagogical domain and Goetz, Zirngilbl, Pekrun and Hall (2003) observed null to very modest correlations between emotions assessed during English lesson (foreign language), German lesson (mother language), music, mathematics, and sport.

That emotions depend on context is hardly surprising if one considers current models of emotion that have been formulated in terms of treatment of information. The emotional process is organized around valence and the importance of the situation for the individual (Frijda, 1987; Scherer, 1984; Lazarus, 1993), and it is important to appreciate the emotional experience in situ. Within such a perspective, Laukenmann, Bleicher, Fub, Gläzer-Ziduka, Mayring and von Rhoeneck (2003) conducted a study integrating both qualitative and qualitative steps. The authors asked 8th grade pupils between 13 and 15 years of age to answer open questions about a lesson (20 sessions) on electricity using a diary, and to participate in semi-structured interviews. Four sets of themes resulted from the qualitative analysis of the answers: interest, boredom, pleasure, and anxiety. In addition, several variables were located with questionnaires: School satisfaction, well-being, anxiety with regard to physics, interest and feeling of competence with regard to the domain (electricity), as well as preliminary knowledge in physics. Positive correlations emerged between performance at the end of the sessions and feeling of competence, interest and well-being. On the other hand, negative correlations also appeared between performance, boredom and anxiety. The strongest relations related to preliminary knowledge and final performance. Because quantitative data analysis was supplemented with the qualitative approach deriving from the diary reports and interviews, it was possible to locate a complex pattern of influence on pupil anxiety. Anxiety features, which showed trans-situational stability, were likely to play an inhibiting role, while state anxiety related to the current situation and was behaviorally mobilizing. Moreover, successful pupils were more clear-sighted about the distinction between fear of failure (an anxiety feature) and being afraid of failure in a learning situation (a reflection of the pressure to succeed and state anxiety). Pupils experiencing difficulties were likely to inhibit their responses related to the pressure to succeed, and thus appeared less anxious in situ but had a more significant level of latent anxiety.

Understanding pupils' perspectives on their own emotional experience has also been the focus of research by Järvenoga and Järvela (2005). These authors have sought to discern the attributions pupils make about the causes of their own emotions while they are learning in interaction and also using the computer-supported collaborative learning projects (TICE). Their research question is formulated in terms of two (presumably) interdependent concepts, emotions and volition, or volitional processes (i.e., behavior regulation according to a goal). Within this framework, they postulate that emotions may affect learning processes in the motivational phase (construction of the goal) as well as in the volitional phase (realization of the goal). Like Laukenmann and al. (2003), the authors privilege a qualitative approach based on interviews of pupils between 12 and 15 years of age engaging in project work. The interviews were centered on the following topics: descriptions of the personal goals, learning strategies, interpretations of the work environment, and beliefs and feelings about oneself. From these topics, five categories relating to the emotions were drawn. They related to oneself (37% of children), the context (32% of children), the task (12% of children), performance (8% of children), and the interaction (8% of children). The category oneself included descriptions of the students' experiences and endeavors, their personal interest and global thoughts about the situation; in particular, their feelings of being able to face the situation and their personal motivations. The context category gathered all the remarks on the work environment. According to the authors, the oneself category was one of the most represented but occurred at the beginning of the activity when the goals were not yet well established. In sum, while the attributions young adolescents make about their emotions in learning situations are diverse and complex, relatively few connect their emotions to the learning goals of specific situations. Instead, they largely focus on their personal resources and experiences, or external factors of the learning environment.

4. Emotions at elementary school

Traditionally, studies of academic emotions have been carried out with secondary school pupils or university students (e.g., Gläser-Zikuda & Mayring, 2003; Pekrun et al., 2002; Järvenoja & Järvelä, 2005). Consequently, the experience of elementary school pupils is poorly understood. Identifying and understanding the role of emotions in school learning from the elementary period is all the more significant because of the potentially long term impact of young children's emotional experiences. In the short term, understanding the emotional experiences of elementary school-aged children is important for better identifying the role of the emotions in school performance (e.g., results, problem solving strategies, etc). With these concerns in mind, we conducted two studies. The first explores characteristics of the emotional experience of 10-year-old children in relation to various work contexts. Children were invited to describe their emotions during work sessions in the classroom, group activities, homework, and also during examinations. The second study aims to identify links between emotional experience, preferences for specific educational subjects, and academic performance in children between eight and 11 years of age.

Study 1. Emotional experience at the elementary school

This study assessed whether children make clear discriminations between emotions in situations that concern their own experiences. Our assessment of what children themselves feel (WCTF) was based on children's evaluations of various important situations. We reasoned that, even if these evaluations occur in a perfectly intimate and personal setting, one will find invariants in the manifestations of various emotions because they impact the child both physically and intellectually, and they color the agreeability of a given situation. We asked 52 children in CM2 (M_{age} = 10;2 , SD = 6 months) to think about emotions they experience in (1) the classroom, (2) during school tests, or (3) during homework. Children were questioned about various aspects of their emotions: agreeability, frequency, and the physiological manifestations and thoughts that accompany them.

Children were questioned on twelve emotions: anger, anxiety, sadness, despair, fear, shame, boredom, pride, relief, surprise, joy and satisfaction. The first seven were regarded as negative valence emotions, and the remaining five were regarded as positive valence emotions.

Each child was provided with envelopes containing a questionnaire that referred to an experienced emotion (WCTF) in a given situation. Each of the 12 emotions was set in each of the three contexts (classroom, school tests, homework), resulting in 36 combinations, and envelope types. Each child only worked on 18 envelopes, however, so that intellectual tiredness would not affect the quality of their answers; particularly given the intense focus on introspection. Thus two groups of children (n_1 = 25 and n_2 = 27) took part in this study. Following a drawing of lots that determined group, each envelope was selected randomly and the child was asked to answer the small questionnaire.

Frequency of the emotion experienced according to contexts.

We compared the frequencies of WCTF (measured on a 1-5 scale) in the three contexts. Frequency of Emotion X Context Differences were examined using a Student t-test. If we first consider differences between the school context (in the classroom or during tests) and home, results showed that fear, despair, anxiety, sadness, boredom and joy were more commonly felt at school, whereas anger and shame were more commonly felt at home, and there were no differences for satisfaction, relief and surprise. Within the school context, emotions related to apprehension (i.e., anxiety) characterized tests, whereas sadness, boredom and joy were more commonly felt in the classroom. Further, in the classroom emotions were more diversified. Leaving aside joy, these emotions (sadness, despair, boredom, and fear) suggest a general feeling of impotence that could have a direct impact on learning, while joy could be related to social contexts (e.g., interactions with peers). The more frequent experience of negative emotions at home may reflect the possibility of letting affects such as anger be expressed. The relatively high level of shame in homework contexts requires further investigations on the nature of this emotion for children. In sum, the results show that the emotions vary in meaningful ways according to context.

The relation between emotional valence and context

Children were also asked to judge the agreeableness (pleasant—unpleasant) of the emotions experienced according to context. This approach was adopted so that we could find out not just what children felt, but how strongly WCTF is moderated by context. For example, is the experience of joy as pleasant during homework as it is in the classroom? Adopting the same approach outlined above, if we first consider differences between the school context and home, results showed that anger, boredom, relief, pride, surprise and joy were experienced as more pleasant, or less unpleasant, in the school context, whereas despair, fear, shame and anxiety were experienced as less unpleasant at home, and there were no differences for satisfaction. Within the school context, pride was experienced as more pleasant in the classroom, while anger, boredom and relief were experiences as more unpleasant in the context of a test. Therefore, it seems that negative emotions are not only identified as more frequent but also more painful at school.

Moreover, the emotions considered to be more pleasant or less unpleasant at school are diverse since they relate as much to anger and boredom as to relief, pride, surprise and joy; covering both positive and negative emotions registers. Concerning different contexts within school, the fact that the children consider anger to be less unpleasant in a testing context appears to be compatible with the fact that anger has a high level of activation and, thus, represents a possible means of facing difficult situations. Further, the fact that boredom and anger are both considered less unpleasant during testing situations confirms the ambiguity already raised by Pekrun et al. (2002): boredom should reflect a difference between actual competence and the target learning outcomes. When this deviation is strong, boredom is likely to fit with a failed avoidance strategy. When the deviation is weak, it is likely to result from the feelings of uselessness about the learning task.

In sum, children differentiated their emotions in terms of frequency and agreeability according to context. Along with the dynamic conceptions described earlier, this initial analysis shows that the emotional experiences of children fall under the individual-situation interaction. The following section presents a fine-grained examination of the content of children's emotional experience of academic emotions, taking into account variations in context.

The content of emotional experiences

The content of the emotional experiences described by children were evaluated with respect to the constellation of responses expected within the cognitive approach framework of emotion. Children were invited to reflect on their experiences (WCTF) in term of thoughts and action tendencies (e.g., a desire for doing something or not), on the one hand, and in terms of bio-behavioral manifestations (vegetative-nervous system activation, tonus, etc), on the other hand. These are described in more detail below.

WCTF. We initially examined variations between positive and negative emotions as described above. For this analysis, we grouped items into three categories according to whether they related to oneself, others or to the interaction between oneself and others or the environment. Of course, sharper distinctions exist inside each category. For clarity, however, we only refer to these categories or items when we think it contributes substantively to understanding.

Table 1 provides an overall representation of the characteristics of the emotional experience described by children. Positive emotions were characterized by an outward orientation to the world, and a pleasant emotion experience. Negative emotions present a strongly contrasting profile, characterized by painful emotional experience, a tendency to withdrawal, mixed with an agonistic, confrontational tendency. A significant element observed for the negative emotions is the need for support, which exists over and above the social sharing tendency.

Table 1. Sub-categories of items more significantly associated with different emotion valence in children's self report (examples and emotions in parentheses)

Categories	Emotion valence	
	Positive	Negative
Oneself	Positive thoughts about oneself (e.g., "I see everything in pink": *joy* and *relief*)	Negative thoughts about oneself (e.g., "I have black thoughts and am no one": *sadness*, *anxiety* and *anger*); Unpleasant affect externalization (e.g., "I feel like shouting/crying": *anger*, *anxiety*, *sadness* and *shame*); Perturbation of psychological activity (e.g., "I can hardly think of anything else and I don't know what to do": *sadness*, *anxiety* and *anger*)
Others	Positive thoughts about others (e.g., "I like everybody": *joy* and *relief*)	Negative thoughts about others (e.g., "I like nobody": *anger*)
Interaction with others or environment	Tendency to approach of others: Social sharing tendency (e.g., "I want everyone to be aware of it": *pride*); Externalization tendency (e.g., "I feel like hopping": *satisfaction*, *pride* and *joy*)	Tendency to withdrawal: Need for support (e.g., "I don't feel like speaking with the others": *sadness* and *anger*); Tendency for agonistic behaviors (e.g., "I feel like getting angry": *anger* and *anxiety*)

Differences according to context were more salient for negative emotions. Thus, in the classroom context, for example, children's emotional experience is organized around, (i) negative thoughts with regard to others (but not towards oneself), (ii) withdrawal tendencies (e.g., "I don't want to speak with the others"; "I feel like falling through the floor", and "I feel like hiding myself"), (iii) agonistic behaviors (e.g., "I want to shout at the teacher") and the externalization of painful affect (e.g., "I feel like crying").

Table 2. Sub-categories of bio-behavioural items associated with positive and negative valence emotions

Categories	Emotion valence	
	Positive	Negative
Tonus/posture	I don't stay still; I gesticulate; I am excited; I am agitated (*Those items above are present for both positive and negative*)	
	I feel cool; I feel relaxed; I am laughing; I breathe a deep breath	I am shaking all over; I feel like a marshmallow; I don't have much energy; I am a little shaking; I feel tense; I feel nervous
Neuro-vegatitive activation	--	I am yawning; I feel nausea; I feel warm; I can feel my heart beating
Agonistic behaviors	--	I insult my buddies; I am brawling
Interruption	--	I feel paralyzed; I can hardly think I say anything; I can hardly do things; I cannot control myself; I am loosing my skills
Externalization	--	I am crying; I use coarse words
Withdrawal	--	I am sulking

Bio-behavioral manifestations. Children's self-reported bio-behavioral manifestations of emotion were categorized using the same principle as the emotion experiences (WCTF). We found the following categories: tonus/posture, neuro-vegetative arousal (e.g., sedation, feelings of heat/cold), agonistic behaviors (e.g., fights, insults), interruption (e.g., thinking, acting difficulties), externalization (e.g., tears, laughing), withdrawal (e.g., sulking, hiding). Manifestations of bio-behavioral consequences associated more strongly with different emotional valences are summarized in Table 2; those characteristics that were significantly more frequent for a given emotion valence, using Chi-squared analyses, are only listed under that valence. Those manifestations appearing independently of valence belong to the tonus/posture category and refer to arousal. Table 2 shows that children's self-reported bio-behavioral manifestations of emotion are consistent with their valences. The unbidden, involuntary character of negative emotions, already documented with emotion experiences (WCTF), also comes through in this analysis.

Summary

These initial analyses show that children are sensitive to the different emotions that arise from closely related academic contexts; they are also sensitive to the variation of intensity in such emotions as a function of context. Further, even at ten years of age, children are clearly able to describe the thoughts and actions that result from positive and negative emotional experiences, and the associated changes in bodily responding. Finally, the descriptions offered by children, whether concerning positive or negative valence emotions, and resulting from contexts that are very similar (all centering on academic emotions), show an impressive level of emotional sophistication. Of course, we could go further and conduct analyses for each emotion specifically but this is beyond the scope of the current discussion. Suffice to say, Study 1 clarifies the content of emotional experiences in children according to emotion valence and context, as revealed by child self-report. The findings show that children make sharp discriminations between their emotional experiences, which are also moderated according to context. The results lead us to think that, at this age, children are very able to discriminate their emotion responses when they are asked to discuss which emotions they feel in various contexts. In the following study, therefore, we examine the wider implications for children's academic emotions in the school context.

Study 2. Emotions in school contexts: Relations with well-being and performance

The objective of this study was to examine relations between academic emotions (see Study 1), academic performance and preference for specific subjects (i.e., Mathematics and French), and children's overall affectivity (positive versus negative affect and emotional control).

Procedure

The study was carried out in an elementary school of the Parisian suburbs, receiving children with a diverse range of backgrounds. Four school levels were assessed, CE1 (2nd grade) through CM2 (5th grade). The sample comprised 122 children, although not all were available for all measures. In the ensuing analyses, because of the distribution of children in the four grades, we sometimes compare 2nd grade children with 3rd through 5th grade children. We have indicated when such an approach has been adopted.

Children were asked to answer a questionnaire on their life at school including items intended to measure their preference for Mathematics and French. They were then asked to answer a questionnaire evaluating their overall affectivity – positive versus negative affect, and emotional control – which was an adaptation of Walden, Harris and Catron's (2003) How I Feel (HIF) scale.

To evaluate academic performance, two books of activities were given to the students, one for Mathematics and one for French. The items in these activity books were extracted from a bank of items provided by the National Evaluations of Competence targeted at the end of French cycle 2 (CE1) and cycle 3 (up to CM2). Once each book was finished, children answered a questionnaire concerning their emotional experiences (academic emotions) in the respective domain. One session was dedicated to Mathematics activities and another to French activities. Each session lasted approximately one hour. It is important to note that the standardized test measures for CE1 (2nd grade) were different and could not be directly compared with CE2-CM2 (3rd to 5th grade). We present the data here in a synthetic way, omitting analyses that were not of theoretical or practical interest.

Positive versus negative affect, emotional control, academic performance and preference for educational subjects (Mathematics and French)

Below, we briefly summarize children's performance in each domain before considering cross-domain relations.

HIF: Positive versus negative affect and emotional control. After carrying out the necessary analyses to check that the psychometric qualities of the French version were compatible with the American version, which they were, we examined the distribution of scores on each of the scales by class. The scores on the positive affect scale were stable, $F_{(3,115)} = 2.01$, ns, suggesting positive affect was equally likely in each grade. In contrast, there was a considerable and significant reduction in average scores for negative affect scale, $F_{(3,117)} = 5.95$, $p < .001$, as well as the control scale, $F_{(3,112)} = 3.08$, $p < .05$.

Academic performance: Examination of the pupils' results on the Mathematics and French tests showed a broad range of distributions, with significant mean increase by grade (between 3rd and 5th) for Mathematics, $F_{(2,87)} = 27.88$, $p < .001$, and French, $F_{(2,66)} = 6.93$, $p < .001$. This difference was particularly marked between CE2 (3rd grade) and CM1 (4th grade). Children's results are summarized in Table 3.

Table 3. Academic performance (mean and standard deviation) in Mathematics and French using standardized school tests

Classroom	French (mother language)			Mathematics		
	Mean	*SD*	Maximum	*Mean*	*SD*	Maximum
CE1 (2nd grade)	55.5	18.00	/112	56.6	20.26	/112
CE2 (3rd grade)	33.2	14.7	/124	25.6	15.45	/168
CM1 (4th grade)	43.8	17.45	/124	53.0	26.87	/168
CM2 (5th grade)	52.3	14.90	/124	76.1	27.97	/168

Preference for academic subjects: With regard to children's preferences for these two subjects, analysis of mean scores showed that a preference for Mathematics was stable across the four classes. For French, however, children's ratings of preference start to reduce from CM1, though it should be noted that the effect was only marginally significant, $F_{(3,118)} = 2.28$, $p = .08$.

Relations between academic competence and preference, and emotional variables (affectivity and academic emotions)

Academic preference and competence. Examination of relations between preference and performance revealed cross-domain relations: The preference for French is correlated with the success in Mathematics for 3rd to 5th grade children, whereas a stronger preference for Mathematics tends to be negatively correlated with performance in French. This relation is depicted in Figure 1.

Figure 1. Correlations between academic preferences (attraction) and performance according to the subject (Mathematics and French) and grade (2nd versus 3rd, 4th and 5th grade)

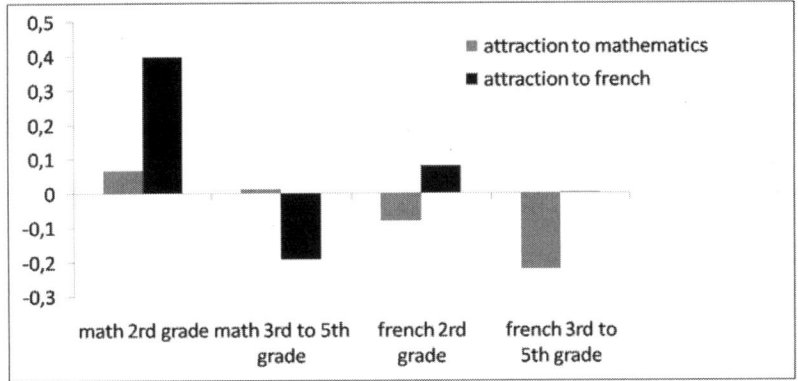

Academic preference and academic emotions. Relations between children's academic preferences and their academic emotions are shown in Table 4, which shows positive and negative correlations between preference and emotion separately for French and Mathematics. Table 4 shows that children's preferences for French were positively, but moderately, associated with positive emotions felt during French activities. In contrast, two negative emotions (anger and boredom) were negatively associated with children's preferences for French: Thus, the more children experience boredom and anger, the lower their preference for French. Or, conversely, the lower their preference for French, the more they experienced boredom and anger.

The pattern of associations differs in the case of Mathematics. Whereas no connection appears between positive emotions and preference for Mathematics, one notes more correlations, also moderate, with negative emotions. Thus, lower levels of anger, sadness and shame tend to be experienced or felt (both in terms of frequency or intensity) when the preference for Mathematics is high.

Table 4. Correlations between children's academic preferences and academic emotions relating to French and in Mathematics

French		Mathematics
Positive correlations	Negative correlations	Negative correlations
Pride		
Frequency: .339 Intensity: .390 Duration: .246 *Agreeability*: .368	--	--
Relief		
Frequency: .301 Duration: .234	--	*Agreeability*: -.201
Hope		
Frequency: .260 Intensity: .262 Duration: .220 *Agreeability*: .357	--	--
Joy		
Frequency: .339 Intensity: .376 Duration: .351 *Agreeability*: .245	--	--
Surprise		
Agreeability: .235	Frequency: -.201	*Agreeability*: -.254
Fear		
Agreeability: .220	--	--
Anger		
--	Frequency: -.248	Frequency: -.170 Intensity: -.233
Boredom		
Frequency: -.239 Intensity: -.233	--	--
Sadness		
--	--	Frequency: -.177
Shame		
--	--	Duration: -.179

Academic competence and affectivity (HIF). Relations between children's affectivity (HIF) sub-scales and academic competence are presented in Table 5. No connection appears between positive affect (i.e., well-being) and academic competence. However, the negative affect scale is negatively associated with performance in French and, for the 3rd to the 5th grade pupils, with performance in Mathematics. Thus, children whose results are weak tend to have higher levels of negative affect scores. This connection is particularly marked in the 2nd grade.

Table 5. *Correlations between children's affectivity (HIF) and academic performance in Mathematics and French*

Subject	Positive emotion		Negative emotion		Emotional control	
	Cycle 2 Grade 2	Cycle 3 Grades 3-5	Cycle 2 Grade 2	Cycle 3 Grades 3-5	Cycle 2 Grade 2	Cycle 3 Grades 3-5
French	.085	.107	-.513**	-.210ᵃ	-.022	-.270*
Mathematics	-.278	-.222	-.266	-.233*	-.046	-.052

ᵃ $p < .10$, * $p < .05$, ** $p < .01$

Academic competence and academic emotions. Finally, we analyzed relations between academic emotions and performance in both Mathematics and French. For simplicity, as in Study 1, academic emotions were first considered merely positive or negative. As can be seen in Figure 2, these relations are rather specific to each subject. In Mathematics, depicted in the left hand side of the figure, positive emotions (pride, relief, joy and hope) vary in the same direction as performance. In contrast, negative emotions (sadness, anger, anxiety and boredom) are conversely connected with success. This phenomenon is observed for all the grades. In French, the frequency of emotions experiences, whether positive or negative, is related to academic performance.

Figure 2. *Mean correlations between performance in Mathematics (left hand side) and French (right hand side) and the frequency of positive and negative academic emotions in 2nd and the 3rd to 5th grade pupils*

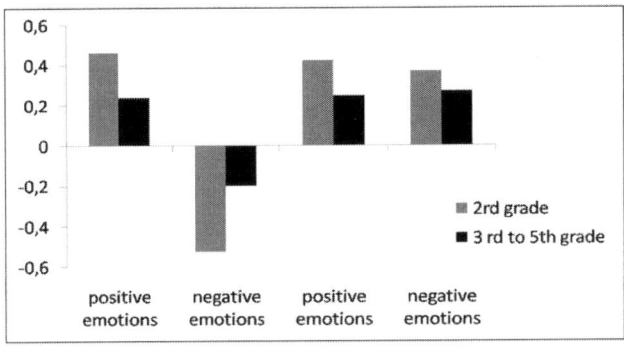

197

Regarding links between poor performance and emotion, a more refined analysis by specific emotions is warranted. Whereas Figure 3 shows, in keeping with Figure 2, that higher levels of sadness and anger are linked with performance in Mathematics and French in contradictory ways, Figure 4 shows that anxiety is associated with poor performance in both subject areas and at both educational levels. From a motivational point of view, it seems that the emotional experience yielding the highest performances in French, anger and sadness, are relatively unpleasant, but the opposite is true for mathematics. By contrast, anxiety, whatever the context, seems to have a negative impact on children's performance.

Figure 3. Correlations between academic performance and negative emotions (sadness and anger) according to subject task and grade

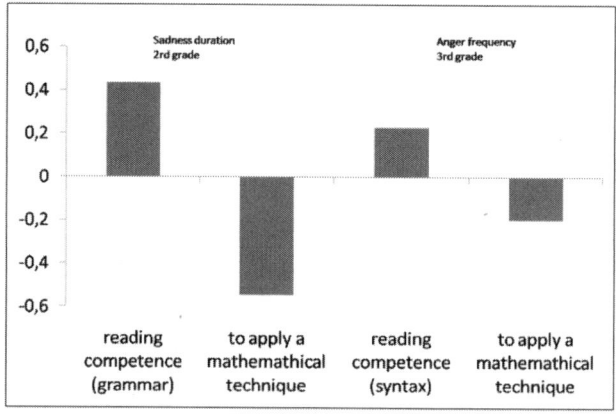

Figure 4. Correlations between frequency of anxiety and academic performance according to grade

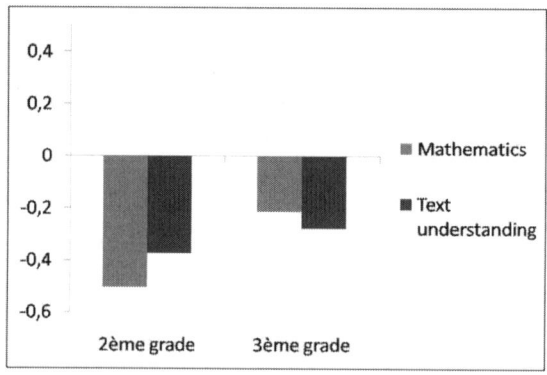

Summary

The academic competence of pupils participating in this study is modest but increases progressively following school progression (see Table 3). Academic competence is only modestly related to children's preferences for French and Mathematics, and these findings are difficult to interpret (see Figure 1). In contrast, more meaningful links appear between children's preferences and their emotional experience in relation to Mathematics and French (see Table 4). In a similar manner, significant links appear between performance and negative affectivity (see Table 5).

Finally, this study shows that the emotional experience of young children has important links with education in a school setting, particularly in the case of negative affectivity. The consistency of relations observed provides a strong incentive for the continuation of other investigations of a similar kind in young child, particularly with a longitudinal focus. Taken together, Studies 1 and 2 show that pupils feel differentiated emotions according to situations. This differentiation not only concerns their emotional repertoire according to the contexts, but the content of the experience for a given emotion according to context as well. Despite extensive testing, particularly in Study 2, the same emotional sensitivity emerged in both groups of children.

5. Discussion and prospects

The studies presented here constitute a first exploration of the emotional experience of elementary school-aged children within the school context. Two complementary goals were pursued: (1) to better understand the ways in which children of this age describe the contents of their emotional experience in school test situations when they work in the classroom and at home; and (2) to study relations between the emotions experienced in these contexts, academic performance and preference (in Mathematics and French), and children's overall affectivity (positive versus negative affect, and emotional control). Several features of these studies deserve comment.

First, it appears that self-reported emotional experiences are highly consistent. This is difficult to explain if we presuppose that children are unable to carry out the necessary introspection for such questioning. Our results, however, converge with other data in the literature on the existence of organized meta-cognitive knowledge relating to the emotions (cf. Pons & Harris, 2005).

Second, the acuteness of children's answers to emotional questioning invites continued investigation of the development of children's meta-cognitive knowledge about emotions, both in terms of their own emotional experiences and those of others. Indeed, our results show that children distinguish the content and the manifestations of their emotions, and they do this according to contexts in an appropriate manner.

Third, affectivity and emotions experienced according to the educational subjects present complex relations with academic performance and preference, and it is important to better understand the causal influences being played out between these domains. In particular, it is important to establish if negative affectivity results from difficulties in educational settings, or if such emotion difficulties/dispositions manifest themselves in the classroom. Of course, it is also possible that another not yet identified variable lies at the origin of these connections.

Finally, it seems important that teachers should be made aware of some of the issues raised in such research within the context of their educational framework. We feel that various points could be communicated to teachers; such as, (1) the richness of children's emotional experience in the school context, (2) the acuity, even for very young pupils, of children's emotional insights, and (3) the ambiguity of the links between emotion and success in school, the nature of which is far from clear. As we would expect, negative emotions are more often associated with difficulties and lower preferences for specific subjects. But, contrary to what would be expected, positive emotions are also sometimes associated with difficulties; which might correspond to the feeling in children of being on a remote setting or even engagement in avoidance strategies. By contrast, negative affects are described by children as more invasive. Thus, the association between feeling positive emotions and poor academic performance would appear to represent a means used by children avoid the negative emotional consequences of learning difficulty and the accumulating negative emotions associated with such difficulties. It is then important for the educator to recognize cases in which the apparently positive emotional presentation of some children belies a painful reality that needs appropriate confrontation. Despite relatively few links with emotional control, future research will need to explore the development of children's emotional regulation in the educational context, and the teacher's contribution to such development.

References

Diener, E., & Lucas, R.E. (2000). Subjective Emotional Well-Being, in M. Lewis, J.-M., Haviland-Jones, (Eds). Handbook of emotions, second edition (pp 325-337), The Guilford Press.

Dunn, J., Brown, J., & Beardsall, L. (1991). Family talk about feeling and children's later understanding of other's emotion. Developmental psychology, 27, 448-455.

Engels, N., Aelterman, A., Van Petegem, K., & Schepens, A. (2004). Factors which influence the well-being of pupils in Flemish scondary schools, Educationnal Studies, 30 (2), 127-143.

Frijda, N.H. (1987). The Emotions, Cambridge: Cambridge University Press.

Gläser-Zikuda, M., & Mayring, P. (2003). A qualitative oriented approach to learning emotions at school, in P. Mayring, C. Von Rhoeneck, (Eds), Learning Emotions (pp.103-127), Peter Lang.

Goetz, T., Zirngilbl, A., Pekrun, R. & Hall, N. (2003). Emotions, Learning and Achievement from an Educational-Psychological perspective, in P. Mayring, C. Von Rhoeneck, (Eds), Learning Emotions (pp.9-29), Peter Lang.

Greene, T.R., & Noice, H. (1988). Influence of positive affect upon creative thinking and problem solving in children, Psychological Reports, 63, 895-898.

Gumora, G., & Arsenio, W.F. (2002). Emotionality, Emotion Regulation, and School Performance in Middle School Children. Journal of School Psychology, 40(5), 395-413.

Huebner, E.S., & McCullough, G. (2001). Correlates of School Satisfaction Among Adolescents. Journal of Educational Research, 93(5), 331-335.

Huebner, E.S., Shannon M.; S. & Smith, L.C. (2004). Life Satisfaction in Children and Youth: Empirical Foundations and Implications for School Psychologists. Psychology in the Schools, 41(1), Special issue: Positive Psychology and Wellness in Children, 81-93.

Isen, A. (2001). An influence of positive affect on decision making in complex situations: theoretical issues with practical implications, Journal of Consumer Psychology, 11(2), 75-85.

Isen, A.M. (1984). Toward Understanding the Role of Affect in Cognition, in R.S. Wyer, & T.K. Srull (Eds), Handbook of social cognition, Vol. 3, London: Laurence Erlbaum Associates Publishers

Järvenoja, H., & Järvelä, S. (2005). How students describe the sources of their emotional and motivational experiences during the learning process: A qualitative approach, Learning and Instruction, 15(5), Oct. Special issue: Feelings and emotions in the learning process, 465-480.

Keenan, T. (2002). Negative affect predicts performance on an object permanence task, Developmental Science, 5(1), 65-71.

Keltner, D., & Ekman, P. (2000). Facial expression of emotion, in M. Lewis, J.-M., Haviland-Jones (Eds), Handbook of emotions, second edition (pp.236-253), The Guilford Press..

Konu, A I., Lintonen, T.P., A., & Ville J. (2002). Evaluation of well-being in schools–A multilevel analysis of general subjective well-being, School Effectiveness and School Improvement, 13, Edition 2, 187-200.

Laukenmann, M., Bleicher, M.; Fub, S.; Gláser-Zikuda, M.; Mayring, P.; & von Rhöneck, C. (2003). An investigation of the influence of emotional factors on learning in physics instruction. International Journal of Science Education, Apr., 25(4), 489-507.

Lazarus, R.S. (1993). From psychological stress to the emotions: A history of changing outlooks, Annual Review of Psychology, 44, 1-21.

Opdenakker, M.C., & Van Damme, J. (2000). Effects of Schools, Teaching Staff and Classes on Achievement and Well-Being in Secondary Education: Similarities and Differences Between School Outcomes. School Effectiveness & School Improvement, (2), 165-196.

Pekrun, R., Goetz, T., & Titz, W. (2002). Academic emotions in students' self-regulated learning and achievement: A program of qualitative and quantitative research. Educational Psychologist, 37(2), 91-106.

Pons, F., & Harris, P.L. (2005). Longitudinal change and longitudinal stability of individual differences in children s emotion understanding. Cognition and Emotion, 19(8), 1158-1174.

Russell, J.A., & Lemay, G. (2000). Emotion Concepts, in M. Lewis, J.-M., Haviland-Jones (Eds), Handbook of emotions, second edition (pp.491-503), The Guilford Press.

Scherer, K. (1984). Les émotions: fonctions et composantes, in B., Rimé, K. Scherer (Eds), Les émotions (pp.97-135), Delachaux et Niestlé.

Scherer, K. (1992). What does facial expression express?, in K. Strongman (Ed), International Review on Studies on Emotion, 2, 139-165, Chichester: Wiley.

Smiley, P., & Huttenlocher, J. (1989). Young children's acquisition of emotion concepts. In : C. Saarni & P. L. Harris (Eds.), Children's understanding emotion (pp.27-49), Cambridge: Cambridge University Press.

Tellegen, A., Watson, D., & Clark, L.A. (1999). On the dimensional and hierarchical structure of affect. Psychological Science, 10(4), 297-304.

Thommen, E., Chatelain, F., & Rimbert, G. (2004). L'interprétation des indices non verbaux par les enfants. Psychologie Française, 49, 145-160.

Walden, T.A., Harris, V.S., & Catron, T.F. A. (2003). How I fell: A self-report measure of emotional arousal and regulation for children, Psychological Assessment. 15(3) 399-412.

Wellman, H. M., Harris, P.L., Banerjee, M., & Sinclair, A. (1995). Early understanding of emotion: Evidence from natural language. Cognition and Emotion, 9, 117-149.

Emotional competence: Development and intervention

Francisco Pons, Marc de Rosnay, Bettina Gamskjær Andersen and Frédérique Cuisinier

1. Introduction

To adapt to the challenges facing them, young children must become increasingly emotionally competent with development. Possessing emotional competence is an essential feature of wellbeing and good social integration; helping us to act and react appropriately in a wide range of situations. Some emotional responses and the situations to which they relate are basic to human experience; such as feeling angry when we are aggressed, or feeling scared when we are in danger. Other responses, which are also fundamental to human experience, seem to lie at the heart of our social existence; such as the emotions we feel that are more appropriate to another person's condition (empathy) or the feelings of attachment that we have for others, which can provoke in us strong feelings of love and affiliation, or terrible feelings of loss. Of course, the emotional challenges facing children on a day-to-day basis are, thankfully, generally less extreme in their nature but they are nonetheless central to the child's feelings of wellbeing and growing sense of autonomy and independence. For example, children must regulate their many anxieties during school, whether interpersonal or performance related, and learn to recognize and respond to a host of complicated socio-emotional situations; they must also learn to express gratitude when receiving a disappointing gift and to understand the origins and consequences of other children's feelings, to which they must respond in a prosocial manner, and so on (see Denham et al. 2003, Harris 1989, Pons et al. 2005, Saarni 1999 for reviews).

The study of emotional competence is necessarily complex because emotions are present in all phases and most aspects of life. Indeed, there is every indication that human beings are very early equipped with a flexible emotion system that is inherently linked to motivation, behavior regulation, signaling and social communication (Izard & Ackerman 2000, Trevarthen &

Aitken 2001). Despite the pervasive nature of emotion in human life and the rich history of emotion research in early childhood, it is difficult to find an integrative review on how the different domains of emotional competence develop in young children. In this chapter we shall present an overview of various domains of children's emotional competence[1] before asking how such competence can be cultivated through intervention. Before entering this overview, it is instructive to consider what is covered by the terms *emotion* and emotional competence.

While it would be preferable to provide a definition of the term *emotion*, it is noteworthy that an uncontroversial definition of emotion continues to eluded philosophers and empirical scientists (Lewis & Haviland-Jones, 2000), and the very category of emotional phenomena does not exist within some philosophical traditions (Ekman et al., 2005). Such complexity perhaps belies the profundity of emotional experience for humans. Nevertheless, we can provide a description of the kinds of experiences and states covered by the term emotion. In this chapter (also see chapter 1), emotion refers to the feelings and moods we have toward our selves, others and the world, whether perceived or imagined. Such feelings can be more or less pleasant or unpleasant, intense or moderate, temporary or permanent, general or specific. They can also be more or less basic or complex, sensorial or symbolic, conscious or unconscious, controlled or uncontrolled, as well as universal or idiosyncratic. In this chapter emotions (and moods) are considered as interrelated states and processes of the mind (i.e. subjective experience), the body (e.g., peptide release, heart rate, respiration rate, blood pressure, muscle tension, etc), and the culture (e.g., the display rules for the expression of emotions; the social and cultural norms related to the experience of emotions).

---

1   The concept of emotional competence is different from the widely used popular psychology concept of emotional intelligence. The former comes from a humanistic and developmental tradition focused on understanding the processes underlying emotional development, the important role of the social environment for emotional development, and the psychological wellbeing of the person (Saarni 1999). The latter is focused on adult psychology and is oriented to social success. Moreover, emotional intelligence is not as inclusive as the concept of emotional competence: Salovey and Grewal (2005), in line with Goleman (1995), define emotional intelligence as the ability to perceive, appraise and express emotions.

In line with the work of Saarni (1999), emotional competence can be sensibly divided into six interconnected domains; the first five can be qualified as being procedural (to do) and the last one declarative (to know). At the most basic level, to be emotionally competent children need to be able (1) to experience emotions (to have the subjective experience feelings such as happiness, anger, fear, sadness, surprise, disgust, pride, shame, etc., as well as emotions that relate to other people's emotional states via empathic processes). It is noteworthy that some children may have specific deficits in the experience of certain feelings such as fear, happiness (a-hedonism) or guilt, the latter of which may pertain to a lack of empathic feelings. The other domains of emotional competence include the capacities to: (2) express subjective emotional experiences (i.e., to show feelings); (3) recognize the expression of subjective emotional experiences (i.e., to identify one's own feelings or those of another person, without necessarily sharing the feeling); (4) control the expression of emotional experiences (i.e., to exert some control over the way a feelings is expressed or express a feeling that one does not experience); (5) regulate subjective emotional experiences (i.e., to have some influence over feelings); and (6) understand emotions, including their nature, causes, consequences, and the possibility of controlling and regulating emotion in the self and others. (See Table 1 for some illustrations by domain of emotional competence.)

Table 1. Illustrations of the six interconnected domains of emotional competence

Domains	Illustrations
To *experience* emotions	To feel happy, sad, angry, scared, disgusted, surprised, etc.
To *express* emotions	To express fear (face, posture, movement, voice, etc.)
To *recognize* emotions	To recognize disgust (face, posture, movement, voice, etc.)
To *control* emotional expression	To hide anger (because of cultural display-rules)
To *regulate* emotions	To stop being sad (by thinking about something positive)
To *understand* emotions	To understand guilt (its origins and consequences)

In the following discussion we shall focus on the development of emotional competence from infancy to preschool-age, a timeframe that many have emphasized (including Donald Winnicott, Jean Piaget, John Bowlby, Daniel Stern and others) because of its importance for healthy psycho-social development.

2. The early development of emotional competence

The development of emotional competence from infancy to middle childhood is influenced by numerous factors, including both genetic and constitutional (Nature) and environmental (Nurture). In line with the seminal work of Charles Darwin, it is still generally accepted that infants have a biological preparedness for emotions; in particular the capacity to express and recognize emotion, which is part of our shared evolutionary inheritance (Ekman, 1999; Izard & Ackerman, 2000; Lazarus, 1991; Malatesta-Magai, 1991). Over and above such shared emotional inheritance, there is also variation in how the individuals within the species habitually respond emotionally, their so-called *temperament*. So whereas virtually all toddlers approach novel situations with some trepidation, there are those who are behaviorally inhibited to the point of inaction, and others who quickly overcome their reticence an embrace the new situation (Kagan, 1999). Despite the appeal of temperamental explanations of individual differences in emotional responding or reactivity to stimuli, temperament constructs have been notoriously difficult to distil in infancy and toddlerhood, precisely when their expression should be the clearest (Fox, Henderson, Rubin, Calkins, & Schmidt, 2001).

At the same time, it is also well accepted that emotional development is facilitated by social interactions with caregivers and the wider social environment. John Bowlby (1969), for example, has provided a rich account of the profound implications of emotional attachments for the development of autonomous emotional regulation and the formation of healthy relationships (see Pons, de Rosnay, Barriol & Zacharopoulu, 2010, for a discussion). Further, Daniel Stern (1985) has described how inter-subjective interactions with the primary caregiver, and the caregiver's capacity to selectively affectively attune herself to her infant's needs, helps a child establish his[2] sense of emotional agency. Indeed, caregivers have an immense influence over the immediate emotional environment for the child on a day-to-day basis (e.g., Izard & Harris, 1995; Tronick, 1989).

Denham (1998) explains how the early caregiving environment is experienced by the child, and the influence it can have on development. First,

---

[2] In this text we adopt the masculine pronoun to refer to the infant or child for clarity and simplicity. Where possbile, we also use the term *caregiver* but it should be noted that the vast majority of research with caregivers has involved mothers rather than fathers.

parents intuitively discern the emotional significance of unfolding events for children through their own expressive patterns and thus show the child which emotions are acceptable in the family and in other specific situations. Second, parents model the display of specific emotions and children learn directly from these patterns. Third, parents show children the common behaviors that are associated with the expression of specific emotions. That is to say, parents show—deliberately or not—their own differing ways of coping with emotional situations; which is the source of great familial and cultural variation. Finally, parents provide an overall emotional environment to which the child is exposed, and the emotional disposition adopted by the child is likely to reflect, to some extent, this overall emotional environment. This latter phenomenon has also been identified by other researchers and theoreticians, and is sometimes referred to as the child's *affective core*, which is akin to temperament but assumes that accumulated social interactions are also to a great extent responsible for the child's habitual emotional dispositions (e.g., Tronick, 1989).

Unfortunately, the child's temperament and affective core are perhaps the most poorly understood areas of emotional development, despite their obvious importance for the emotional competence and wellbeing of the individual. Nevertheless, development brings competence in many domains and although the child's temperament / affective core might form the backdrop against which other aspects of emotional competence unfold, these burgeoning capacities and skills change the nature of the child's relationship to the world, providing new challenges and also new opportunities for individuation and growth. We turn now to each of these domains of competence by providing a description of what abilities and capacities children generally have and, where appropriate, how they change with development. Such a description should assist pedagogues and teachers conceptualize the capabilities and limitations of infants and toddlers at various ages, and also understand when it is likely that an infant or child is likely to be atypical in their developmental trajectory.

The expression of emotions

One of the major questions concerning the emergence of emotions in infants is to what extent they are born with the ability to express emotions? Whether infants express discrete emotions (Izard & Ackerman, 2000) or merely negative or positive arousal states is still subject of debate. A recent cross-cultural study suggested that the early emotional life of infants primarily consists of two universal arousal states, attraction to pleasant stimuli (positive) and avoidance from unpleasant stimuli (negative) (Camras et al., 2003, Camras et al., 2007). We elaborate on these below (see Table 2 for a summary).

Expression of negative emotions is characterized by various facial features typically associated with the expression of specific negative emotions (e.g. sadness, anger, and fear). Some of these characteristics are lowered brows, lip corners pulled to the side, variable degree of mouth opening; head turning, etc. (see Messinger, 2002; Sroufe, 1995)[3]. The facial expression of negative emotions varies and differentiates with age but undifferentiated crying-sad-face (containing a blend of expressions) is the most common reaction of the neonate to unpleasant stimuli such as hunger, pain, sudden changes in body temperature, under- or over-stimulation, and so on.

Table 2. Examples of positive and negative emotional expressions in infants and toddlers

Age	Expression of emotions	
	Negative	Positive
0-3 months	Generalized distress/crying-sad-face as reaction to unpleasant stimuli	Momentary smiles during sleep, often considered associated with biological stimuli rather than social stimuli. Reflexive smiles to social stimuli
3-6 months	Precursors for fear (wariness) and anger (frustration) are shown	Expression of happiness (including smiles) and engaged interest in both social and non-social contexts
6-12 months	Emotional expressions of fear and anger are clearly observed. Stranger and separation anxiety.	Infants begin to smile selectively at familiar faces and show sustained interest in both social and non-social stimuli
1-2 years	The expression of sadness, anger and fear becomes more frequent and clear	The infant has several social smiles and differences in the smiles given to familiar people and friendly strangers are present
2-3 years	Expression of negative self-conscious and socio-moral emotions such as embarrassment, shame (and guilt)	Expression of positive self-conscious and social emotions such as pride and self-satisfaction
3-5 years	Development of the ability to simulate positive and negative emotions (e.g. exaggerate the emotional expression related to a minor injury to receive comfort; smile when getting an undesired gift)). Emergence of the understanding of the difference between the appearance (expression) and reality of emotions (experience).	

3 Most studies conducted on the expression of emotions in young children are based on observational data; hence the expression of emotion is primarily based on facial expressions. However, as noted by Lewis (2009), the failure to observe an emotional facial expression in response to a particular elicitor does not mean the expression is not present at that age, since it might appear under other circumstances and might be expressed in another way (posture, movement, prosody, etc.)

In the latter part of the first six months infants begin to show wariness (as a precursor for fear) and frustration (as a precursor for anger). Around six to seven months of age, emotional reactions of fear and anger are clearly observed (Sroufe, 1995). It is also around this age that the fear of strangers becomes evident, and this typically lasts until the child is approximately two years of age (Sroufe, 1995). As the infant develops toward toddlerhood, the expressions of sadness, anger and fear become more frequent and clear. By two to three years of age, children have some degree of self-awareness and they begin to express self-conscious and social-moral emotions, such a guilt, shame and pride (Denham, 1986).

The first expression of positive emotions in newborn infants is smiling. During the first month of life they show momentary smiles in their sleep, often during the REM phase of sleep. These smiles are often considered to be associated with biological stimuli rather than social interaction (Sroufe & Waters, 1976), although it has been argued that social smiling can occur at this time as well (Trevarthen & Aitken, 2001). By around two to three months of age, however, infants can certainly show happiness in both social situations (e.g., interactions with people may elicit joy) and non-social situations (e.g., shaking a rattle or banging a toy against the floor may elicit joy). From around six months of age, infants begin to smile specifically at familiar people and, in the first year, the child has developed several social smiles; smiling differently to parents and a friendly stranger (Sroufe & Waters, 1976). Some authors have also drawn attention to interest as a positive emotional expression, which emerges relatively early in development (see Izard & Ackerman, 2000; Trevarthen & Aitken, 2001); this has been reflected in table 2.

The recognition of emotions

Whereas infant facial configurations can be filmed or photographed, and classified as specific kinds of emotional expressions on the basis of pre-existing criteria (Camras et al., 2007), it is altogether less clear when an infant, or any person for that matter, has recognized a discrete emotion or the emotional quality of an interaction. According to many close observers of infants (e.g., Stern, 1985; Trevarthen & Aitken, 2001), it is clear from 12 weeks that most infants can recognize and respond appropriately to the emotional expressions and affective features of a partner's communications in a face-to-face interaction. That is not to say infants understand the full range of discrete emotions but it certainly appears to be the case that their proto-conversational exchanges with caregivers can be tightly emotionally calibrated; indeed, the emotional exchanges in these interactions appear to supply the underlying motivational structure for their continuation and elaboration.

In an ingenious and now classic study of infant recognition of emotional expressions, Haviland and Lelwica (1987) showed that, in face-to-face interactions, infants were sensitive to three discrete emotional expressions from their mothers (on which the mothers had been trained): joy, sadness and anger. Each expression had a distinctly different impact on the infant, which was non-random and, importantly, only contained some potentially imitative elements (particularly for joy). That is to say, each expression had a different organizing influence on the infant that could not be dismissed as imitation. Further, infants' responses to each of the emotions suggested that they understood the motivational salience of each expression (e.g., they showed signs of fear in the face of maternal anger). More recent research has to a great extent replicated these important findings. For example, Kahana-Kalman and Walker-Andrews (2001) found that when emotional expressions were portrayed by the mother, infants as young as 3.5 months were able to differentiate emotional expressions such as happiness and sadness in their behavioral responses.

Despite such early, embodied understanding of discrete, salient expressions, it is well established that children's abilities to discriminate facial expressions of emotion and their abilities to recognize emotions from facial expressions improve with age. Sadness and anger are the first among the negative emotions to be recognized, followed by the recognition of fear. Happiness, as discussed above, is recognized very early (see Gross & Ballif, 1991, for review). By and large, the capacity to recognize the basic expression unfolds before two years of age, as can clearly be seen in the social referencing literature. There is now very solid evidence that by 18 months, and probably earlier, toddlers can use facially communicated emotional signals to modify their behavior with respect to specific objects (persons, things or situations) in the environment in appropriate ways; they understand that other people can provide information about the environment and this information is communicated via emotional expressions (Baldwin & Moses, 1996; Harris, 2006). Notwithstanding the remarkable nature of such social communication, it is not until children are much older that they can reliably label emotion expressions, a point to which we will return below.

The control of emotional expressions

The control of emotional expressions is closely linked to the regulation of feelings in young children and can be applied as a strategy for emotion regulation. For example, a child can be effortfully looking happy even though he fears the first day at school in a new class. Looking happy, or not looking fearful, in such a situation may actually act to overcome the fear to some extent (e.g., it may increase the likelihood of positive social encounters), and thereby contribute to a change in the child's emotional experience (i.e., feeling less fear and, perhaps, happiness).

The development of emotional expression control begins at a very early age. Children start to inhibit or exaggerate the expression of certain emotions in specific situations in the second year. One of the earliest examples is when children exaggerate the emotional expression related to a minor injury, to receive comfort and attention. When children are slightly older, this gets played out in a more sophisticated manner; they are more likely to cry after injuring themselves if a caregiver is present, and less likely to cry if they think they are unattended (Saarni, 1999). Furthermore, it is clear at two years of age that toddlers will exhibit reduced tantrum behavior in the face of an unsolvable problem when compared to the behavior of an 18 month old. Indeed, between two and five years of age, children's defiance and non-compliance is reduced and replaced with negotiation and simple refusal (see Sroufe, 1995).

In the existing literature there is also a distinction between self-protective display rules—applied to avoid negative consequences for the child and to preserve self-esteem—which even very young children engage in, and prosocial display rules—applied to protect relationships and to maintain standards of behavior—which occur a little later in childhood (Saarni, 1999). The precise ages at which children engage in these kinds of emotion expression control varies greatly but it is clear that even in preschool children can 'put on a happy face' to protect their self-esteem, and many five-year-olds can smile when they receive a disappointing gift. The success with which children carry off such deceptions also varies considerably and it is not uncommon at five years of age to find that a child simultaneously shows disappointment and attempts to smile when presented with an undesirable gift (Saarni, 1999). Indeed, the extent to which individual children inhibit their (negative) emotion expressiveness has been given considerable attention in the emotion regulation literature, where it has been shown that high levels of negative emotion expression between three and five years of age is associated with relatively poor social outcomes (Saarni, 1999; Miller et al., 2006). Thus, the deliberate control of emotion is likely to be tied up in children's self-regulatory processes, and it is something that distinguishes well from poorly regulated children.

The regulation of emotional experiences

Emotion regulation is essential both for individual functioning (e.g., to diminish the intensity of your anxiety before an exam) and social interactions (e.g., to diminish the intensity of your anger while arguing with somebody). Emotion regulation can be briefly defined as the strategies we employ to influence which emotions we experience (Gross, 1998). To understand the nature of emotion regulation it is important to accept that it is not defined by which emotions are activated but by systematic changes associated with the activated emotions; thus emotion regulation targets positive (pleasant) as well as negative (unpleasant) emotions and is applied for diminishing, heightening and maintaining levels of emotional arousal (Cole, Martin & Dennis, 2004; Thompson & Goodvin, 2007).

Babies are easily overwhelmed by unpleasant stimuli such as hunger, pain and loud noise, and have limited ways to regulate their feelings (e.g., gaze avoidance). They have to rely on their caregivers to control their exposure to stimuli and, to a very great extent, to calm them down. In fact, it has been argued that the main challenge facing mother-infant dyads is the successful regulation of infant's emotional states; within an attachment theory perspective the infant's increasing capacity to self-regulate their emotional experiences begins with effective dyadic co-regulation in the caregiving relationship (see Sroufe, 1995). Thus, based on external caregiver regulation, infants gradually move toward increasingly autonomous emotion regulation. This is a process that continues into childhood and takes in behavioral and psychological aspects of regulation. In line with Bowlby and Wallon, one may say that infant's emotional self-regulation emerges from mother-infant hetero-regulation, which is an inter-subjective process because it involves both psychological and behavioral coordination between the caregiver and the infant. Van Der Veer (1996) explains,

"It seems that Wallon's theory that the child's emotional states are accompanied by global motor behavior which becomes interpreted by the social others [e.g. the mother] as if it were the expression of mental states and that it is this interpretation by the social others [e.g. the mother] which turns the initially purely physiological process into the expression of a genuine mental state is still basically valid. The work of researchers such as Brazelton, Emde, Kaye, Stern, Trevarthen, and others who, incidentally, had no knowledge of the work of Wallon, has validated this view" (pp. 381 & 386).

Emotions are psychological and visceral states that are often experienced powerfully by infants, more so than adults, and when experienced as such, infants as well as older children typically require the support of their parents to manage and integrate such experiences. When the link between the child and the caregiver breaks down, children are very vulnerable (Bowlby, 1969; Denham, 2007; Saarni, 1999; Sroufe, 1995).

From about eight to 10 months, the infant starts to achieve mobility, learning to crawl and subsequently walk. Mobility allows the infant to withdraw himself from distressing stimuli and, critically, seek out the caregiver at times of stress or fear. At about this time, when the infant has a growing appreciation of the social world and there is an upsurge in stranger wariness, the attachment relationship between the infant and a specific caregiver comes into sharp focus. In this relationship, under normal circumstances, the infant finds reliable care in his secure base, so long as that person is a constant companion (i.e., mother, father, guardian, grandparent). Over the period of the second year, although independence is increasing, the toddler still needs his secure base at times of stress, and the prompt, sensitive attention and protection of the caregiver will help the toddler develop a sense of himself as an emotionally independent, autonomous person (Bowlby, 1969; Sroufe, 1995)

With the emergence of communicative competence from about 2½ years of age, children start to label and identify emotional events, not merely current events but also past and future events; they want to talk about emotionally charged events with a receptive conversational partner (Bretherton, Fritz, Zahn-Waxler, & Ridgeway, 1986). These discussions help young children to better understand how emotional circumstances arose (antecedents) and how they will be resolved or dealt with (consequences). Emotion centered verbal communications with caregivers can help the child to express his feelings and also to broaden his emotional repertoire; conversations about feelings, desires and motives are a powerful mechanism by which the child can come to understand himself and others, and thereby regulate and integrate emotional experiences (e.g., Cole, Amstrong, & Pemberton, 2010; de Rosnay & Hughes 2006; Leibowitz, Ramos-Marcuse, & Arsenio, 2002).

By three to four years of age, young children are able to use specific emotion regulation strategies, such as talking to themselves, clinging to a beloved toy or security blanket or playing on their own when they are distressed, thereby allowing themselves to calm down. Other strategies include covering ears or eyes to exclude sensory stimuli, which is relatively immature, or changing their goals when they find themselves in a difficult situation, which is a relatively sophisticated strategy. Using these latter strategies helps children avoid counterproductive behavior, such as throwing temper tantrums. Over time, children become better able to select strategies (emotional, behavioral or cognitive) that are appropriate for the situation they are experiencing and thereby adapt to situations as they encounter them rather than needing to change the situation or seek external support. Of course, young children still need support, but that support is increasingly oriented to helping them manage their own behavior (see Saarni, 1999). Young children slowly begin to understand the relationship between their emotion regulation strategies and the changes in how they feel, and thus their understanding of emotion regulation strategies and their use of deliberate control of emotional expressions increase steadily over childhood (Harris 1989).

For children of preschool-age the mastery of appropriate emotion regulation strategies represents a major stage-relevant developmental achievement, which is particularly important in relation to their school integration. For example, Blair, Denham, Kochanoff and Whipple (2004) showed that young children's emotional coping strategies are linked to pro-social behaviors. In older children, between five and eight years of age, Rydell, Berlin and Bohlin (2003) showed that emotion regulation ability was a better predictor of behavioral adaptation at school than *emotionality*; emotion regulation being construed as a skill and emotionality as a dimension of temperament.

Children's emotional regulation is also a good predictor of academic success. Teacher reports on children's self-regulation show a substantial correlation with academic achievement in the domains of mathematics, literacy and listening, and a similar pattern has been observed with parental reports (Graziano, Reavis, Keane, & Calkins, 2007; Howse, Calkins, Anastopoulos, Keane, & Shelton, 2003). It seems that positive emotions can give confidence to pupils and stimulate their learning whereas negative emotions can provoke feelings of helplessness, boredom or withdrawal. For instance, measures of negative affectivity in pupils between the 6th and 8th grades corresponds with poorer academic achievement, as well as lower self-perceived academic competence (Gumora & Arsenio, 2002), and this relation continues well beyond childhood (Pekrun, Goetz, & Titz, 2002; Schutz & Pekrun, 2007).

In sum, the disruptive effect of emotions on learning varies according to the skills children have to regulate their emotions. According to the Resource Allocation Model, emotions, either positive or negative, can affect the availability of cognitive resources (Ellis & Ashbrook, 1988). Given that the impact of negative emotion on school performance is already well established, it seems that the influence of emotion regulation on school adaptation and success is an important domain of future research (see chapter 7 for further discussion of this point). Unfortunately, there is no research to date specifically devoted to the cognitive cost of emotional processes at school but the importance of such research, especially for younger children entering formal schooling, would seem self-evident.

The growth of emotion understanding: Development, individual differences and relations with social conduct

Within the framework of clinical child psychology and child psychotherapy, the significance of the child's understanding of emotion and the value of interventions seeking to improve this understanding has long been acknowledged. By contrast, those working in education have only recently started to give systematic attention to young children's emotion understanding. In this section, therefore, we first give a general description of the development of emotion understanding during infancy and childhood. We also include a short description of the individual differences in this development, as these are wide-ranging. With this general developmental framework in place, we then discuss the impact of individual differences in children's emotion understanding on the quality of their social relationships in kindergarten and at school.

The underlying and apparently universal capacity of normally developing infants to recognize and respond appropriately to emotional facial expressions, albeit in limited terms (Haviland & Lelwica 1987, Termine & Izard 1988, Tronick 1989), is an essential foundation for emotion understanding. As we have noted earlier, research on social referencing, for example, provides strong evidence that toward the end of the first year, and certainly in the second year, infants utilize emotional input from social partners to inform their own responses to ambiguous situations, objects and persons. Relatedly, within the context of the attachment relationship, it is commonplace to see affective sharing through affiliative gestures, whereby infants actively share pleasurable experiences with the caregiver, such as the discovery of a new toy: It is clear, therefore, that in the second year toddlers understand that emotion is communicative. The second year also witnesses rapid developments in children's empathic understanding. Whereas infants do not initially attempt to comfort another person in distress, by 18 months of age many toddlers make simple but appropriate efforts to alleviate such distress. By 24 months of age many toddlers understand what others are distressed about, provided it is readily interpretable from current circumstances, and they begin to take more sophisticated interventions to placate (or torment) others. Thus, by the end of the second year, toddlers tacitly understand that discrete emotional displays have referents (objects, persons and situations), they understand the motivational salience of these displays, and they engage in social interactions based on such an understanding. It is from this foundation, in the context of children's rapidly developing linguistic and communicative capacities, that emotion understanding grows. Emotion understanding implies the child's ability to treat emotion as an object of knowledge, to think about emotion (de Rosnay, Harris & Pons 2008).

The last 30 years have seen extensive and detailed studies in many areas of children's emotion understanding that span toddlerhood to late childhood (Pons, Harris, & de Rosnay 2004). These studies have enabled the identification of nine or ten more or less complex components of emotion understanding (see Pons, Daniel, Lafortune, Doudin, & Albanese 2006, for a review). Within the framework of this chapter, we propose a three-stage division of emotion comprehension development from early childhood to preadolescence: external, mental and reflective. Each stage expresses a deeper understanding by the child of his own emotions and those of others, of their nature, causes, consequences and the possibility of control.

During the first, external, stage (approximately two to four years of age), three relatively simple components of emotion comprehension emerge. At this time, children begin to identify certain apparent emotions and to understand the effect of some external causes and desires on emotions. From approximately two years of age, when language begins to take form, children start to label basic emotions such as happiness, sadness, fear, and anger. In making these identifications, children are not confined to present reality; they can label imaginary emotions and they can talk about emotions that were experienced in the past and may be experienced in the future. Later, children naturally continue to learn more labels for different emotions (such as guilt, shame, pride, happiness, disgust, contempt, shyness, and embarrassment) but in this early stage they master the idea of labeling. From three years of age, children also begin to recognize certain external causes of emotions. For example, they recognize that losing a cherished object can cause sadness and that receiving a gift can cause joy. Children also understand that the external causes of emotion apply in imaginary contexts. For example, they realize that being chased by a monster can cause fear. Also, from about four years of age, children begin to understand the influence of desires on emotions. Whilst children are able to make links between desires and emotions from an earlier age (e.g., they may recognize that someone is happy if they get what they want), they have more difficulty accommodating conflicting desires: It is not until about four years of age that they understand that two people in the same situation (e.g., who are both thirsty and find a bottle full of milk) but with different desires (one person likes milk whereas the other hates milk) can experience very different emotions (pleasure and displeasure, respectively).

During the second, mental, stage (approximately five to seven years of age), four new components of emotion comprehension emerge (described below). These components indicate that the child has begun to think about emotion in light of psychological causes and phenomena; they are moving from an external to an internal, mentalistic orientation. In keeping with this development, children at this time show considerable mastery of the external components of emotion and they continue to draw on external modes of explaining emotion despite their burgeoning awareness of emotion in relation to genuinely psychological processes. From around five years of age, children begin to understand the effect of memories on emotions. For example, they realize that the intensity of anger decreases over time; that looking at a picture of a lost loved one can cause sadness or that thinking about a positive past event can cause happiness. From approximately six years of age, children also begin to understand the role of knowledge (beliefs, perceptions, etc.) on emotions. For example, they understand that a person feels sad because he thinks a favorite object has been lost, when in reality it has just been misplaced. They also start to understand the impact of emotions, especially when they are negative, on performance, including academic performance; although they still have difficulties explaining this impact. Starting a little later, between six and seven years of age, children also begin to understand the distinction between real and apparent emotions: they realize that it is possible to simulate or conceal an emotion. Thus, someone can cry when in reality he is not sad, or smile even if he is unhappy. For most children, comprehension of second stage components is a necessary condition for the emergence of third stage components.

During the third, reflective, stage of emotion comprehension development (approximately eight to 12 years of age), children begin to understand more complex relationships between internal states, states of the world and emotions. This stage is characterized by an increasing awareness of the ways in which an individual can reflect upon a given situation from various perspectives, and thereby trigger different feelings either concurrently or successively. Once again, this stage encompasses three new components of emotion comprehension: the nature of mixed emotions; the effect of moral rules on certain emotions; and the possibility of controlling experienced emotions with mental strategies. By about eight years of age, and certainly earlier in many cases, children understand the effect of moral rules on certain emotions. For example, they realize that a person may feel guilty after doing something morally reprehensible, such as stealing a desired object or lying, and they also realize that a person may feel proud after doing something morally valued, such as resisting temptation or giving something up for another person. Also around this time, children begin to understand the nature of mixed or ambivalent emotions: they understand that a person can simultaneously experience different or even conflicting emotions. For example, a person can be happy to have found his favorite pet and at the same time sad to find out the pet is hurt. Finally, toward the end of childhood, and even sooner under certain conditions, children begin to understand how to effectively control experienced emotions using psychological strategies. For example, they understand that thinking about something pleasant can help a person stop feeling sad, thinking about something sad can help a person stop laughing, and speaking about an unpleasant emotion can decrease its intensity.

Most of the work we have reviewed to this point has focused on identifying the average ages at which each component of emotion comprehension emerges. These studies have aimed to capture the universal character of emotion comprehension development rather than recognizing individual differences in this development. Recently, some authors have begun to systematically investigate these differences. One of the basic epistemological postulates of such research is to no longer consider individual differences in emotion comprehension development as measurement error or random deviation; occurring, for example, because of the concentration, motivation, and fatigue levels of the subject. Rather, such variation is increasingly seen as the expression of characteristics specific to the child. At least five key findings have emerged from these works (see Pons & Harris 2005, for a review).

First, individual differences in emotion comprehension are observable very early in children's development, almost from their very first conversational interactions. For example, the quantity of utterances with emotional content varies enormously in two-year-old children: some generate more than 25 emotional reference statements per hour (e.g., 'naughty', 'nice', 'good', 'sad', etc.), whereas others generate none.

Second, individual differences in children's emotion comprehension are observable throughout their development, not only in pre-school children, but also in elementary school children. For example, some children between four and five years of age have a level of emotion comprehension that is superior to other children aged between 10 and 11 years. Consequently, children's emotion comprehension development is characterized not only by a very important age effect (see previous discussion of the mastery of different components of emotion understanding), but also by very important individual differences at every age.

Third, individual differences in emotion comprehension are stable over time. Longitudinal studies over a one-year and three-year period show great stability in these differences. For example, two- to three-year-old children that generate the fewest utterances with emotional content are also those that have the lowest level of emotion comprehension at six years of age. Also, Three- to four-year-old children who most readily communicate spontaneously about emotions are those who show better comprehension of emotions a year later. Further, the level of emotion comprehension of children at seven, nine, and 11 years of age corresponds to their level of emotion comprehension a year later; there is, of course, a general improvement.

Fourth, individual differences in emotion comprehension are not the expression of a specific delay or advantage in the comprehension of emotion (i.e., one or another of the nine components described above). Rather, it appears that children have general delay or advantage across various components of emotion comprehension.

Finally, leaving the family environment to enter pre-school between three and four years of age or elementary school between five and six years of age brings on important emotional and cognitive changes, such as meeting new people with whom children will have an opportunity to communicate and participate in new emotional experiences. However, the transition from the family environment to pre-school, and later to school, does not seem to have a significant impact on the extent of individual differences in emotion comprehension; these transitions neither decrease nor increase such individual differences. For example, young children that have a higher than average comprehension of emotions prior to entering elementary school continue to show a higher comprehension after entering the school system; although, of course, the correspondence is not perfect. Continuity of individual differences in emotion understanding as children move through various environments suggests that there may be a sensitive period during which their level of emotion comprehension becomes relatively fixed. Does this mean that at a certain age, around two or three years of age for example, individual differences in emotion comprehension become irrevocable? At this time this question cannot be answered but given the stability of individual differences, it certainly deserves attention.

We have presented a view of emotion understanding that extends naturally from classical developmental research and has started to extend into the domain of individual differences. In part, the focus on individual differences has emerged because of interest in the impact of emotion understanding on children's social conduct. Therefore, we turn to the growing research corpus which points to the significance of emotion understanding for children's social behavior and their friendships.

In the same way that children's understanding of intellectual states and processes (i.e., metacognitive knowledge or theory of mind) have emerged as some of the most important factors for children's intellectual development (see Hacker, Dunlosky, & Graesser 2009, for a review), so has children's emotion understanding emerged as one of the most important factors of their social development (see Pons, Hancock, Lafortune, & Doudin 2005 for a review). Indeed, there is accumulating evidence to suggest that children's comprehension of emotions (and more generally their understanding of the mind) has an impact on the quality of their social relationships with peers in kindergarten and at school. Emotion understanding has been linked with pro-social behaviors, friendship, resolution of inter-personal conflict, popularity, empathy, cooperation, aggressive and antisocial behaviors. Further, this relationship appears to be direct, although there is some concern that it is mediated by linguistic ability (see de Rosnay et al., 2008, for a discussion).

In an early study, Denham et al. (1990) showed that young children who better understood the impact of situational causes of emotions (e.g., feeling happy when receiving a gift or sad when breaking a toy) were also more likely to be popular with their day-care counterparts. In a further study with children aged three and four years of age, Hughes, Dunn, and White (1998) discovered that children with more developed emotion comprehension were less likely to have behavioral problems such as antisocial behavior, aggressiveness or limited empathy. Conversely, Dunn and Cutting (1999) observed that social games involving more co-operation, inter-individual communication and other positive transactions, were associated with more advanced comprehension of emotions amongst four-year-olds. Also, Denham (1986), with children between two and three years of age, and Iannotti (1985), with children between four and five years of age, found that children who are better able to take the emotional perspective of another person are also more likely to initiate and engage in pro-social behavior in various contexts.

In a longitudinal study, Edwards, Manstead, and MacDonald (1984) discovered that four- and five-year-old children who were better able to recognize emotions based on simple expressions, were also the most popular with their classmates one or two years later. Similarly, Dunn, and Herrera (1997) were able to link a high capacity for resolving interpersonal conflicts with schoolmates at six years of age to superior emotion understanding three years earlier. Using a different methodology, Cook, Greenberg and Kusch (1994) identified young primary school children who had high or moderate levels of disruptive behavior problems (an extreme groups analysis) and showed that these children also had relatively poor understanding of their own emotional experience and the cues for recognizing basic emotion. Thus, poor emotion understanding is predicting poor social outcomes in future years, and children currently experiencing problems in their classroom are likely to have poorer emotion understanding.

If we consider sibling relations, similar patterns emerge. In a study by Stewart and Marvin (1984) children between three and five years of age were left in a waiting room with a younger sibling. Upon the departure of the mother, all the younger siblings responded with varying degrees of distress.

Approximately half of the older siblings offered some type of comfort to their younger sibling. Comforting strategies ranged from verbal reassurance to hugs, and they were often appropriately pitched to the distress experienced by the sibling. The majority of those older siblings offering comfort to their younger sibling were at the same time those with the highest level of socio-cognitive understanding. These findings suggest that advanced socio-cognitive understanding (which encompasses emotion understanding) furnishes more flexible and accurate understanding of others' emotions, and helps children to respond empathically to a sibling's distress.

Indeed, the link between emotion understanding and social competence seems to entail throughout childhood. Cassidy et al. (1992) have shown that a good level of emotion comprehension in children during their first mandatory school year went hand in hand with popularity amongst classmates. McDowell, O'Neil, and Parke (2000) showed that nine-year-old children (particularly girls) with a good understanding of strategies for controlling negative emotions were considered the most socially competent by their schoolmates and teachers. Finally, Bosacki and Astington (1999) found a positive link between emotion comprehension in preadolescents aged 11 to 13 years and teacher evaluations of their level of social competence.

In sum, the existing literature documents a robust relationship between children's emotion comprehension and the quality of their social relationships in the kindergarten and at school. This relation is not without consequences for children's intellectual development or school achievement. For example, children that show deficiencies in their comprehension of emotions are less receptive academically. These children can also have a negative impact on the atmosphere in the classroom and, in more extreme cases, they cannot be taught. In educational systems that resort to structural differentiation, these weak pupils, from the viewpoint of emotion comprehension, risk becoming classroom scapegoats and perhaps even being excluded from regular classes. Indeed, some recent studies are also starting to show a link between children's emotion understanding, such as knowledge of emotion regulation strategies, and their school achievement (Govaerts & Grégoire, 2004; Laforturne & Pons, 2005).

It is now well established that the measurement of individual differences emotion understanding opens a window on children's capacities and limitations within the social and perhaps also educational environment of the school, although it is only part of a complex story. In future research it may prove interesting to examine students' perceptions of their teacher's emotions. A literature review on this point by Sutton and Wheatley (2003) suggests that students may use their teacher's facial expressions like indicators of their own performance; associating their successes or failures with positive or negative teacher expressions. Given the obvious significance of emotion understanding and emotion regulation in the educational context, in the next section we review interventions designed to promote children's emotional competence.

3. Emotion based interventions for children

Normally, children's emotional competence develops gradually in an age appropriate manner. However, as is the case with almost all development in children, even within a typical developmental range, large individual differences can be found (Cutting & Dunn, 1999; Farina, Albanese, & Pons 2008; Pons & Harris 2005). For example, while some children do not easily get upset or are good at calming themselves down, others can be very emotional and experience great difficulties in calming themselves. It therefore seems reasonable to consider how the development of good emotional competence can be facilitated. In the following sections, we will consider two perspectives on how to promote a good emotional competence development in children; here in section 3 we focus on direct attempts to promote children's emotion understanding by intervention and in section 4 we consider interventions with pedagogues as an important avenue for future intervention. These approaches can be seen as complementary and may therefore be applied together to advantage.

Although the introduction of emotion competence facilitation in teachers' training and in school programs is still the object of debate, an increasing number of educational systems have attempted to facilitate the development of such competence in children over the last few years. However, scientific research that concerns interventions intended to help children develop their emotional competence, and thus compensate for possible deficiencies, are still too rare. To understand how these interventions can be realized, in practical terms, we present three studies below in a relatively detailed manner. These three studies each aim to improve children's understanding of emotions.

Emotion understanding in autistic children

Autistic children show a delay in their comprehension of emotions. For example, they find it difficult to recognize emotions such as surprise and to understand the influence of beliefs on emotions. Hadwin et al. (1996) have studied the possibility of teaching four components of the first (external) and second (mental) stages of emotion comprehension to autistic children. The four components of emotion comprehension that were taught within the framework of this intervention were: (a) the recognition of basic emotions (e.g., joy, sadness, anger, and fear); (b) the situational causes of emotions (e.g., receiving a gift causes joy); (c) the impact of desires on emotions (e.g., a person will be sad if a wish does not come true); and (d) the effect of beliefs on emotions (e.g., a person will be happy at the thought of receiving a present when in fact he will receive none). Experimental and control groups were compared using a pre-test/intervention/post-test paradigm. During the pre-test phase, children from both groups were evaluated in relation to their comprehension of the four components mentioned above. During the intervention phase, only the experimental group children were taught the components they were unable to understand during the pre-test phase (children from the control group were not taught during this phase). For example, if the child failed in his/her comprehension of the effect of desires on emotions, the experimenter said: "Look, Thomas sees clowns at the circus. He really likes clowns. How does Thomas feel when he sees clowns?" After the child has answered wrongly (because he/she did not understand the impact of desires on emotions) the experimenter added: "Let's see how Thomas feels. Look, Thomas is happy. He is happy because he sees clowns. When you do something you like, then you feel happy!" Finally, the children in both groups were examined once more immediately after the intervention phase and again two months later.

The results of this intervention revealed a significant and stable development of emotion comprehension between pre-test and post-test phases with autistic children who used the teaching program during the intervention phase. By contrast, there was no noteworthy change in children who did not use the program. Overall, autistic children who used the teaching program immediately mastered an additional component of emotion comprehension and retained their insights two months later. This research illustrates that interventions can help autistic children make up for their deficiencies in emotion comprehension and that the impact of this help is stable over time.

Understanding mixed emotions in children between four and seven years of age

Peng et al. (1992) studied the possibility of teaching children between four and seven years of age a relatively complex component of emotion comprehension, namely the comprehension of mixed emotions (e.g., understanding that a person can feel happy because he/she found his/her favorite pet, and at the same time, feel sad because the pet is hurt). Recall from section 2 that it is from about eight years of age that children begin to understand the existence of mixed emotions (which may be more or less conflicting) and to correctly understand situations that cause these kinds of emotions. Younger children are either incapable of understanding the fact that two different emotions can be experienced at the same time or they are unable to imagine a situation that could cause mixed emotions.

In order to implement the intervention, an experimental group and a control group were formed and children were tested using a pre-test/intervention/post-test paradigm. During the pre-test and post-test phases, children in both groups were asked: (1) "Do you think you can feel happy and sad at the same time?" (2) "In which circumstances can you feel both happy and sad?" During the intervention phase, only the experimental group children were coached to understand the different situational elements that cause mixed emotions (control group children receive no coaching during this phase). For example, after telling children a story that described how a lost dog found its way home, but was discovered to be hurt, children were asked: (1) "How does the dog's owner feel when his dog comes home?" (2) "How does the dog's owner feel when he realizes his dog is hurt?" and (3) "How does the dog's owner feel overall?" Finally, children in both groups were tested again immediately after the teaching phase.

The results of this research showed significant development in mixed emotion comprehension between pre-test and post-test phases with children who experienced the teaching program during the intervention phase. No significant change was observed in children that did not use the program. During the post-test phase, children that used the program were better at recognizing the existence of mixed emotions. They were also better able to provide examples of situations that cause this type of emotional response than they had been during the pre-test phase. However, this improvement was only observed in older children between six and seven years of age. At five years of age the improvement was marginal and it did not exist at four years of age. These findings demonstrate that speaking about the nature and the causes of mixed emotions can have a positive effect on children's comprehension but the fact that younger children do not profit from the intervention indicates that teaching comprehension of mixed emotions necessitates some prerequisite abilities.

A classroom based intervention with nine-year-olds

Pons, Harris, and Doudin (2002) examined the possibility of teaching various simple and complex components of emotion comprehension in a school context and the impact of this intervention on individual differences in emotion comprehension. Children tested were nine years of age on average (5th year of elementary school) and receive regular schooling; none of the children were held back a year or in specialized programs. The children's general level of emotion comprehension was evaluated twice with the Test of Emotion Comprehension (TEC)[4] (Pons & Harris 2000); first during the pre-test phase and second during the post-test phase, three months later. The children were divided into experimental and control groups. During the three-month intervention phase, only children in the experimental group used the School Matters In Lifeskills Education (SMILE) (Harrison & Paulin 2000) teaching program dispensed by their usual teacher on a half-hour a day basis. Control group children did not receive any type of emotion comprehension teaching during this period.

The TEC provides a general measure of emotion comprehension in children from two to three years of age, to early adolescence. It measures nine components of emotion comprehension: I. Categorization of basic emotions (joy, sadness, anger, etc.); II. The influence of external causes on emotions; III. The effect of memory on emotions; IV. The role of diverse desires on emotions; V. The effect of knowledge (belief, ignorance) on emotions; VI. The distinction between an apparent emotion and an experienced emotion; VII. The possibility of controlling an experienced emotion; VIII. Mixed emotions; IX. The role of moral rules on emotions. The more components the child masters, the higher is the child's general level of emotion comprehension.

The objective of the SMILE intervention program is to help children de-

---

4 To date, the TEC has been translated into 18 languages: Arabic, Catalan, Chinese, Danish, Dutch, English, Fongbé, French, German, Greek, Icelandic, Italian, Norwegian, Portuguese, Quechua, Spanish, Turkish, and Polish.

velop their comprehension of the nature, causes, and consequences of emotions. It can be used with children from four to 12 years of age and is divided in four parts: Self, Family, Friends, and Others. In each part, several themes are addressed including emotion comprehension. SMILE suggests a certain number of activities to help children develop their comprehension of emotions: (1) relate past and present emotions, and attempt to understand their source; (2) identify people that are liked and disliked; (3) understand the nature of a real or an imaginary friend; (4) recognize and express positive and negative emotions and understand their source; (5) understand the distinction between apparent and experienced emotion and the social usefulness of pretending; (6) identify sources of sadness, anger and fear, and learn to manage them; (7) identify emotions in situations of loss, separation, abandonment, exclusion and harassment, and learn to manage them; (8) identify and understand sources of pride and guilt; (9) identify what we like and dislike in ourselves and in others; (10) identify similarities and differences in emotions experienced by various people and understand the source of these differences; (11) place one's self in a mistreated person's place and identify his/her experiences; (12) identify the influences and consequences of drugs on emotions; (13) understand how adolescence can influence emotions (e.g., the experience of desires, depression, rage, omnipotence, etc.) and how to manage this change. These activities can be carried out either on an individual or group basis, and they can consist of readings and discussions or role-play. SMILE is a mixed teaching program; it attempts to provoke emotions in children, in the here and now, and to remind them of past emotions. It also encourages children to speak and think about their own emotions or those of others, whether they are real or imaginary, past, present or future.

Two important results emerged from this research. Firstly, there was a significant development in the general level of emotion comprehension in children that use the SMILE program and no significant development in children that do not use this program. Most of the children that used the SMILE program (83 %) improved their overall emotion comprehension, whereas relatively few children who did not use the SMILE program improved (22 %). Among the children that used the SMILE program and showed progress, 60 % mastered at least one more component of emotion comprehension, whereas 40 % mastered two. This progress is not trivial. In pre-test, the general level of emotion comprehension in both groups of children was similar to that observed in previous research with children between eight and nine years of age (level 7 on average). In post-test, the general level of emotion comprehension in children that used the SMILE program was similar to that observed in previous studies with children between 10 and 11 years of age (level 8 on average).

Secondly, individual differences in emotion comprehension were profound in both groups during pre-test; there was a dispersion of answers between 5 levels. During post-test, the spectrum of individual differences remained the same in children that did not use the SMILE program but decreased, although not significantly, in children that used the SMILE program (from 5 to 3 levels of dispersion). However, during post-test, weaker children who used the SMILE program showed a general level of emotion comprehension that was equivalent to the majority of typically developing nine-year-olds (level 7); they no longer lagged behind their age group. This was not the case for weaker children who did not use the SMILE program; during the post-test phase they maintained a general level of emotion comprehension (level 5) that was below the majority of typically developing nine-year-olds.

The findings of Pons and colleagues demonstrate that in a regular schooling context, a teacher can help children develop their general level of emotion comprehension. This research also shows that an intervention program such as SMILE only has a relative impact on the spectrum of individual differences in emotion comprehension: children that showed a relative deficit in their general level of emotion comprehension maintained a level that was inferior to their classmates' average after the intervention. Nevertheless, after the intervention these children were shown to function at a level that is equivalent to the average in their age group; they no longer show a delay or a deficiency. Similar results have been obtained with pre-school children of 5 years of age using the Philosophy for Children (P4C) as an intervention program (Pons, Daniel, Schleifer & Auriac, in preparation).

In sum, through adequate intervention, it is possible to help children develop their comprehension of emotions and their emotional competence. Furthermore, individual differences are not irrevocable in spite of the facts that they appear fairly early in children's development, are present throughout development, are stable over time, and are general rather than specific. Kindergartens and schools can play a significant role in the development of children's emotional competence.

4. Interventions with pedagogues

We believe that the relationships between children and those who care for them in educational settings, whether pedagogues or teachers, have an important emotional dimension. Consequently, we conclude our discussion by underlining the importance of focusing in the future on the emotional competence of those involved in the education of children in early childhood and school settings, and on the possible influence of this on the development of the emotional competence in children at kindergarten and primary school.

Today, kindergarten, preschool and school have an increasingly important role in the lives of many children; it therefore make sense that pedagogues and teachers in these facilities should act as important role-models in the children's lives, in line with caregivers/parents. Indeed, this is often the case already. Of course parents and pedagogues-teachers have different roles in the lives of the children, however children spend a great many hours with both and knowing that the children learn about emotions in interaction with their parents, there is no reason to believe that this should not also be the case with teachers in kindergarten, preschool and school.

Traditionally, emotion based interventions have been applied when developmental, social or behavioral problems have been suspected or identified; the focus in these interventions is typically directed at the child and not much attention is given to the wider social environment in which the child functions, such as the relationships with pedagogues and teachers. To date such interventions are rare. However, Webster-Stratton, Reid and Stoolmiller (2008) have conducted an all-inclusive intervention within a school setting. They applied a universal intervention-program, the Incredible Years Teacher Classroom Management, which included training of teachers' positive classroom management skills, and Child Social and Emotional Curriculum (Dinosaur School) training for building social competence and emotional self-regulation, as well as decreasing conduct problems. Matched pairs of high-risk[5] schools were assigned to either intervention- or control-group. Thus, for the schools in the intervention-group, all children enrolled in Head-Start, kindergarten or first grade were part of the intervention. Families, teachers and

---

5 The schools were considered high-risk due to multiple poverty-related risks, which were considered to increase the risk for children to demonstrate less social competence and self-regulation and more behavior problems than more economically advantaged children.

children in the control classrooms continued their regular Head Start and elementary school curriculum and services.

Intervention teachers participated four days (28 hours) in monthly workshops, following the How to Promote Social and Emotional Competence in Young Children (Webster-Stratton, 1999) manual. Approximately half of the training focused on classroom management strategies (e.g., ways to develop positive relationships with the children and their parents, proactive teaching methods, effective use of praise and encouragement and incentive programs for targeted pro-social skills). Teachers learned how to promote children's self-regulation through persistence, emotion and problem-solving coaching, as well as ways to promote social competence through social peer coaching. Teachers were also encouraged to involve parents in home-school behavior plans, using regular parent letters about Dinosaur School, weekly Dinosaur homework for children to be completed with parents, and so on.

For the children, The Dinosaur Social Skills and Problem Solving Curriculum was designed to promote children's social competence, emotional self-regulation (e.g., engagement with class-room activities, persistence, problem solving and anger control) and school behavior (e.g. following teacher directions and cooperation). The Dinosaur Curriculum used 30 class-room lessons per year and had preschool and primary grade versions. The content consist of seven units; (a) learning school rules (b) how to be successful in school (c) emotional literacy, empathy and perspective taking (d) interpersonal problem solving (e) anger management (f) social skills and (g) communication skills. Teachers followed lesson plans that covered each of these content areas at least 2 times a week using 15-20 minute large group circle time followed by 20 minutes of small group skill-practice activities. A certified research staff member co-led all the lessons with the teachers to ensure each classroom received the full intervention.

Webster-Stratton et al. (2008) found that intervention teachers used more positive classroom management strategies and their students showed more social competence and emotional self-regulation, and less conduct problems compared to control. Furthermore, intervention teachers reported more involvement and bonding with parents than control teachers. These findings support the efficacy of all-inclusive preventive intervention, however in socio-economically disadvantaged children. The efficacy of such preventive interventions among children who are not socio-emotionally disadvantaged remains to be studied. There is, however, no reason to believe that the program would not be successful with typical children.

5. Conclusion

On the present basis, it is not yet possible to outline general guidelines for how to facilitate good emotional competence development in children. Nevertheless, the interventions outlined above make it clear that the ways in which we talk to children about emotion, and the ways in which we structure their environments, can greatly facilitate the growth of emotion understanding and the acquisition of emotion regulation skills. It is now well established in the developmental literature that families who engage in communication about psychological states, and who do so in a way that is sensitive to the child's development, promote the child's understanding of emotion (see de Rosnay & Hughes, 2006, for a review). It is perhaps to be expected, therefore, that by helping pedagogues/teachers to engage with children in emotion-oriented ways, we should expect to see positive outcomes for the children under their care. Beyond emotion understanding, it is entirely plausible that the pedagogue/teacher role is one that can be a model for children, fostering self-regulation, emotional accessibility and engagement, and empathy.

References

Baldwin, D., & Moses, L. (1996). The ontogeny of social information gathering. Child Development, 67, 1915-1939.

Blair, K., Denham, S., Kochanoff, A., & Whipple, B. (2004). Playing it cool: Temperament, emotion regulation, and social behavior in preschoolers, Journal of School Psychology, 42, 419-443.

Bowlby, J. (1969). Attachment and Loss: Vol. 1 Attachment. New York: Basic Books.

Bosacki, S., & Astington, J. (1999). Theory of mind in preadolescence: Relations between social understanding and social competence. Social Development, 8, 237-255.

Bretherton, I., Fritz, J., Zahn-Waxler, C., & Ridgeway, D. (1986). Learning to talk about emotions: a functionalist perspective. Child Development, 57, 529-548.

Camras, L., Oster, H., Campos, J., & Bakeman, R. (2003). Emotional facial expressions in European-American, Japanese and Chinese infants. Annals of the New York Academy of Sciences, 1000, 1-17.

Camras, L., Oster, H., Bakeman, R., Meng, Z., Ujiie, T., & Campos, J. (2007).

Do infants show distinct negative facial expressions for fear and anger? Emotional expression in 11-month-old european American, Chinese, and Japanese infants. Infancy, 11, 131-155.

Cassidy, J., Parke, R., Butkovsky L., & Braungart, J. (1992). Family-peer connections: The roles of emotional expressiveness within family and children's understanding of emotions. Child Development, 63, 603-618.

Cole, P., Martin, S., & Dennis, T. (2004). Emotion Regulation as a scientific construct: methodological challenges and directions for child development research. Child Development, 75, 317-333.

Cole, P., Armstrong, L., & Pemberton, C. (2010). The Role of language in the development of emotion regulation. In S. Calkins & M. Bell (Eds.), Child Development at the intersection of Emotion and Cognition. Washington: American Psychological Association.

Cook, E., Greenberg, M., & Kusche, C. (1994). The relations between emotional understanding, intellectual functioning, and disruptive behaviour problems in elementary-school-aged children. Journal of Abnormal Child Psychology, 22, 205-219.

Cutting, A., & Dunn, J. (1999). Theory of mind, emotion understanding, Language, and family background: Individual differences and interrelations. Child Development, 70, 853-865.

Denham, S. (1986). Social cognition, prosocial behavior, and emotion in preschoolers: Contextual validation. Child Development, 57, 194-201.

Denham, S. (1998). Emotional development in young children. New York: The Guilford Press.

Denham, S. (2007). Dealing with feelings: How children negotiate the worlds of emotions and social relationships. Cognition, Brain, Behavior 11, 1-48.

Denham, S., McKinly, M., Couchoud, E., & Holt, R. (1990). Emotional and behavioral predictors of preschool peer ratings. Child Development, 61, 1145-1152.

Denham, S., Blair, K., DeMulder, E., Levitas, J., Sawyer, K., & Major, S. (2003). Preschool emotional competence: Pathway to social competence? Child Development, 74, 238-256.

de Rosnay, M., & Hughes, C. (2006). Conversation and theory of mind: Do children talk their way to socio-cognitive understanding? British Journal of Developmental Psychology, 24 (1), 7-37.

de Rosnay, M., Harris, P., & Pons, F. (2008). Emotion understanding and developmental psychopathology in young children. In C. Sharp, P. Fonagy &

I. Goodyer (Eds.), Social Cognition and Developmental Psychopathology (pp. 343-385). Oxford: Oxford University Press

Dunn, J., & Herrera, C. (1997). Conflict resolution with friends, siblings, and mothers: A developmental perspective. Aggressive Behavior. 23, 343-357.

Dunn, J., & Cutting, A. (1999). Understanding others, and individual differences in friendship interactions in young children. Social Development, 8, 201-219.

Edwards, R., Manstead, A., & MacDonald, C. (1984). The relationship between children's sociometric status and ability to recognize facial expression of emotion. European Journal of Social Psychology, 14, 235-238.

Ekman, P. (1999). Basic Emotions. In T. Dalgleish & M. Power (Eds.), Handbook of cognition and emotion. Sussex: John Wiley.

Ekman, P., Davidson, R., Matthieu, R., & Wallace, A. (2005). Buddhist and psychological perspectives on emotions and well-being. Current Directions in Psychological Science, 14, 59-63.

Ellis, H., & Ashbrook, P. (1988). Resource allocation model of the effects of depressed mood states on memory. In K. Fiedler & J. Forgas (Eds.), Affect, cognition and social behavior. Hogrefe.

Farina, E., Albanese, O., & Pons, F. (2008). Making inferences and individual differences in emotion understanding. Psychology of Language and Communication 11, 3-19.

Fox, N. A., Henderson, H. A., Rubin, K. H., Calkins, S. D., & Schmidt, L. A. (2001). Continuity and discontinuity of behavioral inhibition and exuberance: Psychophysiological and behavioral influences across the first four years of life. Child Development, 72(1) 1-21

Govaerts, S., & Grégoire, J. (2004). Stressful academic situations: Study on appraisal variables in adolescence. European Review of Applied Psychology, 54, 261-271.

Goleman, D. (1995). Emotional intelligence. New York: Batman.

Gross, J. (1998). The emerging field of emotion regulation: An integrative review. Review of General Psychology 2, 271-299.

Gross, A., & Ballif, B. (1991). Children's understanding of emotion from facial expressions and situations: A review. Developmental Review 11, 368-398.

Graziano, P., Reavis, R., Keane, S., & Calkins, S. (2007). The role of emotion regulation in children's early academic success, Journal of School Psychology, 45, 3-19.

Gumora, G., & Arsenio, W. (2002). Emotionality, emotion regulation, and school performance in middle school children, Journal of School Psychology, 40, 395-413.

Hacker, D., Dunlosky J., & Graesser A., (2009). Handbook of metacognition in education. New York: Routlegde.

Hadwin, J., Baron-Cohen, S., Howlin, P., & Hill, K. (1996). Can we teach children with autism to understand emotions, beliefs, or pretence? Development and Psychopathology, 8, 345-365.

Harris, P. (1989). Children and Emotion. Oxford: Blackwell.

Harris, P. (2006). Social cognition. In D. Kuhn & R. Siegler (Eds.) Handbook of child Psychology (Sixth Edition), Volume Two: Cognition, perception, and language (pp. 811-868). New Jersey; John Wiley.

Harris, P., Donnelly, K., Guz, G., & Pitt-Watson, R. (1986). Children's understanding of the distinction between real and apparent emotion. Child Development, 57, 895-909.

Harrison, P., & Paulin, G. (2000). School Matters in Lifeskills Education. a framework for PSHE and citizenship in primary schools. Oxford: Oxford County Council.

Haviland, J., & Lelwica, J. (1987). The induced affect response: 10-week-old infants' responses to three emotion expression. Developmental Psychology, 23, 97-104.

Howse, R., Calkins, S., Anastopoulos, A., Keane, S., & Shelton, T. (2003). Regulatory contributors to children's kindergarten achievement. Early Education and Development, 14, 101-119.

Hughes, C., Dunn, J., & White, A. (1998). Trick or treat? Uneven understanding of mind and emotion and executive dysfunction in "hard-to-manage" preschoolers. Journal of Child Psychology and Psychiatry, 39, 981-994.

Iannotti, R. (1985). Naturalistic and structured assessments of pro-social behavior in preschool children: The influence of empathy and perspective taking. Developmental Psychology, 21(1), 46-55.

Izard, C., & Ackerman, B. (2000). Motivational, Organizational, and Regulatory Functions of Discrete Emotions. In M. Lewis & J. Haviland-Jones (Eds.), Handbook of Emotions. New York: The Guilford Press.

Izard, C. E., & Harris, P. L. (1995). Emotional development and developmental psychopathology. In: D. Cohen, & D. J. Cohen (Eds.), Developmental psychopathology: volume I. Theory and methods (pp. 467–503). New York: Wiley.

Kagan, J. (1999). The concept of behavioral inhibition. In L. Schmidt & J. Schulkin (Eds.), Extreme fear, shyness and social phobia: Origins, biological mechanisms, and clinical outcomes (pp. 3-13). Oxford: Oxford University Press.

Kahana-Kalman, R., & Walker-Andrews, A. (2001). The Role of person familiarity in young infants' perception of emotional expressions. Child Development 72, 352-369.

Lafortune, L., & Pons, F. (2005). The role of anxiety in metacognition in mathematics. In F. Pons, D. Hancock, L. Lafortune & P.-A. Doudin (Eds.). Emotions in learning. Aalborg University Press.

Lazarus, R. (1991). Progress on a cognitive- motivational-relational theory of emotion. American Psychologist 46, 819-834.

Leibowitz, J., Ramos-Marcuse, F., & Arsenio, W. (2002). Parent-child emotion communication, attachment, and affective narratives. Attachment & Human Development, 4, 55-67.

Lewis, M. (2009). The Emergence of Human Emotions. In M. Lewis, & J. Haviland-Jones (Eds.), Handbook of emotions. New York: The Guilford Press.

Lewis, M., & Haviland-Jones, J. (Eds.) 2000. Handbook of emotions. New York: The Guilford Press.

Malatesta-Magai, C. (1991). Development of emotion expression during infancy: General course and pattern of individual difference. In J. Garber & K. Dodge (Eds.), The development of emotion regulation and dysregulation. Cambridge University Press.

McDowell, D., O'Neil, R., & Parke, R. (2000). Display rule application in a disappointing situation and children's emotional reactivity: Relations with social competences. Merril Palmer Quarterly, 46, 306-324.

Messinger, D. (2002). Positive and Negative: Infant Facial Expressions and Emotions. Current Directions in Psychological Science, 11, 1-6.

Miller, A., Fine, S., Gouley, K., Seifer, R., Dickstein S., & Shields, A. (2006). Showing and telling about emotions: Interrelations between facets of emotional competence and associations with classroom adjustment in Head Start preschoolers. Cognition and Emotion, 20, 1170-1192.

Pekrun, R., Goetz, T., & Titz, W. (2002). Academic emotions in students' self-regulated learning and achievement: A program of qualitative and quantitative research. Educational Psychologist, 37, 91-106.

Peng, M., Johnson, C., Pollock, J., Glasspool, R., & Harris, P. (1992). Training young children to acknowledge mixed emotions. Cognition and Emotion, 6,

387-401.

Pons, F., & Harris, P. (2000). Test of Emotion Comprehension – TEC. Oxford: University of Oxford.

Pons, F., Harris, P., & Doudin, P.-A. (2002). Teaching emotion understanding. European Journal of Psychology of Education, 17, 293-304.

Pons, F., Harris, P., & de Rosnay, M. (2004). Emotion comprehension between 3 and 11 years: Developmental periods and hierarchical organization. European Journal of Developmental Psychology 1, 127-152.

Pons, F., & Harris, P. (2005). Longitudinal change and longitudinal stability of individual differences in children's emotion understanding. Cognition & Emotion, 19, 1158-1174.

Pons, F., Doudin, P.-A., Harris, P. L., & de Rosnay, M. (2005). Helping children to improve their emotion comprehension. In F. Pons, D. R. Hancock, L. Lafortune & P.-A. Doudin (Eds.), Emotions in learning. Aalborg University Press.

Pons, F., Hancock, D., Lafortune L., & Doudin P.-A. (Eds.) (2005). Emotions in learning. Aalborg University Press.

Pons, F., Daniel, M.-F., Lafortune, L., Doudin, P.-A., & Albanese, O. (Eds.) (2006). Toward Emotional Competences. Aalborg University Press.

Pons, F., de Rosnay, M., Barriol, C., & Zacharopoulou, M., (2010). Origins of attachment theory: subjectivity and interdisciplinary encounters. Impuls, 2, 10-22.

Rydell, A.-M., Berlin, L., & Bohlin, G. (2003). Emotionality, emotion regulation, and adaptation among 5- to 8-years-old children, Emotion, 3, 30-47.

Saarni, C. (1999). Development of the emotional competence. New York: The Guilford Press.

Salovey, P., & Grewal, D. (2005). The science of emotional intelligence. Current Directions in Psychological Sciences, 14, 281-285.

Schutz, P., & Pekrun, R. (2007). Emotion in education. London: Elsevier.

Sroufe, L., & Waters, E. (1976). The ontogenesis of smiling and laughter: A perspective on the organization of development in infancy. Psychological Review, 83, 173-189.

Sroufe, A. (1995). Emotional Development: The organization of emotional life in the early years. Cambridge: Cambridge University Press.

Stern, D. (1985). The interpersonal world of the infant. New York: Basic Books

Stewart, R., & Marvin, R. (1984). Sibling relations: The role of conceptual perspective taking in the ontogeny of sibling caregiving. Child Development,

55, 1322-32.

Sutton, R., & Wheatley, K. (2003). Teacher's emotions and teaching a review of literature and directions for future research, Educational Psychology Review, 15(4), 327-358.

Termine, N., & Izard, C. (1988). Infants' responses to their mothers' expressions of joy and sadness. Developmental Psychology, 24, 223-229.

Thompson, R., & Goodvin R. (2007). Taming the tempest in the teapot; emotion regulation in toddlers. In C. Brownell & C. Kopp (Eds.), Socioemotional development in the toddler years; transitions & transformations. New York: The Guilford Press.

Trevarthen, C., & Aitken, K. (2001). Infant intersubjectivity: Research, theory, and clinical approaches. Journal of Child Psychology and Psychiatry, 42, 3-48.

Tronick, E. (1989). Emotions and emotional communication in infants. American Psychologist 44, 112-119.

Van Der Veer, R. (1996). Henri Wallon's Theory of early child development: The role of emotions, Developmental Review, 13, 364-390.

Webster-Stratton, C. (1999). How to promote children's social and emotional competence. Thousand Oaks: Sage.

Webster-Stratton, C., Reid, M., & Stoolmiller, M. (2008). Preventing conduct problems and improving school readiness: Evaluation of the incredible years teacher and child training programs in high-risk schools. Journal of Child Psychology and Psychiatry, 49, 471-488.

Chapter 9

Violence at school: Emotional control and risk of burnout in teachers[1]

Pierre-André Doudin, Denise Curchod and Bernard Baumberger

Introduction

Child abuse by and within the family environment represents a significant factor of risk to the social, emotional, and cognitive development of these children, also to the quality of their integration at school (see Erkohen-Marküs & Doudin, 2000 for a review). Ideally, school should act as an important compensation factor for these children, in particular by giving them access to teachers who can represent a positive identification model. Moreover, school offers these children the opportunity of benefiting from a positive social anchoring, in particular concerning the development of their interpersonal skills. School may thereby favorably influence the child's development, reducing risks of developmental disorders resulting from mistreatment.

Institutional violence is one of the factors that can negatively affect school's protective role with respect to abused children. Indeed, such children tend to integrate violent interaction models into their own behavior and to repeat these within the school environment, both when dealing with their peers and/or with the educational staff.

Faced with the distressing and unpleasant nature of such behavior, teachers can be at risk, in turn, of responding with violent behavior (for instance violent attitudes, or in extreme cases physical violence), resulting in further abuse for the child. In such cases school would fail in fulfilling its protective role: unable to present and maintain compensation factors it would reinforce risk factors associated with abuse. Abuse suffered at school adds to abuse suffered in the home. Unknowingly, school and educational staff enter a vicious circle of violence, to which it is difficult to put an end.

---

1 We thank R. F. Martin for the translation of this text.

Prevention of institutional violence should focus on consolidating the positive role played by school for all pupils, and in particular for mistreated children, so that they may develop in an optimal manner. Taking into account the issue of institutional violence at school, the necessity and obligation to recognize the problem and to prevent it, are part of a tertiary prevention strategy, offering abused children the opportunity of developing under the best possible conditions.

2. Abuse

The attention given by clinical practitioners and researchers to child abuse in general, and in the family environment in particular, is relatively recent in the history of psychology and educational sciences. Kempe, Silverman, Steele, Droegmuller et Silver (1962) were among the first to address the issue of child abuse. They described what they called the "battered child syndrome", taking into account the issues of diagnostic, etiology, and treatment. The authors focused on abused children and their abusing parents. Many studies have since added to our knowledge of the different types of abuse and risk factors they entail with respect to children's development, as well as to the quality of their integration at school (Erkohen-Marküs & Doudin, 2000).

As noted by Christoffel, Schiedt, Agran, Kraus, McLoughlin and Paulson (1992), abuse refers to behaviours that transgress generally accepted behavioral norms, presenting a risk of jeopardizing the children's physical, cognitive and socio-emotional development, or of transgressing their rights. Such behaviors include acts that are perpetrated and/or those that are neglected (Zuravin, 1999), whether these are voluntary or not. This covers a wide and diversified range of behaviors that can be classified into 4 categories:

1. physical abuse, for example hitting someone with the hand or using an object;
2. sexual abuse, for example incest, attempted rape, fondling, exposing children to indecent acts, sexual rites or pornography;
3. psychological abuse, recently recognized as a form of "victimization" of children; this includes verbal abuse and depreciation, symbolic acts intended to terrify the child, and also the lack of emotional availability of the parents or other carer;
4. neglect, a deficit in care given to the children that is detrimental to their psychological and/or physical health.

Institutional violence

The attention given to institutional violence started essentially in the early 1990s, and relatively few studies have addressed this issue. However, the pioneering work by Gil (1975) already identified 3 types of abuse: intra-familial, institutional and societal.

Thomas (1990) proposes a general definition of institutional violence: the author considers that any professional decision and action that can alter a child's identity and abilities falls within the scope of institutional violence. Moreover, this author notes that this type of violence also occurs when it is not possible to prove that the child is developing appropriately as a result of the professionals' actions. This definition places the emphasis on the quality of the child/teacher interactions and on the educational staff's responsibility. Tomkiewicz (1997, p. 310) proposes a wider definition of institutional violence as being "any violence perpetrated in, or by, an institution, or any lack of action, that can cause undue physical or psychological suffering to the child and/or that can hinder his/her future development"[2].

As noted by Jésu (1998, p. 286),"it would be illusory to believe that children, parents and education professionals can constantly be united around perfect, absolute and flawless "well-treatment""[3]. This does not mean however that these different partners are locked in a spiral of mistreatment. Detecting institutional violence is essential in order to ensure children's existential rights, and to satisfy their needs in terms of development, as well as their physical, emotional and mental safety.

As previously mentioned, school brings together many children, some of whom may display violent behaviors. In certain cases, the educational staff may adopt "mirroring behaviors" (Morrison, 1996) subconsciously reproducing the violent behaviors:

- when dealing with the children, responding to violence with violence (punishments, exclusion, insults, rejection…). This type of violence, perpetrated by professionals responsible for the children's education, would explain in part why most abuses are due to individuals who are close to the child and who the children are supposed to trust (Jones & Myers, 1997);

-when dealing with their colleagues; according to Mitchell (1996), vio-

---

[2] Adapted from the French

lence amongst colleagues (also between management and staff) is frequent. Relations between professionals can become highly antagonistic and focusing on personal or collective conflicts can lead to neglecting the pupils' needs (Tomkiewicz & Vivet, 1991). As neglect is a form of mistreatment, this results in pupils becoming the victims of conflicts amongst professionals.

Moreover, in the wake of studies demonstrating the extent of intra-family mistreatment, the school institution has become entrusted with the task of identifying potential abuse on pupils and of reporting such situations. This task can elicit significant anxiety in teachers. In order to face such anxiety, they might subconsciously have recourse to defense mechanisms (Killén, 1996) such as denial, minimizing, doubt, inhibition of the will to know. These mechanisms reduce guilt and encourage non-action.

Along the same lines, faced with abuse from children, professionals can choose to ignore such behavior, minimize the seriousness of the acts or assimilate them to "normal" aggressiveness related, for example, to teenage development (Roberts, Dempster, Taylor & Milian, 1992 ; La Fontaine, 1991).

Emotional burnout can be considered to be an important element for understanding institutional violence. Bradley (1969) was the first to identify a type of stress specific to the professional environment which he coined as "burnout". Today, there is still no consensus as to the definition of burnout. However, following Freudenberger (1974), most authors place the emphasis on 3 main characteristics of burnout:

(1) a feeling of professional exhaustion with the impression of having depleted ones' energy and having nothing left to contribute on the professional level;

(2) a tendency toward dehumanizing (or depersonalizing) relationships, associated in particular with a depersonalized and negative representation of pupils, parents and colleagues. The relationship is cold, distant, even cynical;

(3) a decrease in personal fulfillment experienced as a failure with respect to personal success in ones' work.

Burnout therefore entails a risk of dehumanization of relationships, with a deficiency in terms of empathy. This phenomena counteracts the ability to consolidate psycho-social skills in children and to create an atmosphere of well-treatment that is all the more essential for children who are mistreated within their family environment.

Many studies, including work by Freudenberger (1974), Maslach (1976) and later by Vézinas and Gingras (1995), and Camana (2002) have shown that teaching professions, like other professions based on a help relationship (nurses, doctors, lawyer, social workers, police agents, psychologists), is particularly exposed to professional burnout. Gonik, Kurt and Boillat (2000) in Switzerland, and Bauer et al. (2007) in Germany have shown that a relatively important proportion of the teacher population suffers from professional exhaustion or burnout.

In order to prevent institutional violence, it is essential that the school establishment pay attention to its staff's health. Social support for teachers faced with complex professional situations, involving violence in particular, is of utmost importance, as is acknowledgment by the establishment of any efforts accomplished (Unterbrink et al., 2007). On the contrary, conflicting relations with colleagues, or on a societal level, loss of authority or professional recognition represent a significant risk of burnout for teachers. Several studies (for example Rindfleisch & Foulk, 1992 ; Dodge-Reyome, 1995 ; Nunno, 1997) have shown that dissatisfaction at work, professional stress and work-related depression can lead to abusing behavior in school professionals.

These different researches on burnout in teachers point to the issue of the vicious circle of violence or, in other words, to the circularity of violence: violent behavior in pupils can arouse violent attitudes in teachers, but violent attitudes in teachers presenting a risk of professional burnout can also cause violent behavior in the pupils.

Research on institutional violence is still in its early stages. Further studies must be carried out in order to broaden our understanding of the issue, in particular concerning certain more insidious forms taken on by violence and the associated risks they represent, both for the pupils (in terms of emotional, social and intellectual development) and for the teacher ("work-related depression" or burnout).

Meta-emotion

A new paradigm is emerging that proposes a theoretical framework and diagnostic and intervention instruments to address the concept of interpersonal skills. It consists in studying the development of meta-emotion (Pons, Doudin & Harris, 2004). The concept of meta-emotion stems from studies on meta-cognition (for a review on the subject see Doudin, Martin & Albanese, 2001) that distinguish the knowledge that subjects have of their own cognitive functioning and/or that of others, from their ability to use a number of functions involved in problem solving tasks, in particular and especially the control and regulation of their own solving processes. By analogy, Pons, Doudin, Harris and de Rosnay (2002) define meta-emotion as being, on one hand, the understanding that subjects have of the nature, causes, consequences and possibility of control over emotions; as such it is a conscious knowledge that a person has concerning emotions. On the other hand, meta-emotion also refers to the subjects' ability to regulate both the perception of emotions and the expression of emotions to others.

Research concerning meta-emotion and the understanding of emotions within the school environment has mainly focused on pupils (for example: Pons, Doudin, Harris & de Rosnay, 2004), the emotional experience of teachers has been largely neglected. This is paradoxical, as the teachers' emotional experience is closely related to their work and has a direct impact on the quality of learning and emotional experience of their pupils. We can however note the pioneering work by Saarni (1999) who studied the role that teachers can play in the development of the understanding of their pupils' emotions. The author (op. cit.) identifies the skills that teachers should have acquired in order to play such a role, in particular, awareness of one's own emotions, recognition and understanding of emotions in others (pupils, parents, colleagues, management...), empathy, and emotional control. As noted by Lafortune, St-Pierre and Martin (2006), these skills should be an integral part of teachers' professional skills and should be addressed in all professional curriculum preparing to the teaching profession.

Research

A small number of studies have began to investigate meta-emotion in teachers within their professional environment. The research presented here adopts this approach. We are currently carrying out a study addressing the risks of circularity of violence or the vicious circle of violence, as well as teachers' ability to regulate their emotions in a professional situation involving violence at school, and their relational ethics with respect to the emotions that a teacher can or cannot express towards his/her pupils. We also investigate the impact that burnout could have on teachers' ability to regulate their emotions and maintain their relational ethics.

We asked 137 teachers to answer a questionnaire after reading the following scenario: "During a playtime break you are in the playground where many children are playing around you. It is your playground supervision week. Your attention is drawn by Roberta, one of your pupils, who pushes another pupil violently and insults her. You walk up to Roberta and ask her what's going on. Her eyes grow narrow, and Roberta insults you, telling you to mind your own business".

Through a series of questions, and from a set of 9 emotions proposed (anger, fear, sadness, distaste, joy, contempt, surprise, guilt, shame), the teachers were asked to identify and assess the intensity[3] of the emotions they would feel in this situation, also those that they would feel toward the violent pupil. As professionals dealing with children and adolescents, teachers are regularly faced with their pupils' impulsiveness. Teachers must be able to manage their own impulsivity by having acquired the skills necessary to regulate their own emotions, in particular emotions such as distaste and contempt, that are potentially detrimental to their pupils' development. This involves regulating the intensity of these emotions: the intensity expressed should be less than that felt. We calculated an emotional cue[4], taking into account intensity for each of the 9 emotions.

We used Maslach's Burn Out Inventory scale (MBI), Maslach (1976) in order to assess the level of professional exhaustion. This is the instrument most frequently used for assessing the risk of burnout. The scale was first developed to measure burnout phenomena in the medical professions. It has been adapted to the teaching profession and has been used in many studies investigating burnout in teachers in the early 80s (for example: Belcastro & Gold, 1983; Mazur & Lynch, 1989) also more recently (for example Burke, Greenglass & Schwarzer, 1996 ; Evers, Tomic & Brouwers, 2004 ; Lau, Tak Yuen & Chan, 2004 ; Unterbrink et al., 2007). This scale is comprised of 3 dimensions: – professional exhaustion (example: "I feel emotionally exhausted by my work"); – professional fulfillment (example: "I have accomplished much that is worthy in my work"); – dehumanization or depersonalization (example: "I have become more insensitive to others since I started this job").

---

3 Nil, low, strong, very strong
4 Nil = 0 ; weak = 1 ; strong = 2 ; very strong = 3

6. Results

Regulation of emotions

As shown in table 1, in this fictitious situation of violence at school the emotions that the teachers reported they felt most strongly were: anger, surprise and sadness. With lesser intensity, the teachers also reported feeling fear (despite the fact that this emotion seems legitimate in such situations), distaste and contempt (potentially detrimental to the pupils' integrity), then shame and guilt (potentially detrimental to the teacher's integrity). As for joy, considering the type of situation involved, it was quite surprising to see this emotion mentioned at all, albeit weakly. Each of these emotions would be expressed toward the aggressor pupil with less intensity than it has been felt by the teacher. The fictitious situation of violence proposed here resulted in a regulation in intensity of the emotions. The two emotions, distaste and contempt, potentially detrimental to the pupil's development were also regulated.

Table 1: Cue measuring the intensity of the emotions that the teachers (n=137) reported they felt and would express toward the aggressor pupil.

Emotion	Index of intensity (emotions felt)	Index of intensity (emotions expressed)
Anger	433	362
Fear	169	67
Sadness	318	275
Distaste	150	74
Joy	6	5
Contempt	118	64
Surprise	358	291
Guilt	61	33
Shame	65	34

Burnout and regulation of emotions

In table 2, we present the results of Pearson's R. correlation test with respect to the relationship between the teachers' level of burnout at each of the three sub-scales of Maslach's test (dehumanization or depersonalization; professional fulfillment; professional exhaustion), and the intensity of distaste and contempt felt and expressed toward the aggressor pupil.

Concerning distaste, no significant correlation was found between the scores at the three burnout scales and the intensity of distaste felt by the teachers. Similarly, the correlation between the score at the professional fulfillment scale and the intensity of distaste expressed was not significant. There was however a significant correlation between the score at the depersonalization and professional exhaustion scales and the intensity of distaste expressed by the teacher toward the aggressor pupil: the higher the scores at the depersonalization and professional exhaustion scales, the more the teacher would express distaste toward the aggressor pupil.

Table 2. Emotions (distaste and contempt) felt and expressed in relation to the teachers' situation with respect to burnout.

Burnout scales	Intensity of distaste felt	Intensity of distaste expressed	Intensity of contempt felt	Intensity of contempt expressed
Score at the dehumanization or depersonalization scale R de Pearson Sig.	NS	.356 p≤.005	NS	NS
Score professional fulfillment scale R de Pearson Sig.	NS	NS	NS	NS
Score at the professional exhaustion scale R de Pearson Sig.	NS	.270 p≤.05	.363 p≤.005	NS
NS= Non-Significant				

NS= Non-Significant

Concerning contempt, no significant correlation was found between the scores at the depersonalization and professional fulfillment scales, and the intensity of contempt felt by the teachers; however, a significant correlation was revealed between the score at the professional exhaustion scale and the intensity of contempt they felt: the higher the score on the exhaustion scale, the higher the intensity of contempt they reported having felt. Finally, no correlation was found between the three burnout scales and the intensity of contempt expressed by the teachers.

These results suggest that some aspects of the risk of burnout can have an impact on the perception of emotions and on their regulation: distaste seems to be more difficult to regulate for teachers presenting a high risk of burnout, as measured using the dehumanization or depersonalization and professional exhaustion scales. Professional exhaustion affects the way teachers feel contempt, whereas dehumanization and professional exhaustion affect the way teachers express distaste.

7. Discussion

Like any profession based on a help relationship, the teaching profession is particularly exposed to professional burnout (Freudenberger, 1974; Maslach, 1976; Vézina, Cousineau, Mergler, Vinet & Laurendeau, 1992 ; Vézinas & Gingras, 1995 ; Camana, 2002). The study presented here aims to investigate the impact that the risk of burnout could have on teachers' ability to regulate their emotions and maintain relational ethics when faced with situations involving violence at school. School can or should play a compensatory role for pupils who are mistreated in their family environment (Erkohen-Marküs & Doudin, 2000). These pupils, more than others are at risk of engaging in violent interactions. If teachers are unprepared to deal with this type of behavior, in particular with respect to their meta-emotional skills, and regulation of their emotions (Pons, Doudin, Harris & de Rosnay, 2002 ; Saarni, 1999 ; Lafortune, St-Pierre & Martin, 2006), the risk of entering a vicious circle of violence will be greater. In this case, school will have failed in one of its missions. It fails to uphold the compensation factors, and actually reinforces the risk factors associated with abuse, with the risk of fuelling institutional violence (Thomas, 1990 ; Tomkiewicz, 1997).

The results show that, for the 9 emotions taken into consideration, the intensity with which the emotions are expressed is always lower than the intensity with which they are felt. This suggests that, in our fictitious situation, teachers regulate the intensity of their emotions, thereby protecting the violent pupil from their own impulsivity, which, coming from an adult in charge of their education, could prove detrimental to their development. Regulating distaste and contempt in particular avoids exposing the children to humiliating emotions and also contributes to avoid entering a spiralling circle of violence in which the teachers could be tempted to respond to the pupil's violence by adopting a violent attitude themselves. The regulation process ensures that the teachers avoid mirroring violence with violence, which would fuel the pupils' violent behaviors (Morrison, 1996). The fact that the teachers regulate their emotions in such a manner attests to their dedication toward maintaining ethical relations in complex situations in which they are confronted with their own limits. The teachers' ability at regulating their emotions could therefore represent an interesting, yet still largely ignored, means for preventing the circularity of violence.

However, not all teachers have the same ability to regulate their emotions and maintain an ethical relationship when confronted with a situation involving violence. Indeed, even though several factors can account for this, the risk of burnout in teachers seems to affect their ability to regulate the intensity of distaste. Regardless of the risk of burnout, teachers reported feeling distaste with the same intensity, however, the teachers most affected by the risk of dehumanization or professional exhaustion were also those who encountered the most difficulty in reducing the intensity with which they expressed their distaste. Our results illustrate one of the aspects associated with the risk of dehumanization of relationships through the management of emotions. Although certain authors such as Freudenberger (1974 ; 1981) or Maslach (1976) had already noted the cynical approach to relationships adopted by some professionals presenting a risk of burnout, our results show that such cynicism is likely due to difficulties at grasping the consequences that expressing an emotion such as distaste can have on others. This is a lack of empathy that works against the creation of a framework of well-treatment, a framework that is essential for children suffering from mistreatment in their family environment (Kempe et al., 1962 ; Erkohen-Markūs & Doudin, 2000).

Concerning contempt, the results show that, regardless of the risk of burnout, teachers display this emotion with the same intensity. However, in teachers presenting a risk of professional exhaustion, contempt is felt more strongly. There appears to be a vulnerability in protecting oneself against invasive emotions. However this does not jeopardize the ability to regulate this emotion, and to maintain an ethics of relationships. However, feeling this emotion more strongly than teachers presenting a lower risk of burnout, whilst expressing it moderately could result in additional stress, feeding the risk of burnout. In the fictitious scenario involving violence at school, although teachers have the time to consider the situation, we already note difficulties in regulating emotions and risks of ethical transgression. It is possible that in real-life situations carrying a high emotional load, this trend could be amplified. This highlights the necessity to better prepare teachers, who are increasingly exposed to complex professional situations, by offering them, as part of initial and continuous training, the possibility of building meta-emotional skills necessary to deal with these crisis situations. Building such skills is part of a tertiary prevention strategy, as it represents a means of preventing institutional violence toward all pupils, and in particular toward those who are exposed to mistreatment in their family environment and who are strongly dependent on a well-treatment relationship with their teacher, even when the pupils adopt antisocial behavior.

References

Bauer, J., Unterbrink, T., Hack, A., Pfeifer, R., Buhl-Grießhaber, V., Müller, U., Wesche, H., Frommhold, M., Seibt, R., Scheuch, K. & Wirsching, M. (2007). Working conditions, adverse events and mental health problems in a sample of 949 German teachers. International Archives of Occupational and Environmental Health, 80(5), 442-449.

Belcastro, P.A. & Gold, R.S. (1983). Teacher stress and burnout : implications for school health personnel. Journal of School Health, 53(7), 404-407.

Bradley, H.B. (1969). Community bases treatment for young adult offenders. Crime and Delinquency, 15, 359-370.

Burke, R.J., Greenglass, E.R. & Schwarzer, R. (1996). Predicting teacher burnout over time : effects of works stress, social support, and self-doubts on burnout and its consequences. Anxiety, stress, and Coping : An International Journal, 9(3), 261-275.

Camana, C. (2002). La crise professionnelle des enseignants : des outils pour agir. Paris : Delagrave.

Christoffel, K.K., Schiedt, P.F., Agran, J.F., Kraus, J.F., McLoughlin E. & Paulson, J.A. (1992). Standard definitions for childhood injury research: Excerpts of a conference report. Pediatrics, 89(6), 1027-1034.

Dodge-Reymone, N. (1995). Sense of competence and attitudes towards abuse interactions with adolescents in residential child care workers. Journal of Child and Youth Care, 10(1), 57-62.

Doudin, P.-A. & Erkohen, M. (2000). Violence à l'école : fatalité ou défi ? Bruxelles : De Boeck.

Doudin, P.-A., Martin, D. & Albanese, O. (2001). Métacognition et éducation.

Berne : Peter Lang.

Erkohen-Marküs, M. & Doudin, P.-A. (2000). Le devenir de l'enfant violenté et sa scolarité. In P.-A. Doudin & M. Erkohen-Marküs (Ed.), Violence à l'école: fatalité ou défi? (pp. 23-52). Bruxelles: De Boeck.

Evers, J.G., Tomic, W. & Brouwers, A. (2004). Burnout among teachers: Students' and teachers' perceptions compared. School Psychology International, 25(2), 131-148.

Freundenberger, H.-J. (1974). Staff burnout. Journal of Social Issues, 30, 159-165.

Freundenberger, H.-J. (1981). L'épuisement professionnel : « la brûlure interne ». Québec : Gaëtan Morin.

Gil, E. (1975). Unravelling child abuse. American Journal of Orthopsychiatry, 45, 346-356.

Gonik, V., Kurth, S. & Boillat, M.-A. (2000). Analyse du questionnaire sur l'état de santé physique et mentale des enseignants vaudois. Rapport final. Lausanne : Institut universitaire romand de santé au travail (IST).

Jésu, F. (1998). Des maltraitances à la bientraitance institutionnelle. In M. Gabel, F. Jésu & M. Manciaux (Ed.), Maltraitances institutionnelles accueillir et soigner les enfants sans les maltraiter (pp. 285-303). Paris : Éditions Fleurus.

Jones, J. & Myers, J. (1997). The future detection and prevention of institutional abuse: Giving children to participate in research. Early Child Development & Care, 133, 115-125.

Kempe, C.H., Silverman, F.N., Steele, B.F., Droegmuller, W. & Silver, H.K. (1962). The battered child syndrome. Journal of American Medical Association, 181, 4-11.

Killén, K. (1996). Invited Commentary: How far have we come in dealing with the emotional challenge of abuse and neglect? Child Abuse & Neglect, 20(9), 791-795.

La Fontaine, J. (1991). Bullying : The child view. London : Calouste Gulbenkian Foundation.

Lafortune, L., St-Pierre, L. & Martin, D. (2005). Emotional competency in accompaniment : Analysis of the manifestation of emotion in a context of change. In F. Pons, M.-F. Daniel, L. Lafortune, P.-A. Doudin & O. Albanese (Eds.), Toward emotional competences (pp. 177-204). Aalborg : Aalborg Universitetsforlag.

Lau, S.Y., Tak Yuen, M. & Chan, R.M.C. (2004). Do demographic characteristics make a difference to burnout among Hong Kong secondary school teachers ? Social Indicators Research, 71(1-3), 491-516.

Maslach, C. (1976). Burned-out. Human Behavior, 9(5), 16-22.

Mazur, P.J. & Lynch, M.D. (1989). Differential impact of administrative, organizational, and pesonality factors on teacher burnout. Teaching and Teacher Education, 5(4), 337-353.

Mitchell, D. (1996). Fear rules. Community Care, 18, 14-20.

Morrison, T. (1996). Staff supervision in social care. Brighton : Pavillon Puplishing.

Nunno, M. (1997). Institutional abuse : the role of leadership, authority and the environment in the social sciences litterature. Early Child Development and Care, 133, 21-40.

Pons, F., Doudin, P.-A. & Harris, P.L. (2004). La compréhension des émotions : développement, différences individuelles, causes et interventions. In L. Lafortune, P.-A. Doudin, F. Pons & D.R. Hancock (Ed.), Les émotions à l'école (pp. 6-31). Sainte-Foy (Québec) : Presses de l'Université du Québec.

Pons, F., Doudin, P.-A., Harris, P. & de Rosnay, M. (2002). Métaémotion et intégration scolaire. In L. Lafortune (Ed.), Affectivité et apprentissage scolaire (pp. 89-106). Sainte-Foy (Québec): Presses de l'Université du Québec.

Rindfleisch, N. & Foulk, R.C. (1992). Factors that influence the occurrence and the seriousness of adverse incidents in residential facilities. Journal of Social Service Research, 16(3-4), 65-87.

Roberts, J., Dempster, H., Taylor, C. & Milian, B. (1992). Research briefing: The sexual abuse of children by other children and young people. Child Abuse Review, 5(3), 10.

Saarni, C. (1999). The development of emotional competence. New York : Guilford Press.

Thomas, G. (1990). Institutional child abuse:The making and prevention of an un-problem. Journal of Child and Youth Care, 4, 1-22.

Tomkiewicz, S. (1997). Violences dans les institutions pour enfants, à l'école et à l'hôpital. In M. Manciaux, M. Gabel, D. Girodet, C. Mignot & M. Rouyer (Ed.), Enfance en danger (pp. 309-369). Paris : Éditions Fleurus.

Tomkiewicz, S. & Vivet, P. (1991). Aimer mal, châtier bien. Enquête sur les violences dans les institutions pour enfants et adolescents. Paris : Le Seuil.

Unterbrink, T., Hack, A., Pfeifer, R., Buhl-Grießhaber, V., Müller. U., Wesche, H., Frommhold, M., Scheuch, K., Seibt, R., Wirsching, M. & Bauer, J. (2007). Burnout and effort-reward-imbalance in a sample of 949 german teachers. International archives of occupational and environmental health, 80(5), 433-441.

Vézina, M. & Gingras, S. (1995). Travail et santé mentale : les groupes à risque. Département de médecine sociale et préventive. Québec : Université Laval.

Zuravin, S.J. (1999). Child neglect : a review of definitions and measurement reserach. In H. Dubowitz (Ed.), Neglected children : research, practice, and policy (pp. 24-46). Thousand Oaks, CA. : Sage.

List of contributors

Bettina Gamskjær Andersen
University of Oslo (Norway)

Lina Arias
Autónoma University of Madrid (Spain)

Emmanuelle Auriac
University Clermont (France)

Bernard Baumberger
Teacher Training University, VD, Lausanne (Switzerland)

Patrick Bender
University of Copenhagen (Denmark)

Karli Beswick
University of Sydney (Australia)

Céline Clavel
University of Paris Ouest (France)

Frederique Cuisiner
University of Paris Ouest (France)

Denise Curchod
Teacher Training University, VD, Lausanne (Switzerland)

Marie-France Daniel
University of Montréal (Canada)

Marc de Rosnay
University of Sydney (Australia)

Pierre-André Doudin
University of Lausanne and Teacher Training University, VD, (Switzerland)

Christian Jantzen
University of Aalborg (Denmark)

Lee Londei
McGill University (Canada)

Mark Meerum Terwogt
Free University of Amsterdam (Netherlands)

Francisco Pons
University of Oslo (Norway) and University of Aalborg (Denmark)

Laura Quintanilla
UNED (Spain)

Encarnación Sarriá
UNED (Spain)

Selene Succar
University of Sydney (Australia)

Hedy Stegge
Free University of Amsterdam (Netherlands)

Mikael Vetner
University of Aalborg (Denmark)